COMPACT DISC PLAYER

MAINTENANCE AND REPAIR

No. 2790
$18.95

COMPACT DISC PLAYER
MAINTENANCE AND REPAIR

Gordon McComb and John Cook

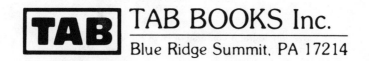

TAB BOOKS Inc.

Blue Ridge Summit, PA 17214

To Thomas Edison, who gave us our first taste of recorded sound. We only
wish he could be around to hear the compact disc.

FIRST EDITION
FIRST PRINTING

Library of Congress Cataloging in Publication Data

McComb, Gordon.
Compact disc player maintenance and repair.

Includes index.
1. Compact disc players—Maintenance and repair.
I. Cook, John. II. Title.
TK7881.75 1987   621.389′33   86-29998
ISBN 0-8306-0190-2
ISBN 0-8306-2790-1 (pbk.)

Cover photograph courtesy of Hunt Audio & Associates,
Long Meadow Shopping Center, Hagerstown, Maryland.

Contents

Acknowledgments

When help was needed (which was often), Jennifer Meredith and Sue Ellis were there to lend a hand. We thank you.

Several companies lent us their time, expertise, and compact disc players to aid us in this difficult writing project, and we are eternally grateful. We specifically wish to acknowledge Marc Finer at Sony, Keld Hannsen at Bang & Olufsen, and the marketing and technical staffs at Denon, Yamaha, Hitachi, and Technics. You came through when others didn't care to contribute.

We are indebted to David Kaye at The Federated Group, who allowed us to disrupt his store in order for us to take pictures and study his assortment of compact disc players. Again, many thanks.

Finally, a warm thank you to Bill Gladstone, our agent, and to our editors at TAB, who believed in this project—and believed in us.

Introduction

Just when you thought all the important things have already been invented, along comes another gadget that changes everything. In 1876 it was the telephone, in 1924 (or thereabouts) it was the television, and in 1975 it was the personal computer.

In 1980, the wonderful invention "that changed everything" was the compact disc, a silver pancake-sized platter that holds—guess what—sound! Actually, the compact disc holds much more than just sound. It holds wonderful sound, better than any other recording medium ever invented.

The compact disc is generations beyond conventional music-recording systems, for it is based on digital computer technology. It uses the computer to record every note, every nuance of the finest music, then play it back with superb fidelity and accuracy. Music recorded on the compact disc sounds exactly as it did when it was first performed.

For the first time ever, compact-disc technology lets anyone—not just trained audio technicians—build the ultimate hi-fi system. Because the high fidelity of the sound is almost guaranteed, the compact disc brings audiophile sound quality to the masses. In fact, the compact disc, or CD for short, offers so much fidelity that it sounds great even when played through bargain-basement amplifiers and speakers.

Compact disc players have been on the consumer market since 1982. They really took off in late 1984, when everyone realized that CD was here to stay. Since that time, millions of compact disc players have been sold, and in the years to come, millions more will find their way into America's homes and cars—not to mention beaches, campsites, cabins, tents, boats, you name it. It might take a while, but industry experts agree that the compact disc will someday completely supplant the cassette player and LP turntable. Take a long look at your existing hi-fi components. Tomorrow they may wind up in the Smithsonian!

Because of the way they work, CD players are both extremely sophisticated and utterly simple. It's an odd but true mixture. Compact disc players represent the latest in computer technology, and the majority of machines use the most recent advances in miniaturization and automated manufacturing. The result: a consumer product that's both easy to maintain and resistant to breakdown.

However, all this doesn't mean that CD players, and the discs played on them, can be abused and still work properly. And it certainly doesn't mean that breakdown isn't a distinct possibility. On the contrary. It'll be a day far in the future when manufacturers perfect the totally repair-free product. Until then, we'll have to fix 'em when things go wrong.

That's where this book comes in. *Compact Disc Player Maintenance and Repair* is designed to help you get the most out of your CD player. It shows you how to set up a CD and connect it to your stereo system, how to keep your player in tip-top shape, and what to do when disaster strikes.

Additional chapters provide a solid theory of operation of compact-disc-player technology, so that you will not only understand how CD works, but better appreciate the truly remarkable innovation that it represents. This book also includes a chapter on understanding CD specifications, as well as several chapters outlining the features, controls, and special servicing notes for over 60 popular players. This information is useful when comparison shopping and while servicing your player.

This book is written for the stereo hobbyist and electronics enthusiast. It is technical in nature, but it does not assume an intimate knowledge of audio, computer technology, electronics, or maintenance-and-repair techniques. You'll find plenty of introductory information and tips that will help you to not only enjoy your CD investment, but save you time and money when (and if) repair time comes around.

Compact disc players are loaded with specialty parts, such as precision optical lenses, lasers, and proprietary surface-mount, integrated circuits. You can't get these things at the local Radio Shack, and most manufacturers don't sell replacement parts to consumers. Even if you could obtain the components, they require special alignment tools and test jigs to test and install properly.

All this means that in the event your compact disc player has a truly serious problem, the home-based technician can do little to affect repairs. Unless you have specific knowledge of servicing your particular brand of player, an oscilloscope to diagnose waveforms, all the specialty tools on hand, and a service manual, you are better off having serious ailments serviced at a repair center. You are free to attempt larger-scale repairs, of course, but they are beyond the scope of this book.

Fortunately, malfunctions in the crucial components of CD players are rather rare, even with the inexpensive models. Most problems are caused by such things as dirty switch contacts, broken wires, smudges on the lens, and damaged or warped discs. In fact, these represent the greatest percentage of service calls to repair centers. You can fix these faults yourself, and with a minimum of tools and time. This book shows you how.

You can greatly minimize repairs—whether done by you or someone else—by keeping your CD player in tip-top shape. This book presents an easy-to-follow, preventative-maintenance schedule that you can use to keep your player working at its fullest.

Even if you can't repair the player yourself, this book serves another important purpose: it helps you to be well informed about the possible causes of compact disc problems. You will be better able to articulate your player's symptoms to the repair technician. By specifically stating what is wrong, you have a greater chance that the problem will be fixed correctly the first time, and at a lower cost.

You will also be in better position to spot unscrupulous repair tactics, like charging for parts that were never replaced or labor above and beyond what had to be done to service a component. Most service centers and repair technicians are honest and fair, but there are exceptions. Be on the lookout for them.

Chapter 1

Introduction to Compact Disc

Thomas Edison was one of the first to develop a way to capture and store sound. Among his many inventions was the phonograph, which he completed in the evening of December 6, 1877. This mechanical contraption transcribed the vibrations of sound into a cylinder made of metal foil. By moving a needle through the grooves made during recording, the sound could be played back. The first "record" was born.

Almost 10 years later, another inventor, by the name of Emile Berliner, designed his version of the phonograph. He called it the gramophone, and it used flat pancake-like records. From both the original Edison phonograph, and the Berliner gramophone, the record player—as we know it today —was born.

The sound quality of the early Edison and Berliner phonographs was scratchy and poor. Edison's original test recording of "Mary Had a Little Lamb," which he made on his prototype phonograph, survives today. It sounds the same as it did over a hundred years ago—bad.

Advancements in audio playback have been scarce since Edison and Berliner's time. Sure, the record player was electrified in 1925, with the introduction of the Brunswick Panatrope, and the quality got a little better because of it. Magnetic tape recorders using plastic tape were perfected during World War II, as part of the German war effort. It took years for tape recorders to reach the home, and the sound they reproduce still isn't all that good.

Audio advancements have been slow in coming, but in 1980 that trend changed. That was the year the compact disc was officially introduced. The compact disc (CD) is unlike any other kind of audio medium ever seen or heard. As shown in Fig. 1-1, the CD looks like a silverized 45-RPM record, but it holds over 74 minutes of crystal clear music.

The CD is played on a compact disc player. It uses digital computer technology to play back music with incredible high fidelity. With little exception, music from a compact disc player is an exact aural mirror image of the original performance. Be-

Fig. 1-1. The compact disc is the most revolutionary sound storage and reproduction system to come out since Edison invented the phonograph.

cause of the way the compact disc works, you can't hear scratches or tape hiss like you can with records and tape recorders.

Let's take a close look at the technology behind compact discs, and find out why they reproduce sound as well as they do. We'll investigate how the discs are recorded, made, and played back on a CD player. This chapter is devoted to the science and technology behind the compact disc. Chapter 2 discusses in detail how compact disc players retrieve the audio from the disc and process it for our ears to enjoy.

THE COMPACT DISC:
AN INTERNATIONAL STANDARD

The compact disc was jointly conceived by two electronics giants: Sony, in Japan, and Philips, in

the Netherlands (audio buffs will remember that it was Philips that also invented the common audio cassette tape cartridge that is in wide use today). Separately, the two companies had been working for years on a way to digitally encode audio information and play it back on an inexpensive home player. Fortunately, they decided to join forces and establish a worldwide digital audio standard.

This standard covers many things—including the way the audio is encoded on the disc, the size of the disc, the speed of the disc during playback, and other factors. See Table 1-1 for more complete specifications of the CD standard.

Philips and Sony license the CD technology to other manufacturers, who follow the standard to the letter (or should at any rate). As a result, any compact disc you buy will play on any compact disc player. If you're into computers, you are well aware

Table 1-1. Compact Disc Specifications.

Disc	
Playing time:	Approximately 74 minutes on one side.
Rotation:	Clockwise, when viewed from top.
Rotational speed:	500 to 200 rpm; 1.2 to 1.4 m/sec.
Track pitch:	1.6 μm.
Diameter:	120 mm (4.7 inches).
Thickness:	1.2 mm.
Center hole diameter:	15 mm.
Recording area:	46 mm to 117 mm.
Signal area:	509 mm to 116 mm.
Coating material:	Any transparent material with 1.5 refractive index.
Minimum pit length:	0.833 μm (1.2m/sec.) to 0.972 μm (1.4 m/sec).
Maximum pit length:	3.05 μm (1.2 m/sec.) to 3.65 μm (1.4 m/sec.)
Pit depth:	Approximately 0.11 μm.
Pit width:	Approximately 0.5 μm.

Optical System	
Standard wavelength:	780 nm (7,800 Angstrom units).
Focal depth:	$\pm$ 2 μm.
Beam diameter/surface:	About 1.0 mm.
Beam diameter/signal:	About 0.8 μm.
Optical source:	Semiconductor laser.
Focusing system:	Astigmatic or Foucault (typ.).

Signal Format	
Number of channels:	2 channels (4 channel recording at twice rotation speed).
Quantization:	16-bit linear.
Quantizing timing:	Concurrent for all channels.
Sampling frequency:	44.1 kHz.
Channel bit rate:	4.3218 megabits per second.
Data bit rate:	2.0338 megabits per second.
Data-to-channel bits:	8:17.
Filtering:	Analog or digital.
Error correction code:	CIRC (with 25% redundancy).
Modulation system:	EFM.
Max. number of tracks:	99.
Max. number of indexes:	99.

Theoretical Audio Specifications	
Frequency response:	5-20, 000 Hz $\pm$ 0 dB.
Dynamic range:	96 dB.
Signal-to-Noise ratio:	97.5 dB.
Harmonic distortion:	Less than 0.003% (at 1 kHz).
Channel separation:	96 dB (at 1 kHz).
Wow/flutter:	Less than measurable limits.

Typical Audio Specifications	
Frequency response:	20-20,000 Hz +0.4, $-$0.2 dB.
Dynamic range:	93 dB.
Signal-to-Noise ratio:	92 dB.
Harmonic distortion:	Less than 0.01% (at 1 kHz).
Channel separation:	90 dB (at 1 kHz).
Wow/flutter:	Less than measurable limits.

of the incompatibility problems between different computer brands (or even models made by the same company). Not so with the compact disc.

A CLOSER LOOK AT THE COMPACT DISC

Physically, the CD doesn't look like much, but appearances can be misleading. The disc (Fig. 1-2) is 12 centimeters in size, or about 4.7 inches. It has a thickness of 1.2mm, and the hole in the center has a diameter of 15mm. The disc itself is composed of a very thin piece of stamped aluminum encased in plastic. The discs sold today have music on one side, but there is no technical reason why a CD could not be made to hold music on two sides.

The original design of the compact disc specifies that the maximum total playing time per side is 60 minutes. Theoretically, this can be increased to 80 minutes, which means that only a single side of a CD would be sufficient for Beethoven's entire 9th Symphony (with applause). A total playing time of about 74 minutes is the current practical limit for compact discs.

The compact disc is capable of containing either 2-channel or 4-channel audio. Four-channel audio consumes twice as much disc space because the disc turns twice as fast. The maximum playing time with 4-channel audio is 37 minutes.

Compact discs can hold up to 99 music selections, or songs, as long as the total running time for the selections do not exceed the maximum capacity of the disc. Each selection can be further divided into index points. When the disc is created, index points can be placed at the beginning bar or other important place in the music.

Information on a compact disc is composed of very small "pits," originally etched into a master by a laser. The pits spiral from the inside of the disc to the outside. Stretched out, the spiral of pits would go on for 3 miles. The flat areas between each pit are called lands. Together, the pits and lands correspond to a sequence of digital data.

The spiral path that the pits and lands take around the disc is the track. *Track* is a better word than groove. There is no continuous groove on a

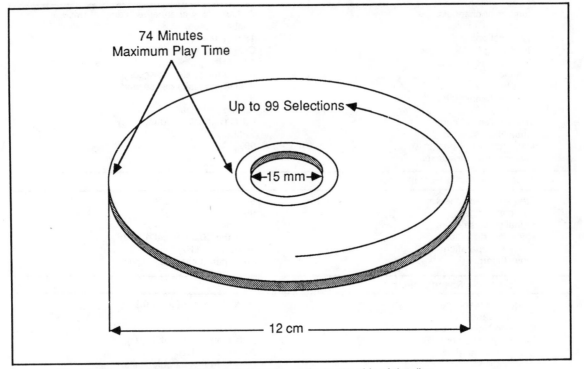

74 Minutes
Maximum Play Time

Up to 99 Selections

←15 mm→

12 cm

Fig. 1-2. CDs hold up to 74 minutes of high fidelity stereo music on one side of the disc.

compact disc, as there is with a record. The term track is also often used to denote a music selection. In this book, to avoid confusion, we will refer to the track of pits and lands on the disc as the *data track* or *information track*. Individual audio selections will be referred to as *music tracks.*

Refer to Fig. 1-3. The pits on the CD are 0.5 micrometers (μm) wide. The tracks are spaced 1.6 μm apart. It's hard to imagine anything this small, but consider this: You can pack 20,000 compact disc tracks to the inch, 60 tracks in the groove of an LP record, 30 tracks on the strand of hair, and about 750 crammed inside a lowercase o!

During playback, the disc rotates clockwise (when viewed from the top) at speeds that range from 200 to 500 rpm. Because the tracks are longer, the rotation of the disc slows when information from the outer edge is retrieved. More pits can be crammed into one rotation, as shown in Fig. 1-4, and the disc slows down to take advantage of the extra real estate. This technique is called *constant linear velocity*, or CLV, and helps increase the playing time of the CD.

AUDIO ENCODING

In a record player, sound is reproduced by a needle traveling in a narrow, bumpy groove, as illustrated in Fig. 1-5. The bumps make the needle vibrate, and the vibrations are transmitted mechanically to a cartridge. The cartridge contains a transducer made of magnetic or crystal material, which translates the mechanical fluctuations of the needle into electrical impulses.

Sound is retrieved from a compact disc in an entirely different manner, as diagrammed in Fig. 1-6. Chapter 2 goes into detail on exactly how a compact disc player works, but here is the general process.

A laser built into the player emits a pencil-thin beam of infrared light that strikes against the pits and lands on the disc. When the beam reflects off the flat lands, most of the light is reflected back into a photodetector. When the beam reflects off the pits, less light is reflected into the photodetector. The result, as seen by the photodetector, is a sequence of very short on-off flashes of light. A circuit inside the player takes the on-off flashes and converts the data from digital format to analog format. Once in analog form, the signal is routed to an amplifier for listening. Let's backtrack a bit and investigate how the music got on the disc in digital format in the first place.

Fig. 1-3. The surface of the CD is covered with billions of microsized pits.

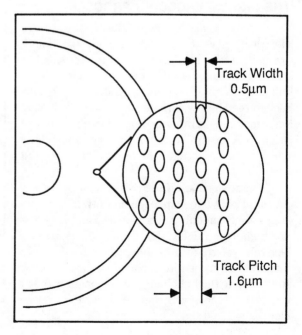

Track Width
0.5μm

Track Pitch
1.6μm

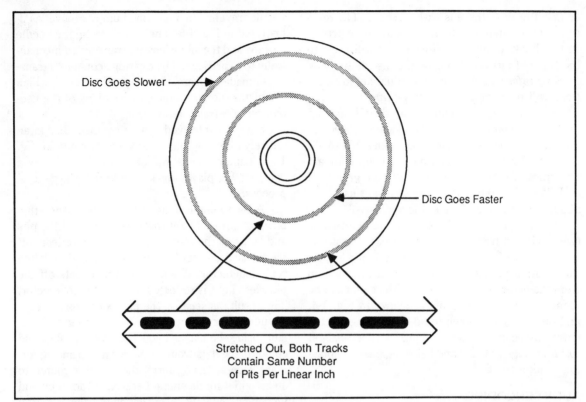

Fig. 1-4. Constant linear velocity packs more music onto a disc.

THE DIGITAL ENCODING PROCESS

Analog signals, as you probably are aware, are electrical waves that continuously change. There are an infinite number of steps between the smallest and largest analog signals. Imagine a light bulb on a dimmer circuit. Apply only a small amount of current to the bulb by turning the dimmer only part way, and the light turns on. But it doesn't glow very brightly. Keep turning the dimmer control and the current increases, until the light glows with full brightness.

Digital signals, on the other hand, are comprised of only two states—on and off. These two states are commonly referred to as 0 and 1, or low and high, respectively. The 0 and 1 digits are collectively referred to as bits, and are the only numerals in the entire binary counting system. Returning to the light bulb, you no longer can dial in any brightness you want. You have only two choices: off and on.

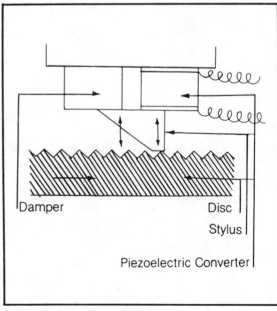

Fig. 1-5. The mechanical stylus of a record player.

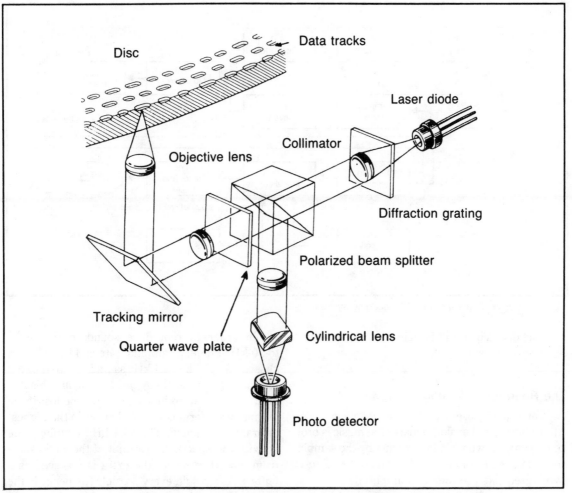

Fig. 1-6. The optical components of a typical compact disc player, and the method of "reading" a disc.

At first glance, it would seem that digital signals are very restrictive. Actually, you can string together a number of binary 1's and 0's and, with a translation circuit, you can turn those numbers into an analog signal. You can also go the other way around. You can take an analog signal and convert it into a digital number. This is exactly what happens in the compact disc audio-encoding process.

Analog-to-Digital Conversion

Before music is recorded on the compact disc, it is translated to its digital equivalent. The entire process is shown in block diagram form in Fig. 1-7.

The conversion first begins with the low-pass filter, sample and hold circuits, and A/D converter. There are two sets of these circuits, one each for the right and left channels. The low-pass filter blocks frequencies above 20 kHz, the cutoff range specified in the CD standard. The sample and hold and D/A converter circuits examine the music and convert it to its digital equivalent. (Not surprisingly, a digital-to-analog converter, with another sample/hold circuit, is located in the CD player.)

The digital data from the two channels is multiplexed (mixed), and then processed with error-correction data, control and display information, and synchronization data. Finally, it is modulated in a unique binary format specifically designed for

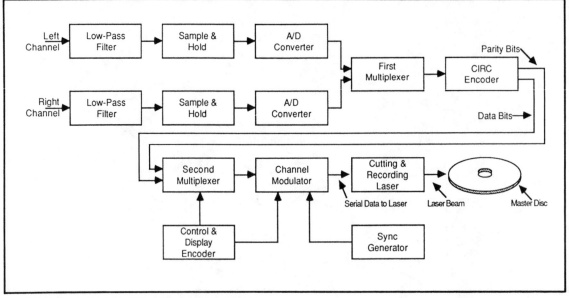

Fig. 1-7. A block diagram of the CD encoding system.

compact disc. The result is etched into a glass master disc by a laser.

The Road From Analog to Digital

Let's take a closer look at the encoding process. After filtering, the analog signal of the music is broken down into two main ingredients by the sample and hold circuits and by the A/D converter. These two ingredients are time and amplitude.

The music changes over time, and the A/D converter examines the sound at regular, predetermined intervals. This process is known as *sampling*. The audio signal is sampled at 44.1 thousand cycles per second, or more commonly expressed as 44.1 kHz. Therefore, the smallest piece of music is only 1/44,100 of a second long.

The sampling process examines discrete moments in the audio signal. Does this mean that periods between these sampling points are missing, and the music in between is lost? No. The reason lies in the fact that the compact-disc system is designed to deliver sound over the entire human hearing range of approximately 5 Hz to 20 kHz. Neither humans—and hence CD players—care much about sound that occurs above 20 kHz.

In order to reproduce sound in the 5-Hz-to-20-kHz range, a sampling rate of 44.1 kHz was chosen. Why? The 44.1 kHz sampling rate is based on what's known as the *Nyquist Theorem*. This theorem states that no information will be lost if the original waveform is sampled at twice the highest desirable frequency. The 44.1 kHz sampling rate is twice the 20 kHz upper limit of the audio spectrum, and then some (the extra is reserved as a buffer). As a result, every possible frequency in the range of human hearing is captured in the sampling process.

As mentioned earlier, the A/D converter breaks the audio signal into two ingredients. We have discussed time. Now consider the other ingredient, *amplitude*. At any given moment, sound has a certain amplitude, or volume, and this volume is translated in the digital process as well. The conversion of volume into digital values is called *quantization*. The word may sound complex, but it's really a simple concept. Quantization determines the quantity—in this case volume—of any given sampling period.

Now refer to Fig. 1-8. For every sampling period, which is time, the A/D converter senses its relative volume level, which is amplitude. The con-

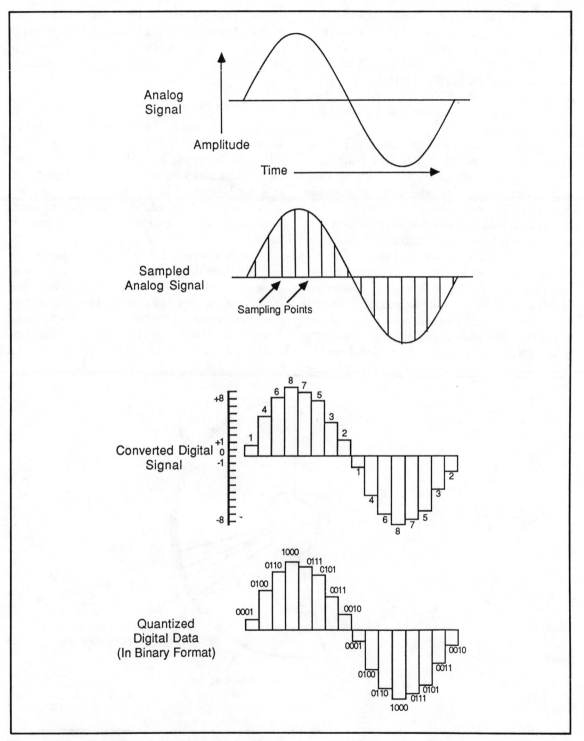

Fig. 1-8. Converting analog sound into digital signals.

verter assigns a digital number to each sampling point. For a compact disc, the number consists of 16 binary digits, something on the order of 1000110101110101. There are 65,536 different combinations of 1's and 0's in a 16-bit "word," so any sampling period can have any of 65,536 values. Figure 1-8 shows just the first four digits in a simplified 4-bit system.

You'll note that, unlike the sampling process, quantization does not yield all of the infinite variations in the amplitude of sound. An analog value of 99.2, for example, is rounded down to the nearest digit, or 99. An analog value of 99.6 is rounded up to 100. Realistically, the 65,536 values is more than enough for the human ear, which cannot discern between more than a few hundred volume levels.

With 16 bits of data for every sampling period, that makes for 705,600 bits of audio information in just one second of music! As you'll see, there is more than just audio information on a compact disc. Given this extra information, and a disc filled to the brim with 74 minutes of music, you'd find over 6.5 billion bits of digital data. In more concrete terms, such vast amounts of data roughly equals 10 copies of the Bible—New and Old Testaments combined! Imagine. All that just to play Benny Goodman.

More Than Music Bits

The music you hear on a compact disc actually accounts for only 32.7 percent of the bits on the disc. The remaining 67.3 percent is composed of modulation, parity, synchronization, merging, and subcode bits (see Fig. 1-9 for a more complete breakdown). All are added during the encoding process, before the disc is mastered and copies are made.

The synchronization, subcode, and parity bits are added to the music data to create discrete *frames*. The frame is the smallest block of data that the CD player manipulates at one time, and a filled disc contains some 34 million of them. Each frame, which holds a total of 588 bits when eventually encoded onto the disc (channel) bits, corresponds

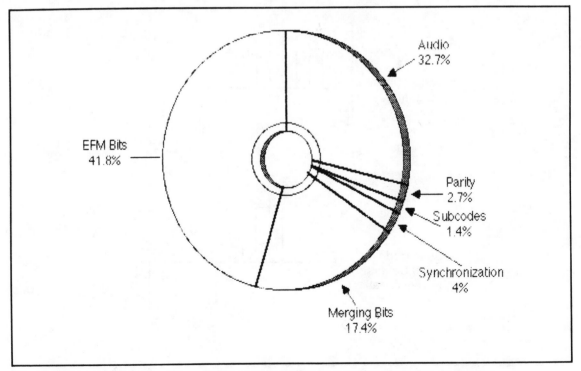

Fig. 1-9. The composition of the CD; audio bits account for only 32.7 percent of the data on the disc.

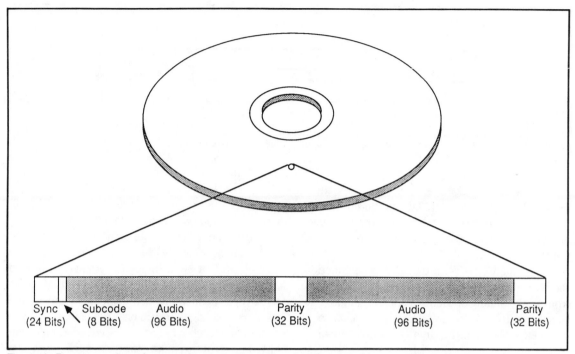

Sync (24 Bits)	Subcode (8 Bits)	Audio (96 Bits)	Parity (32 Bits)	Audio (96 Bits)	Parity (32 Bits)

Fig. 1-10. Frames consists of sync, subcode, audio, and parity bits, placed in a specific order.

in time to 136 μsec. Figure 1-10 shows a pictorial representation of the contents of each frame.

In some technical CD literature, the bits in the frame are sometimes referred to as *symbols*. A symbol is simply a set of eight bits. So, if you read that a certain piece of data contains four symbols, it means it is made up of 32 bits ($8 \times 4 = 32$). At the start of the frame is a pattern of 27 synchronization bits, specifically 100000000001000000000010. This series of uniquely arranged bits does not occur in any other part of the frame, and it tells the player that a new frame has begun. The synchronization bits are necessary so that the player can assign all of the other bits in the frame to their proper functions.

The following eight bits comprise subcode data, which provide useful information to the player and possibly the person operating the player. There are eight subcodes in all, and they are technically designated P through W. The P and Q subcodes, which are the only ones currently used, contain the following information:

☐ Lead-In and Lead-Out Signals. The lead-in signal is located just in front of where the signal area on the disc starts; the lead-out signal appears right after the end of the signal area. These two signals are used to control the movement of the optical pickup in the player.

☐ Table of Contents. Written in the lead-in area is the time information on control codes, including the start time of each selection on the disc as well as the total number and playing time of selections.

☐ Control Codes. These codes distinguish between 2-channel and 4-channel recording. The codes can also be used to indicate if a particular recording was made with preemphasis. In most players, the preemphasis circuitry is automatically switched on when preemphasis is required. Additionally, the codes can be used to change the circuit connections inside the player, if the machine is so designed. Presently, no players are engineered in this fashion.

☐ Music Start Flag. The music start flag is provided in the blank space between selections. By counting this flag, the player can locate any desired

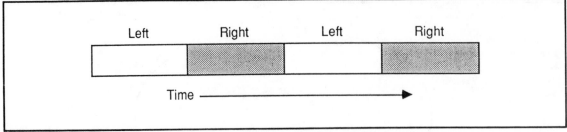

Left　　　　　　Right　　　　　　Left　　　　　　Right

Time ————————————————————————————————————▶

Fig. 1-11. The right and left stereo channels are encoded on the disc one after the other.

selection on the disc.

☐ Track Number and Index. Selections recorded on the disc can be numbered from 1 through 99. These are tracks. Each bar in a piece of music can also be addressed from 1 to 99. These are index points.

☐ Time Code. With the time code function, the player can process and display the time lapse from the beginning of each selection in minutes, seconds, and 1/75 of a second. During the blank space between selections, the time is counted down.

The remaining subcodes aren't used in most discs and players, but can hold a variety of information. A number of CD manufacturers currently make players with separate data outputs for processing the extra six bits of subcode data. More players with this feature are on the way. This subcode data can include things such as album liner notes, sheet music, color photographs, and more.

An entire video picture can be created by collecting only five seconds worth of subcode data (that's the equivalent of approximately 20,000 to 30,000 audio frames). After the data has been collected, the picture is displayed on a suitable monitor, and the information for another frame is slowly gathered. One compact disc can hold up to 700 still pictures, in addition to the 74 minutes of audio data.

After the subcode data comes 96 bits of audio information. These 96 bits are broken down into 12 "blocks" of eight bits each. As shown in Fig. 1-11, the first eight bits comprise the audio for the left stereo channel, the next eight bits comprise the audio for the right stereo channel, and so on. Because the stereo information is encoded individually, one right after the other, channel separation on CD players is theoretically 90 dB or better. Unlike turntables, cassette decks, and FM tuners, you'll hardly ever hear crosstalk between the two stereo channels.

The compact disc system includes a sophisticated error-correction system that uses parity checking. Simply stated, parity data is mathematical "totals" that the player uses to determine if any music information has been lost. Should information indeed be missing, the parity data is used by the player to reconstruct the loss.

You can more readily understand how parity

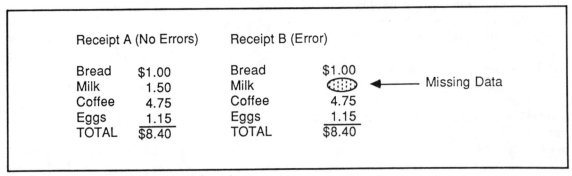

Fig. 1-12. Parity data reconstructs lost information.

works by referring to Fig. 1-12. Imagine the music recorded on the disc as grocery receipts. Each item has a specified price, and the prices are totaled. The prices themselves are like the audio data; the totals are like the parity data. In Receipt A, there are no errors, and the total data is not used by the player. In Receipt B, one of the prices is missing, but it can be retrieved by examining the total. By applying some simple arithmetic, it's possible to calculate the exact price of the missing value (in this case $1.50).

Two sets of parity data are added to each frame of audio. The first parity set, called P (not to be confused with the P subcode), is used to detect and correct errors due to lost data. The other set of parity bits, labeled Q, allows a player to determine whether an error has occured. The Q parity bits serve the same general purpose as the parity bits used in computer telecommunications.

Interleaving

The use of parity bits is only one of the error correction schemes used in the compact disc system, the other is *interleaving*. This technique is based on the Cross-Interleave Reed-Solomon Code, or CIRC, and is performed to the entire frame of synchronization, subcode, audio, and parity information.

With CIRC, the bits of audio information are scattered among several different frames—sort of like shuffling a deck of cards. However, the scattering is not random but follows a set of strict rules. Circuitry in the player knows how to decode the interleaved data and place the bits back into their proper sequence. With interleaving throughout many frames, there is much less chance of losing a large chunk of data.

Figure 1-13 illustrates the interleaving process and how errors can be more readily concealed. Without interleaving, a dropout (from a smudge, speck of dirt, scratch, etc.) might cause a very large, contiguous piece of audio data to be lost. The result of this lost data is an audible error—a click or pop—during playback. With interleaving, the data is jumbled so that a dropout affects noncontiguous bits of encoded audio data. When re-interleaved,

the player can better approximate, through a process known as interpolation, the smaller portions of lost information. The result is that most errors due to data dropouts are completely concealed.

Encoding the Data

With the synchronization, subcode, audio, and parity data assembled in frames—and interleaved to minimize audio errors in playback—it is modulated to create a unique 14-bit code (Fig. 1-14). Despite the addition of more bits, this 14-bit code actually saves space on the compact disc. Without EFM, the compact disc would hold roughly 25 percent less music.

The 14-bit code is called EFM, which stands for Eight-to-Fourteen Modulation. With it, every eight bits of frame data is converted to 14 brand new bits.

Because of the way the pits and lands on the disc represent binary 1's and 0's, three merging bits are added between each set of 14 EFM bits. With the merging bits added, there is never an instance when there is more than one binary 1 for every three bits of data. Similar, the EFM process assures that there is a binary 1 for at least every 11 bits. This is also required because of the way the data is etched on the disc by the laser.

During playback of a disc, the CD player strips off the merging bits, demodulates the data, and separates the subcode, data, and error correction information using the synchronization bits. Once separated, the sync bits are tossed aside. Table 1-2 compares data bits (used in the actual reprocessing of the audio signal) and the channel bits, which comprise the data encoded on the disc.

MAKING THE DISC

With the audio data fully encoded, it is finally ready to be made into a compact disc (whew!).

Cutting the Master

The first step in the disc-making process is to create the metal master. This process is shown in Fig. 1-15. This is done by taking a very smooth and highly polished glass plate and coating it with plas-

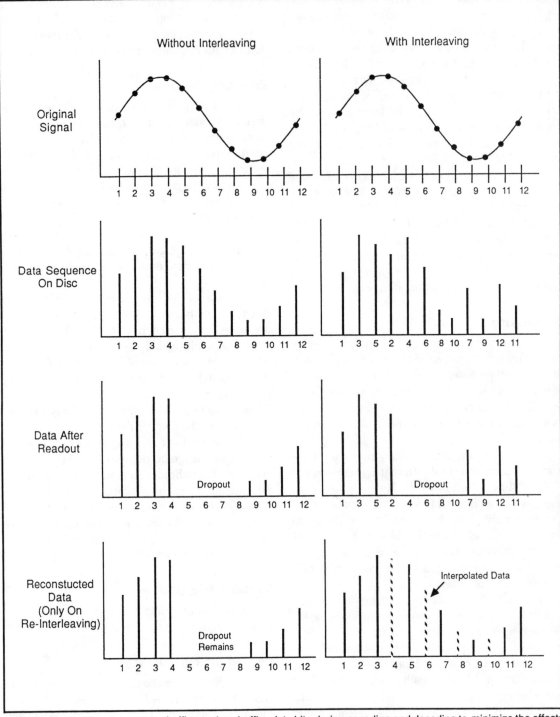

Fig. 1-13. The interleaving system shuffles and unshuffles data bits during encoding and decoding to minimize the effects of dropouts.

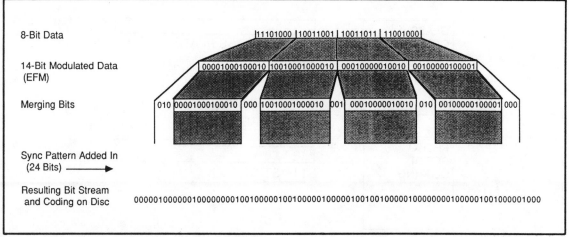

Fig. 1-14. The Eight-to-Fourteen encoding process, with merging and synchronization bits added to the mix.

tic on one side and photo resist on the other. The plastic acts to protect the glass disc, and the photo resist creates a light sensitive layer.

The coated disc is placed on the cutting rig (sometimes called the optical lathe). A turntable spins the disc while a precision laser exposes portions of the photo resist. The laser light is modulated by the encoded digital data. After exposure to the laser light, the disc is developed. Pits are formed where the laser was turned on.

Contrary to popular belief, the pits do not represent binary 1's and the lands binary 0's. Rather, a binary 1 occurs at every pit/land and land/pit transition. Everything else is a binary 0. Figure 1-16 graphically shows this.

This encoding process is infinitely more workable that using pits and lands to separately represent 1's and 0's. It is also why the audio data is converted to EFM format and why merging bits are added. The EFM/merging bit process ensures that there will never be a pit shorter than the time it takes to encode three binary digits, and no longer than 11 binary digits. You'll sometimes see the CD data encoding format expressed as 3T-11T, with the letter "T" meaning time intervals (one time interval is equal to one bit).

After the master has been developed, it is silvered, and then nickel plated. The metal master is now complete, and is carefully inspected to ensure that there are no surface blemishes.

Duplicating Discs

The metal master is used to make an intermediate master or "mother." The mother is then used to make the stampers. It is the stampers that create the distribution copies that are purchased in record stores. See Fig. 1-17.

Table 1-2. Frame Format.

	Data Bits	Channel Bits
Sync bits		24
Control/indication bits	$1 \times 8 = 8$	$1 \times 14 = 14$
Data bits	$12 \times 2 \times 8 = 192$	$12 \times 2 \times 14 = 336$
Error correction bits	$4 \times 2 \times 8 = 64$	$4 \times 2 \times 14 = 112$
Merging bits		$32 \times 3 = 102$
Total	261	588

15

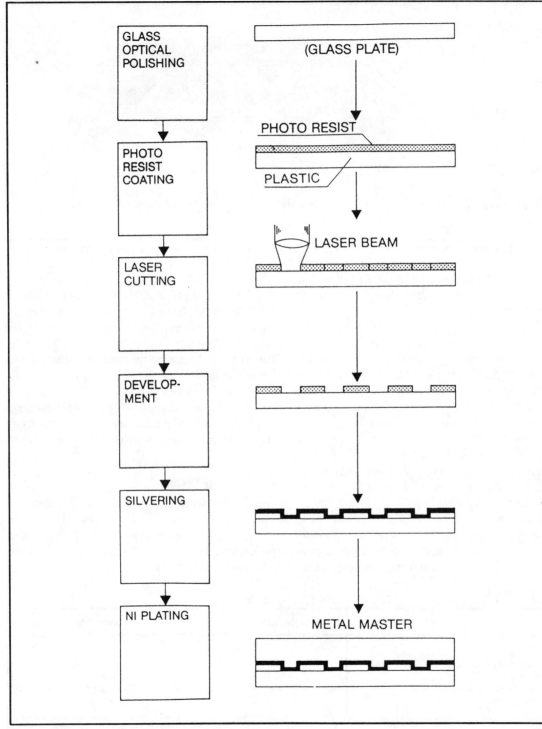

Fig. 1-15. Cutting a disc—from the glass plate to the metal master.

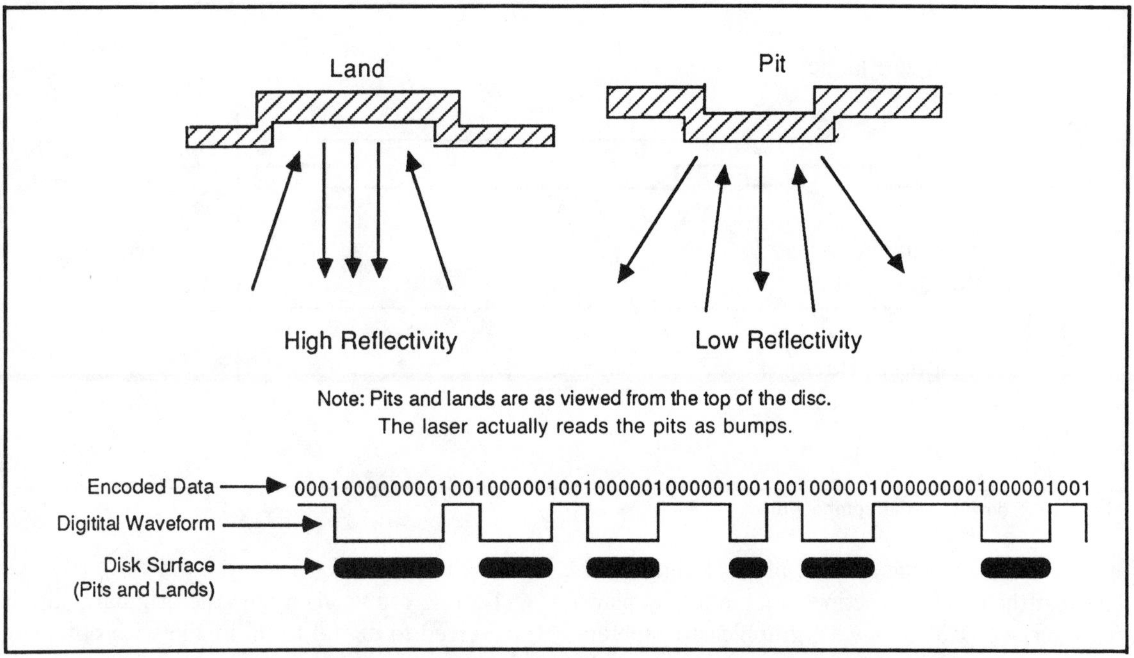
Land
Pit
High Reflectivity
Low Reflectivity
Note: Pits and lands are as viewed from the top of the disc.
The laser actually reads the pits as bumps.
Encoded Data
00010000000001001000001001000001000001001001000001000000001000001001
Digitital Waveform
Disk Surface
(Pits and Lands)

Fig. 1-16. The transitions between pits and lands represent binary 1; everything else represents binary 0.

A stamped disc, called the signal layer, is nothing more than a thin 0.1 μm sheet of aluminum, coated with plastic on the top and bottom. The bottom coating is about 1.1mm thick and serves as the medium through which the laser in the player reads the aluminum stamping (Fig. 1-18). The top coating is much thinner—on the order of 10 to 20 μm.

Imperfections such as bubbles in the bottom plastic coating can cause data dropouts. If the imperfection is large enough, the resultant data error can be heard as a click or pop. A very serious defect makes the player skip, just like an LP record. But fortunately, such audible defects are rather rare.

At the surface of the disc, the beam from the laser in the player is about 1mm in diameter. By the time the beam reaches the aluminum stamping, it has been reduced to 0.8 μm in size. A 1mm bubble near the surface of the disc is actually only a millionth in size on the signal surface—about the same as one or two pits. That's not nearly enough to cause any serious trouble to the player.

Additionally, the parity and CIRC error correction schemes used in the compact disc system can

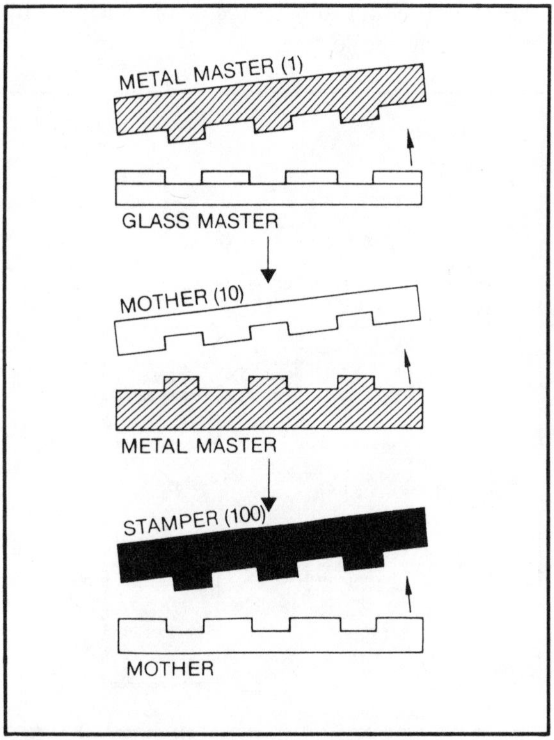
METAL MASTER (1)
GLASS MASTER
MOTHER (10)
METAL MASTER
STAMPER (100)
MOTHER

Fig. 1-17. Duplicating discs with intermediate stampers.

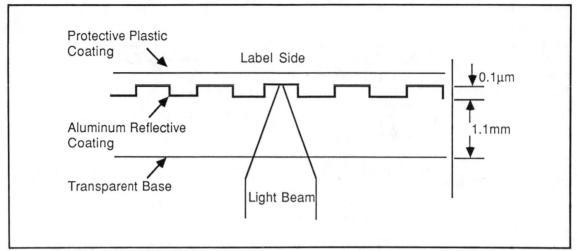

Fig. 1-18. Sideview of the compact disc.

handle errors as large as 3584 bits at a time. You can test the error correction capabilities by placing a piece of 1/32-inch-wide graphics art tape on the bottom of the disc. The tape acts to totally block out data, but the effects can't be heard on playback. The error is either fully corrected or concealed by interpolating the lost data.

DISC PLAYBACK

So far, you've seen how the original audio is transferred to digital form, mixed with other important pieces of data, and used to make a master disc and subsequent copies. To complete the picture, we resume our brief discussion on how the sound is recreated in the compact disc player.

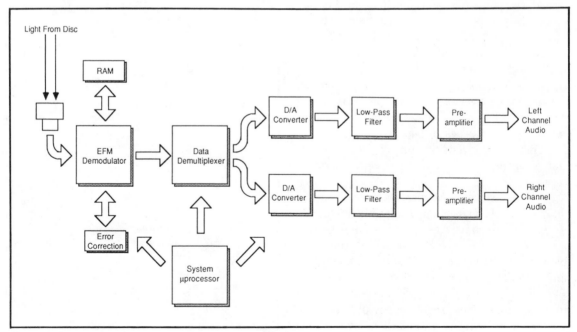

Fig. 1-19. Basic block of the main circuit blocks in a CD player.

Data Conversion

You already know that a laser is used to shine a beam of light on the disc, and that the pits and lands make the reflected beam flash on and off into a photodetector. At the photodetector, the light beam is converted into a high frequency signal.

The signal is first routed to an EFM decoder (as shown in Fig. 1-19) where the merging bits are stripped off, and the 14 bits of data are reduced back to their original 8 bit-at-a-time form. The process is controlled by a system microprocessor—a computer on a chip. The microprocessor is connected to most of the other systems on the player as well, so that everything is timed to ensure proper decoding and playback.

The player then processes the data by looking for the synchronization bits that occur at the beginning of each frame. The subcode bits are read and stored in random access memory (RAM), and the audio data is collected for processing. If a dropout or loss of signal is detected, the parity bits are used to recreate the lost information, if possible.

From here, the design of many compact disc players vary greatly, but here is one method of converting the digital data to analog sound (other methods are covered in greater detail in Chapter 2). The audio bits are first sent to a demultiplexer circuit that separates the one stream of digital data into the two stereo channels.

The audio bits are applied to a pair of digital-to-analog (D/A) converters (sometimes built into one integrated circuit). It is in the D/A converters that the digital data is transformed back into the original analog music. The D/A converter duplicates the process performed by the A/D converter prior to making the disc, but in reverse order. The D/A converter in the player samples the digital data at the 44.1 kHz rate, taking in 16 bits at a time. The numeric value of the 16 bits is translated into amplitude, corresponding to the original value of the music.

The signal coming out of the D/A converter is sound, but it is not yet very pleasing to the ear. The sampling process introduces strong voltage spikes, which are audible. These are removed by a low-pass filter. The filter chops off frequencies beyond the audible range of 20 kHz (this is an analog filter; digital filters are covered in Chapter 2). The output of the filter is connected to a low-power preamplifier. The preamp boosts the audio signal to a level that can be better handled by the amplifier in your stereo system.

THREE KINDS OF PLAYERS

There are three general kinds of compact disc players on the market today: ac operated home models, portable models, and car models. Examples of each are shown in Figs. 1-20 through 1-22.

Home CDs

Ac operated home models represent the largest

Fig. 1-20. A typical front loading ac operated home player.

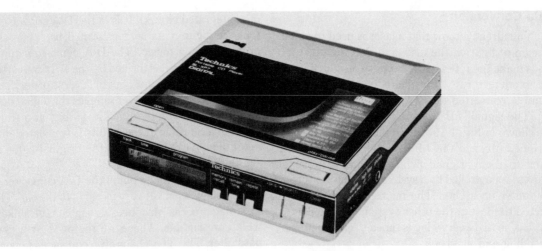

Fig. 1-21. Battery-powered portable players let you listen to discs while on the go.

group of CD players, and are the most diverse. Home models can be further divided into top loaders and front loaders. There are two forms of front loading mechanisms—drawer and door (more about these in Chapter 2). A few home models have automatic disc changers. You load from five to 60

Fig. 1-22. This automotive CD player fits in the trunk and holds up to 10 discs. You control it from inside your car.

(yes, sixty) discs and play some or all of them.

Portable CDs

Portable models are designed for on-the-go listening, and although most come with an ac adapter, they are specifically designed for battery operation. With some models, the batteries are an integral part of the player; with most others, the batteries are included in a special case. To use the player as a portable, you place it in the carrying case, where electrical contact to the batteries is made. You listen to the player through a set of stereo headphones.

Car CDs

Car CD players are gaining in popularity. Most models are now sold with an integral AM/FM stereo, although you can buy a stand-alone CD player for use with your existing tape deck. A player for use in a car lacks an amplifier. You need to connect it to an amp to listen to the sound.

With most car CDs, you load the disc manually into a slot in the front of the player. As with the high-end home players, a few models for the road have automatic disc changers. The whole contraption fits in your trunk, out of sight. You can select the specific disc and track you want to listen to by pushing buttons on a wired remote control.

Chapter 2

How CD Players Work

Joining the ranks of great expressions such as "The check is in the mail," and "We service what we sell," is "All compact disc players are alike." The statement simply isn't true. In fact, no two CD player models are designed or manufactured exactly the same. That means the music one player reproduces might sound considerably different than the sound from another.

While it is true that the digital nature of compact disc helps ensure a kind of mass standardization among CD players, the standardization does not inhibit technological advances in player design. Compact disc players differ greatly in the way they retrieve information from the disc, process it, and reconstitute it into analog sound. For a full appreciation of the compact disc medium, and to better understand the varied mechanics of player design and maintenance, read this chapter on how CD players work.

DISC LOADING

Outwardly, CD players differ the most in their method of disc loading.

Home Players

The ac-operated home players can be either front or top loading. Top loading CDs are the simplest of the bunch. You just open the top door, like the hood of a car, slip the disc in, push the door closed, and start the disc. On a mechanical level, the simplicity of the design means there is no disc loading mechanism to foul up so less can go wrong. On a purely ergonomic level, top loaders are not generally as desirable as front loaders because you can't stack the player in with your other hi-fi gear.

Front loading players are either the drawer or door variety. The drawer loading type is shown in Fig. 2-1. Both use internal motors to open a sliding tray or receptacle for the disc. You insert the disc on the tray or receptacle, which then closes, automatically placing the disc into play position. Door loaders consist of a hinged door that pops down when you push the Open/Close switch, much like the loading door of a cassette deck. You slip the disc into the slot and shut the door Open/Close switch once again (on some models you manually

Fig. 2-1. The drawer-type front loading home CD players are currently the most popular design.

push the door closed). Inside, a clamping mechanism presses the disc against the spindle. The disc spins vertically.

Drawer loaders are a bit different. Pushing the Open/Close switch makes a tray-like drawer slide out of the player. You place the disc horizontally on the tray, then push the Open/Close switch again. A clamper pushes the disc down into the drive spindle during play. The disc spins horizontally.

While there is really no technical advantage to drawer loaders over door loaders, most current CD models are the former. A few door loading compact disc players still exist, but they are generally made with more mechanical parts and are harder to service.

A fourth type of home CD player is the changer. This is actually a subset of the drawer loading variety, but instead of inserting one disc at a time, you insert a special cartridge that holds five or more discs. You can play the discs individually by pushing the proper function buttons on the front panel of the player, or set the machine for continuous play.

Portable Players

All current portable players are considered top loaders, even though the playing mechanism may be located on the top front of the unit. With a portable CD, you push a button which releases a loading hatch. You manually lift the loading hatch and place the disc in the player. Press the hatch back down and press Play. A typical portable CD is shown in Fig. 2-2.

Car Players

Car players are front loaders, but they don't

Fig. 2-2. Portable CDs are considered top loaders.

employ the use of drawers or doors. With one type of car player you insert the disc into a wide slot in the front of the unit. Internally, the player grasps the disc and pulls it into play position. A clamper keeps the disc snugly against the drive spindle. After playing, the unit ejects the disc, you remove it from the slot and return it to its jewel storage box.

With the other type of car player, you first place the CD in a special cartridge and insert the cartridge into the player. Manufacturers of players that use cartridges claim there is less chance of damage to the disc, but you must spend extra for the cartridges. Some cartridge-load car CD players can accept up to 10 discs at a time. You select the disc you want to hear by pressing a wired remote control.

PICKUP TECHNIQUES

Compact disc players vary the greatest in ways

that you can't see. To begin, there are two general designs for the optical assembly, which contains the laser diode, the photodetectors, and all the associated optics for relaying the beam from the laser to the photodetectors. The whole assembly is generally referred to simply as the optical pickup, or just pickup. The two types of pickups are the 1-beam and the 3-beam. A cutaway view of the 3-beam type is shown in Fig. 2-3.

Contrary to what you may think, both types of pickups use only one laser. The difference lies in how the laser beam is split into smaller beams, and how the beams are manipulated within the pickup assembly. The 1-beam system was the first to come out, but most players use 3-beam pickups these days. There really is no technical advantage to the 3-beam system, at least not anything that can be proven.

With both systems, the pickup is mounted on a transport mechanism that moves it from the in-

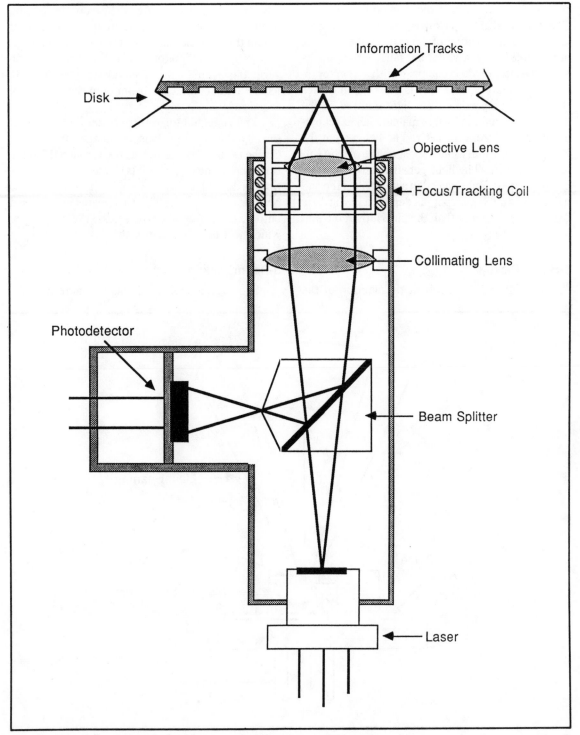

Fig. 2-3. A cutaway view of the optical pickup system in a typical CD player.

side of the disc towards the outside during play. The laser used in the pickup is a semiconductor device with a light output of 3-5 mW—not enough to burn a hole in Darth Vader but fairly strong for its size. The laser diode is equipped with a monitor diode, shown in Fig. 2-4. This is a detection device that receives a portion of the light emitted by the laser. The monitor is used to maintain an exact output light level from the laser. The beam from the laser is about 1 mm as measured on the plastic surface of the disc. The light penetrates through the plastic coating, and reduced in size, strikes the signal layer as a 0.8 μm spot, as depicted in Fig. 2-5. This is slightly wider than the pit width of 0.5 μm.

1-beam pickup system. At the heart of the 1-beam pickup is the laser diode. Its light is reflected off a semi-transparent mirror, where the beam bounces up through a collimator. The collimator acts to diverge the beam—make all its rays parallel. The objective lens focuses the beam onto the surface of the disc.

The reflected (or return) beam bounces back through the objective lens, collimator, and mirror. On the return trip, the beam goes through the semi-transparent mirror, where is strikes against an optical wedge. This curious form of lens splits the one beam into two parts. The two beams are focused onto a set of four photodetectors, the purpose of which will be discussed in the next section.

1-Beam Pickup

See Fig. 2-6 for a schematic diagram of the

3-Beam Pickup

See Fig. 2-7 for a schematic diagram of the

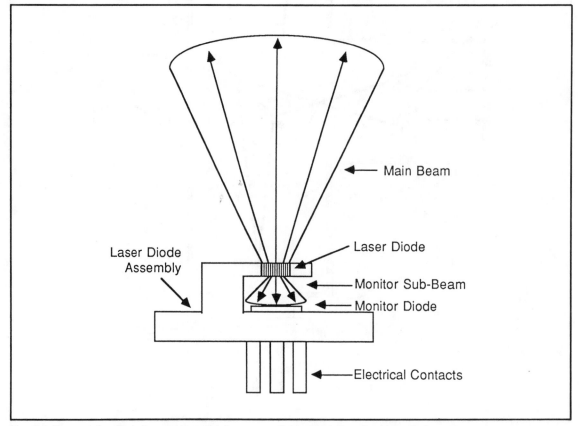

Fig. 2-4. The monitor diode is used to maintain an even light output from the laser diode.

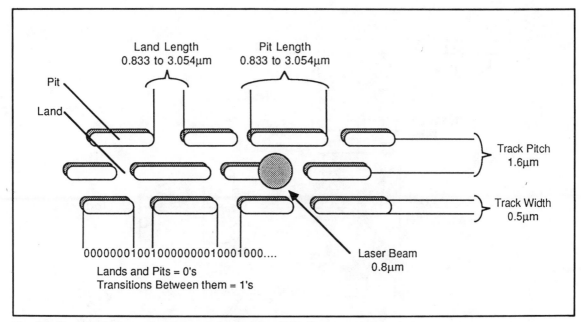

Fig. 2-5. The laser beam as it appears on the surface of the disc.

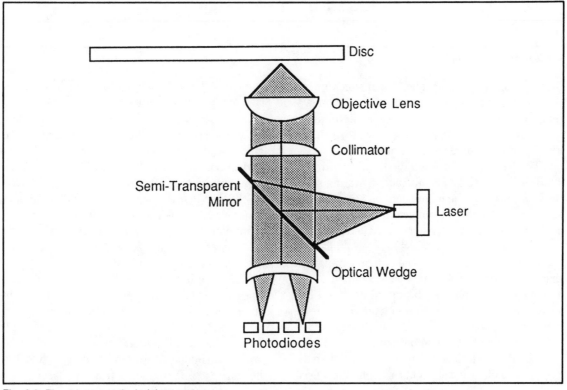

Fig. 2-6. The 1-beam optical pickup system.

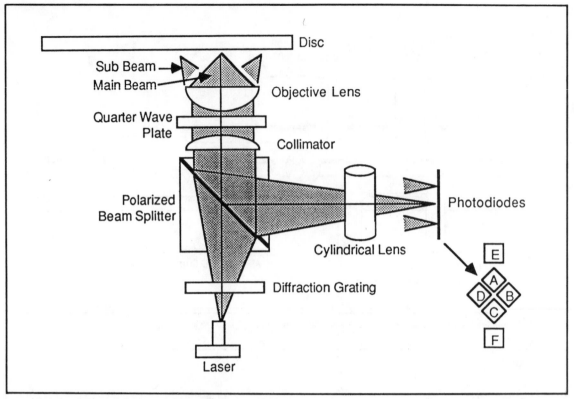

Fig. 2-7. The 3-beam optical pickup system.

3-beam pickup system. The 3-beam pickup has some of the same components as the 1-beam system, but is more complex. It necessarily requires a little more explanation, but it is well worth it— it's the most common system in use today.

The beam from the laser diode shines through a diffraction grating. The diffraction grating splits the light, making one main beam and two smaller sub-beams. Additional sub-beams are also generated, but these are weak and not used in the system.

The three beams then pass through a polarized beam splitter. This is a special optical component that consists of two prisms with a common 45 degree face. The polarized beam splitter (or PBS) serves to pass the beam emitted from the laser diode to the signal surface of the disc, then direct the reflected beam to the photo diode.

The PBS is designed so that it *passes* light polarized in one direction straight through, but *reflects* light that is polarized in the other direction. For the

time being, the PBS passes the light from the laser diode straight through.

Prior to focusing the beams onto the disc, they are passed through a collimator and quarter wave plate, or QWP. The QWP component shifts the polarization of the laser light by 90 degrees. After going through the QWP, the beams are focused onto the disc by the objective lens. Three distinct beams appear on the disc: one main beam that's 0.8 μm in diameter, and two slightly smaller and weaker ones ahead and behind the main beam, as shown in Fig. 2-8.

The three beams are reflected off the surface of the disc, where again they pass through the objective lens and through the QWP. On the second time around, the QWP twists the light another 90 degrees. The light is now 180 degrees out of phase from the incoming beam, and is polarized in the other direction. If the beam from the laser diode is polarized horizontally, for example, passing the

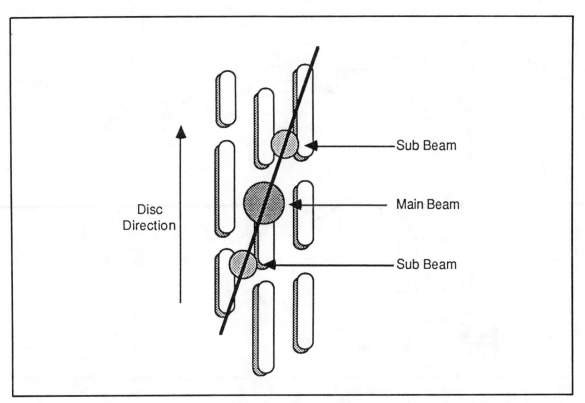

Fig. 2-8. The three beam system projects one large spot and two smaller spots on the surface of the disc.

light through the QWP twice polarizes the light vertically. The polarized beam splitter reflects the vertically polarized light to the photodetector section of the pickup.

Once through the PBS, the beams are passed through a cylindrical lens. This kind of lens magnifies or reduces an image in one plane only. It's the same kind of lens used in movie cameras and projectors to make wide screen pictures. The main beam falls on a set of four photodetectors; the two sub-beams fall on detectors of their own. The multiple role of these photodetectors is discussed in the next section.

FOCUSING AND TRACKING SYSTEMS

Directly linked to the pickup system is the way the compact disc player tracks the information pits on the disc, and at the same time keeps the laser beam in perfect focus. Again, the discussion will be divided between 1-beam and 3-beam systems.

Tracking and focusing systems are critical to compact disc player design, because of the small tolerances involved. The extremely narrow pitch of the information track is much like a tightrope to a circus performer. In a compact disc, the information track pitch is only 1.6 μm, several hundred times smaller than the wobble that's present in all discs! Focusing is just as critical, with an equally small room for error. The laser pickup has a depth of focus of only $\pm$ 2 μm. Yet discs commonly deviate as much as $\pm$ 0.6mm because of warpage.

1-Beam Tracking/Focusing

See Fig. 2-9 for a schematic diagram of the 1-beam focusing/tracking system. As discussed above, the return laser light from the disc is split into two beams by the optical wedge. The two beams fall on a set of four photodetectors, which serve a three-part purpose:

☐ The photodetectors sense the on-off high

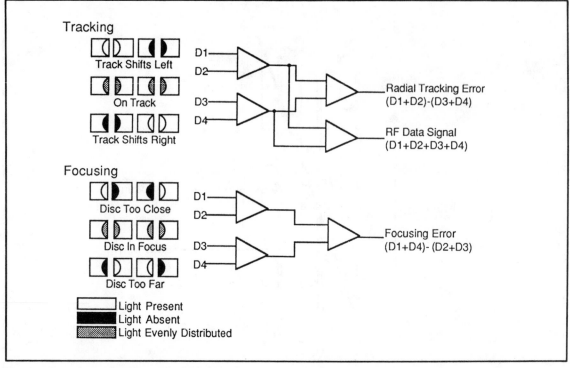

Fig. 2-9. The 1-beam focusing and tracking system.

frequency EFM signal from the disc, and pass it along to the player's circuits for decoding into music.

☐ The photodetectors sense when the laser beam wanders off the track, and provides an error signal so that the tracking control circuits can keep the beam on target.

☐ The photodetectors sense when the laser beam goes out of focus in relation to the disc surface, and provides an error signal so that the error control circuits can keep the beam in focus.

All four photodetectors work in tandem to generate the high frequency data signal that the player uses to make music. As designed, it doesn't matter if all the laser light falls on one detector or evenly on all of them. The player still receives the data signal.

For tracking control, the two light beams coming from the optical wedge are evenly distributed if the laser is precisely following the information

tracks. If the laser beam wanders off to the right of the spiral of pits, too much light reaches the rightmost two diodes. The player detects this and advances the pickup to the left. The reverse occurs if the laser beam wanders off to the right of the information tracks.

Focusing is handled in a similar manner. When the disc is too close to the objective lens, the two light beams traveling through the wedge move closer together, thanks to an optical phenomenon first observed by J.B.L. Foucault in the 1850's. The two inner diodes get the bulk of the light intensity, and the player corrects this by moving the objective lens down, and away from the disc. The reverse occurs when the disc is too far away from the objective.

3-Beam Pickup

See Fig. 2-10 for a schematic diagram of the 3-beam focusing/tracking system. As you will recall, the 3-beam pickup employs six photodetectors.

The main set of four photodetectors serve double duty, and are usually referred to as A, B, C, and D:

☐ The photodetectors sense the on-off high frequency EFM signal from the disc, and pass it along to the player's circuits for decoding into music.

☐ The photodetectors sense when the laser beam goes out of focus in relation to the disc surface, and provides an error signal so that the error control circuits can keep the beam in focus.

The remaining two photodetectors, labeled E and F, are for tracking control. If the laser beam begins to veer off the information tracks, as shown in Fig. 2-11, the detectors provide an error signal so that the error control circuits can keep the beam on target.

All four photodetectors (A, B, C, and D) work in tandem to generate the high frequency data signal that the player uses to make music. As designed, it doesn't matter how much laser light falls on the individual detectors, the player still receives the data signal.

For focusing, the cylindrical lens forms an oval on the four detectors when there is a focus error. If the oval predominantly touches the A and C detectors, for example, the disc is too close to the objective lens. The detectors generate an error signal that causes the player to move the lens further away from the disc. If the oval predominantly touches the B and D detectors, the disc is too far, and the player works to correct it. If the light makes a circle, it touches all four detectors evenly, and the disc is in focus.

The tracking control is a bit more involved. The two sub-beams strike the E and F photodetectors. If tracking if off, the light reaching the detectors is uneven, and the detectors generate an error voltage that the player uses to keep the beam on track. For example, if the beam wanders off to the right, the F detector receives more light, and the player responds by inching the pickup to the right to correct for the error.

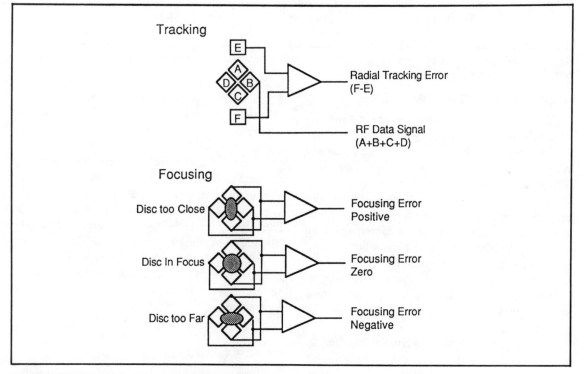

Fig. 2-10. The 3-beam focusing and tracking system.

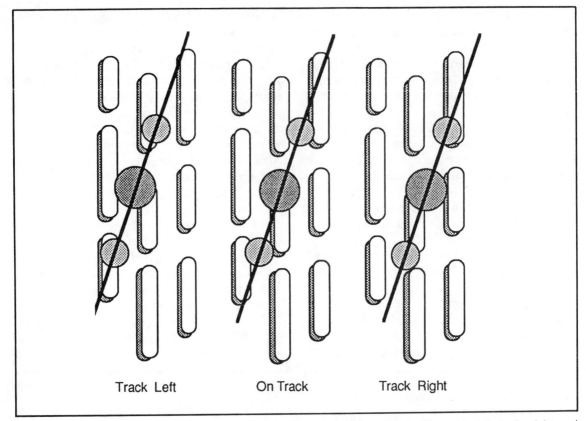

Track Left   On Track   Track Right

Fig. 2-11. The appearance of the laser spots in a 3-beam system, on a disc when tracking to the left, to the right, and evenly down the track.

FOCUSING AND TRACKING COILS

The pickup is mounted on a transport mechanism, which moves it radially along the disc surface. As the disc is played, the pickup slowly moves from the inside of the disc to the outside. The transport is powered by a single motor.

The transport motor is not used for maintaining proper focus and tracking. Tracking and focus correction require changes on an extremely small scale that the transport motor cannot provide. As an example, the disc is considered out of focus if its distance from the objective lens changes by as little as ± 2 μm. Since all compact discs have some warpage, they all go out of focus several hundred times each revolution.

Tracking and focus correction is handled by precision coils. The tracking and focus coils in a CD player are much like the voice coils in a speaker.

A small amount of current creates a magnetic field. This field then moves the lens, which is mounted in a ferrous ring. When current is applied to the focus coils, the lens moves up and down. When current is applied to the tracking coils, the lens moves back and forth. With some players, the tracking coil is mounted to a mirror. The mirror shifts slightly from side to side when current is applied to the coil. The mirror directs the reflected beam to precisely follow the information track on the disc.

Figure 2-12 shows a closeup view of a 3-beam pickup equipped with a two axis *actuator*. This actuator has two voice coils, one for focus, the other for tracking.

PICKUP TRANSPORTS

There are two kinds of transport mechanisms

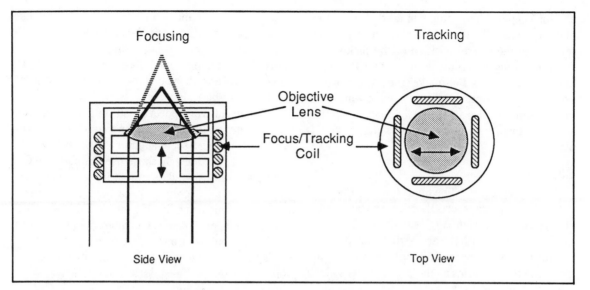

Fig. 2-12. The two-axis actuator moves the objective lens up and down and right to left.

used to move the pickup across the disc: swing arm and slide.

Swing Arm

Players with 1-beam pickups often use a sim-ple swing arm transport mechanism, shown in Fig. 2-13. The laser is mounted on one end of a low-inertia balanced arm. On the other end, at the pivot point, is a motor. This motor swings the arm, moving the pickup in an arc across the surface of the disc. The swing arm also incorporates a tracking

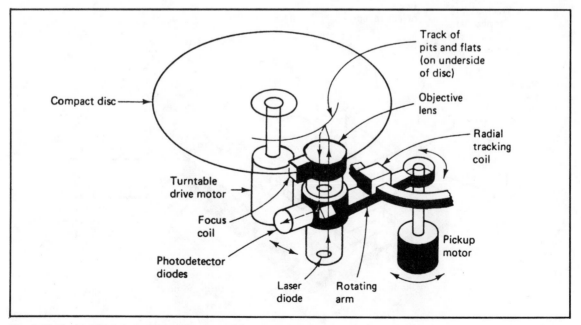

Fig. 2-13. A simplified view of the swing arm pickup transport.

coil for keeping the pickup centered on the information tracks. The tracking coil makes small corrections in the lateral position of the pickup.

With swing arm transports, the only true moving part is the pivot. This makes the swing arm system relatively immune to wear. Swing arm mechanisms are also small and lightweight, so they are ideal for use in portable and automotive CD player use.

Slide

The design of the 3-beam pickup can't be used with swing arm transports, because the beam must always be kept at right angles to the tracks on the disc (remember, with the arm swing transport, the pickup is swept across the disc in an arc, so the angle of the tracks varies as the pickup moves along the radius of the disc).

The 3-beam systems (Fig. 2-14) use a slide transport where the pickup is moved across the disc on a double-rail platform. The slide (sometimes called the sled) is perhaps the most common trans-

port used today, and is a favorite among Japanese CD player manufacturers. American and European manufacturers tend to favor the swing arm transport, but as more machines are designed with 3-beam pickups, the use of the swing arm transport will greatly be reduced.

Most slide transports consist of a motor-driven lead screw and matching gear that slowly moves the pickup along a set of alignment rails. A few slide transports, particularly those used in portable CD players, are designed as miniature linear motors. There is no lead screw and gear; rather, the transport mechanism is in itself a motor. Coils attached to the transport frame act as motor windings. The coils are mounted around a set of special laminated rails, which serve as the motor armatures. A second set of rails act as guides to keep the transport in proper alignment.

PROCESSING CIRCUITRY

The circuitry inside the player that processes

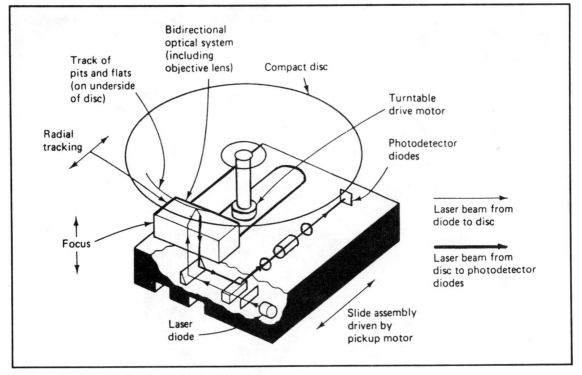

Fig. 2-14. A simplified view of the slide (or sled) pickup transport.

Fig. 2-15. VLSI chips play an important role in compact disc players.

the high frequency signal, insuring that all the music data is present—or if it isn't, correcting the missing information—comes in many forms. In some players, particularly the early models, these circuits are comprised of a large volume of off-the-shelf ICs and components.

The latest players incorporate LSI (Large Scale Integration) circuitry to greatly reduce the electronic components. LSI chips are custom designed integrated circuits that combine the functions of a number of ICs and other components.

A typical LSI chip used in CD players is shown in Fig. 2-15. It bristles with 80 pins and uses surface-mount technology. The pins aren't inserted into holes in the printed circuit board (PCB); rather the pins are soldered directly onto solder pads on the underside of the board. Surface-mount components, which also include such common items as di-

odes, resistors, capacitors, and transistors, are soldered onto the PCB using automated robot assembly equipment.

LSI chips are often used as building blocks in the design of the CD player, with each block being a complete circuit. The main building blocks in a CD player are the preamplifier, EFM demodulator, tracking and focus servo, system microprocessor, and D/A converter. In some players, these functions may be the domain of just one or two ICs; in others, the functions may spread among a half dozen or more integrated circuits.

The low parts count in the latest compact disc players reduces the chances of component failure, but it also makes servicing a real problem. The LSI chips are proprietary designs that are closely guarded by CD player manufacturers. You can't go to the neighborhood electronics store, for example, and pick up an extra EFM decoder. And since LSI chips can't be easily soldered and desoldered using manual soldering techniques, they are nearly impossible to replace if bad. Manufacturers recommended replacing the entire PCB if one of the LSI chips is defective. It may sound extreme, but it's often cheaper and easier to exchange the whole board than tediously replace the LSI chip.

A Closer Look at CD Player Circuits

The following is a brief rundown of the general purpose of the main building block circuits of the compact disc player, and how they work with one another. Refer to Fig. 2-16 for a block diagram of these circuits as used in a typical player.

Preamplifier

The preamplifier receives the signals from the photodetectors and amplifies them for use by the rest of the player. Amplified signals are sent to the system microprocessor, EFM decoder, and servo circuits.

EFM Demodulator

The EFM demodulator (also called the EFM decoder) decodes the high frequency EFM signal generated by the photodiodes and boosted by the preamplifier. The decoding process is performed in the reverse order as data encoding, described in detail in Chapter 1. Briefly, the EFM demodulator detects the synchronization bits that mark the beginning of each audio frame and strip the merging bits from the 14 bit code. The EFM signal is then reconverted to its original 8 bit digitized format.

In many players, the EFM demodulator also serves as the dropout error detector. If EFM data is lost due to a data dropout, the parity and CIRC correction circuits in the EFM decoder recreate or conceal the error.

The output of the EFM demodulator feeds into the D/A converter.

Tracking and Focus Servo

In both 1-beam and 3-beam systems, the photodetectors serve to capture the EFM signal for the

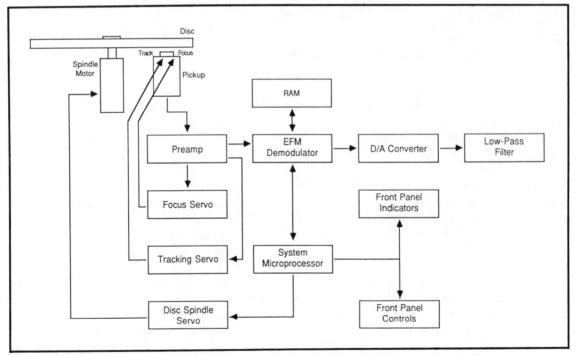

Fig. 2-16. The main blocks of the CD player. The system microprocessor maintains smooth operation.

EFM demodulator, and also to provide tracking and focus error signals for the tracking and focus servo. The signals from the photodetectors is first boosted by the preamplifier, then passed to the tracking and focus servo (which can be one circuit or separate circuits). The servo generates control voltages for operating the tracking and focus coils.

System Microprocessor

The system microprocessor assures that all the components in the compact disc player operate in tandem. The processor also serves as the communications link between the front panel controls and indicators, as well as player electronics.

On models with a programmable memory function, the system microprocessor accepts programming entry and stores it for execution. Advanced players employ electrical erasable programmable read only memory (EEPROM) for permanently storing "favorite selections" for retrieval at any time. The EEPROM retains its memory, even when the player is unplugged, until reprogrammed.

Support Electronics

All CD players are operated by a system clock running at 4.3218 MHz. The clock is governed by a quartz crystal oscillator for precise timing. Some players incorporate additional "sub clocks" for controlling different components. However, the recent trend is to design players with one master clock. The pulses from the clock are divided into other frequencies for use by the various components. The master clock prevents multiple clock pulses from interfering with proper D/A conversion.

CD players employ random access memory (RAM) for temporarily storing EFM data (the RAM can be built into the EFM demodulator). The function of the RAM is to act as a data reservoir during playback. It assures that the D/A converter receives a steady stream of data, even if the rate of data retrieved from the disc fluctuates. (Chapter 3 supplies more information on the function and operation of the RAM.)

A disc spindle servo and associated voltage controlled oscillator circuits keep the disc spinning at the proper speed. The disc spindle servo is under the control of the system microprocessor. If the disc begins to spin too fast, the microprocessor tells the servo to decrease the speed. Conversely, if the disc spins too slow, the microprocessor tells the servo to increase the speed.

The front panel controls and indicators let you command the player. Pushing a button on the panel command the microprocessor, which in turn decides how to act on your instruction. Some players have a separate microprocessor that handles just the front panel controls. This microprocessor works under the supervision of the system microprocessor. Playback information is shown on the front panel indicators.

D/A CONVERSION

The D/A converter is one of the most important electronic components of the compact disc system. As with the laser pick-up mechanism, players use a variety of D/A converter designs.

The overall function of the D/A converter is to take the 16 bits of digital data output by the EFM demodulator, sample the data, and provide an analog signal based on the value of the binary digits decoded from the disc.

It sounds simple enough but there is a flaw in the basic design of all D/A converters, one that has the potential to ruin the sound of the CD player. The sampling circuit in the D/A converter creates a voltage spike at each sampling interval, as depicted in Fig. 2-17A. This isn't desirable by any means, and it isn't music, so the D/A converter includes another internal component called the hold circuit. The hold circuit maintains the voltage level of the sample until the next sampling period. As shown in Fig. 2-17B, the result is a stairstep-shaped wave, which follows the contours of the analog output.

Significant frequency components, or harmonics, of the original sampling spikes still remain, despite the smoothing action of the hold circuit. These harmonics are particularly strong in the 25 to 44 kHz range, but continue on up the frequency spectrum to infinity. The harmonics are centered around multiples of the sampling frequency. That

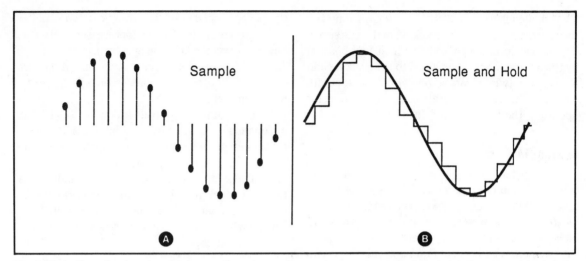

Fig. 2-17. A. Sampling introduces voltage spikes. B. A hold circuit maintains the voltage level of each sample until the next one arrives, to help reduce the spikes.

is, there is a series of harmonics centered around 44.1 kHz, 88.2 kHz, 132.3 kHz, and so forth.

Most of the frequencies are inaudible (called "out-of-band"). But some harmonics can extend into the normal hearing range, or at least affect those frequencies that we can pick up with our ears. A filter, either built into the D/A converter or added just prior to the audio preamp in the player, blocks unwanted frequencies above 20 kHz.

There are two general types of D/A converters in common use in CD players—normal sampling and oversampling—and they use different kinds of filtering techniques. Let's take a look at each one below.

Normal Sampling

The typical D/A converter, using normal sam-

pling, examines the data originally encoded on the disc at the CD standard of 44.1 kHz (see Fig. 2-18). The sample and hold circuit(s) in the D/A converter samples each 16 bit word from the EFM decoder and holds it until the next sampling period. As explained above, the sampling spikes are partially supressed by the hold circuits in the D/A converter as the waveform is converted to its blocky stairstep shape.

The spikes are further reduced by the addition of a low-pass filter at the analog output of the D/A converter. The low-pass filter is a necessary component of the normal sampling D/A converter. When used with just a low-pass filter, the player is said to have analog filtering.

Figure 2-19 shows a simplified block diagram of the signal path from the EFM demodulator to

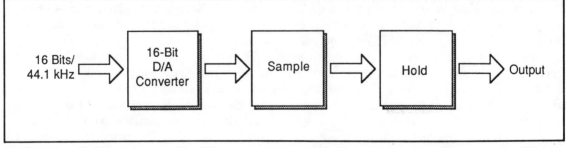

Fig. 2-18. Simplified block diagram of the D/A converter and sample/hold circuits in a player that uses analog filtering.

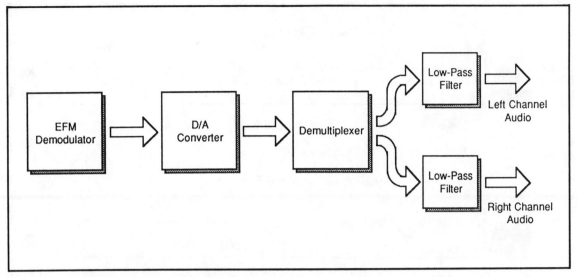

Fig. 2-19. Simplified block diagram of analog filtering.

the stereo low-pass filters. In this diagram, the converted analog signal is passed through a demultiplexer, a fast acting electronic switch that alternates the right and left stereo information into the two channels.

The design of the low-pass filter is an important one, and it determines the overall frequency response of the player. The filter is designed to leave frequencies below 20 kHz untouched, but supress everything above it. To obtain such a sharp dropoff, the filter is designed as a type of electronic brick wall.

Try as they might, however, engineers cannot make an analog filter that chops off all frequencies above 20 kHz, without affecting at least some of the frequencies below. The response curve of most analog filters employed in CD players starts to drop 0.5 dB or so after 16 or 17 kHz, then fall dramatically to 1 dB or more as it approaches 20 kHz.

To be effective, the filter must totally supress all frequencies at or above 25 kHz, where the sampling frequency components are their strongest. Figure 2-20A illustrates the action of the analog filter. The black portion is the range (or "pass") of the filter. Note the slope of the filter as it approaches 25 kHz. The harmonics of the sampling spikes still remain, centered at 44.1, 88.2, 132.3, 176.4, 220.5 kHz, and so on.

Oversampling

One solution to the problem of sampling spikes and steep filter cutoff is oversampling. With this technique, sampling spikes are effectively removed in the frequency range spanning from 25 kHz up to the oversampling frequency, which is usually 88.2 kHz or 176.4 kHz (see Fig. 2-20B). Oversampling is often referred to as digital filtering, because the sampling spikes are suppressed digitally, before they are converted to analog form.

Here's how oversampling works: Instead of sampling the incoming data 16 bits at a time every 44.1 kHz, the digital data is multiplied two times or four times—to 88.2 kHz or 176.4 kHz, as shown in Fig. 2-21. Most D/A converters in present day compact disc players oversample four times. With 4X oversampling, for example, the noise power originally confined to a band from 0 Hz to 22 kHz is now spread out over a band four times as wide, or 0 Hz or 88 kHz. So the sampling spikes are only one quarter their original strength. A digital noise filter built into the D/A converter acts to limit the sampling spikes even more.

Sampling noise still occurs, but the bulk of it is confined to a region around the oversampling rate, well out-of-band. Here, conventional low-pass analog filtration, when used at all, can easily remove the harmonics from the sampling spikes.

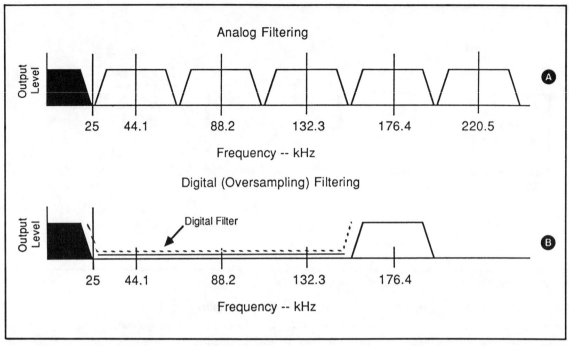

Fig. 2-20. A. Analog filtering does not reduce the voltage transients above 20 kHz but attempts to block them. B. Digital filtering reduces and blocks voltage transients beyond 20 kHz.

Figure 2-22 shows a simplified block diagram of the signal path from the EFM demodulator to the stereo channel low-pass filters. In this diagram, the digital filter is the portion of the circuit that oversamples the incoming data. It is then separated into in its right and left stereo components, and passed through separate D/A converters.

14 Bit Vs. 16 Bit

The first oversampling systems, developed by Philips, used a 14 bit D/A converter that simplified the digital filtering components, but still maintaining a reasonably high dynamic range of 84 dB or greater (the theoretical dynamic range of compact disc players, which is determined by the number of bits in the quantized sample, is 96 dB or greater).

In this system, the 16 bit/44.1 kHz data from the EFM demodulator is passed through a digital oversampling filter. It comes out as 28 bits sampled at 176.4 kHz. A noise shaper and passive digital filter reduce the output to 14 bits at 176.4 kHz.

This output is applied to the sample and hold circuits of the D/A converter. The 14-bit system has fallen into disuse, however, by the development of true 16 bit oversampling D/A coverters, which are now used in most present-day CD players.

ONE OR TWO CONVERTERS

CD players can have either one or two D/A converters (some have even more). With one-converter players, the audio information from the EFM decoder is received as combined right and left channel information. The D/A converter processes the single stream as usual, and passes the resulting analog signal to an electronic switch. The switch sequentially toggles between right and left channels.

One-coverter players are capable of superb sound, and they are less expensive to manufacture, but they are susceptible to switching distortion. They are also prone to interchannel phase distortion, which is when the sound from the right and left channels do not exactly match up in time. (See

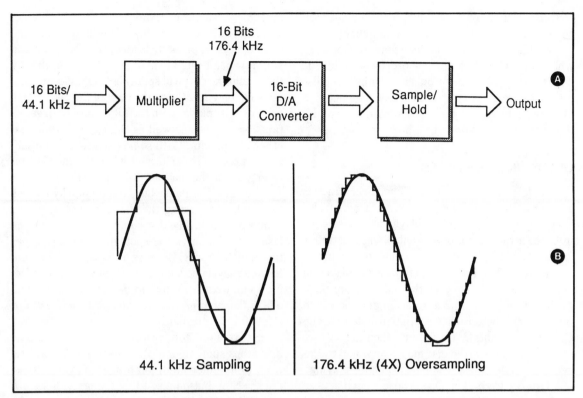

Fig. 2-21. A. Simplified block diagram of the D/A converter and sample/hold circuits in a player that uses digital filtering. B. Normal (44.1 kHz) sampling and 4X (176.4 kHz) oversampling.

Chapter 3 for more information about interchannel phase response.)

Players with two D/A converters lick this prob- lem. Before digital-to-analog conversion, the data stream from the EFM demodulator is broken down into its right and left channel components. One D/A

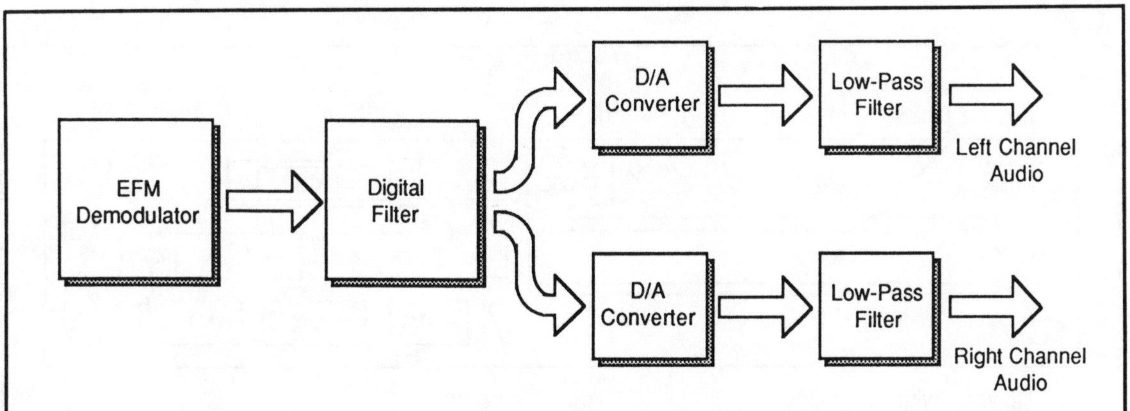

Fig. 2-22. Simplified block diagram of digital filtering.

converter is used for the left audio channel; one D/A converter is used for the right audio channel.

Problems can occur in dual-converter players when the converters are not precisely matched. Their outputs may vary from one another and distortion can result. Many of the latest compact disc players get around this limitation by using one IC that has two D/A converters built-in.

OPERATING CONTROLS

Models of compact disc players vary in the number and type of front panel operating controls. The typical drawer loading player has these controls (the actual names of the controls, as illustrated in Fig. 2-23, may vary from machine to machine):

Power. The Power switch turns the player on and off. Push once to turn the machine on; push again to turn it off. Unlike stereo amplifiers, which often operate better when continuously left on, the CD player should be turned off when not in use. With some models, the disc motor spins and the laser emits light, even when a disc is not playing.

Open/Close. The Open/Close switch acts as a toggle to open the disc loading drawer or to close it. Push once to open; push again to close. Many players have sensing switches inside the loading tray. These switches detect pressure on the tray so the drawer will retract if manually closed. This prevents possible damage to the loading drawer. Pushing the Play button (described below) on most

machines also closes the drawer.

Play. The Play button initiates playback of the disc. If a disc is properly loaded, the optical pickup will advance to its inner limit (if it is not already there) and the disc will spin. The pickup locates the table of contents area on the start of the disc, which provides the player with the total number of selections on the disc as well as the running time and other useful data. With some players, this initialization process is performed when the disc is first inserted and the loading drawer is closed.

Pause. The Pause button temporarily freezes playback. Depressing the Pause button again resumes playback. The disc continues to spin and the laser stays at the same spot, maintaining proper tracking and focus. Because of this, you should not leave a player in Pause for extended periods. Doing so may cause premature failure of the laser diode (5,000 hour normal life) and disc spindle motor (10,000 hour normal life).

Stop. The Stop button ceases playback. The disc stops spinning and the optical pickup will retract to its inner limit. With most players, pressing the Stop button also turns the laser diode off.

Track Up. The Track Up button advances the pickup through each selection, or music track, one at a time. Repeatedly depressing the Track Up button, or keeping it depressed, advances sequentially through all the tracks.

Track Down. The Track Down button serves the opposite purpose of the Track Up control.

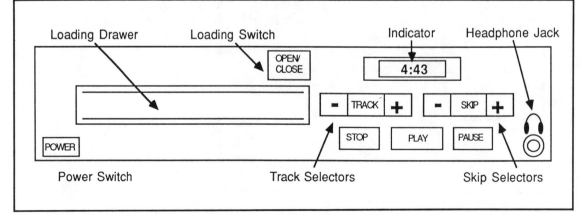

Fig. 2-23. The front panel controls and indicators on a typical home CD player.

More advanced models may have additional features, which are controlled by these front panel switches:

Skip Up. Skip Up is used to fast forward through a selection, usually at 4X to 8X normal speed. The pitch of the music is not affected, because the disc speed is not changed. Rather, the pickup advances through the information tracks at higher than normal speed, skipping many tracks at once.

Skip Down. Skip Down serves the opposite purpose of the Skip Up control.

Program. The Program switch enters a specific music track into memory for automatic playback. The method of programming varies from machine to machine, but with many players, you select the desired track with the Track Up and Track Down buttons, then depress the Program switch to enter the selection into memory. You repeat the process until all desired tracks are entered. The maximum number of program tracks is typically 15 or 16, although some players allow you to program up to the 99 selections, the maximum number of music tracks that a compact disc can contain.

Repeat. The Repeat control allows you to play a disc through twice.

Display Mode. The indicator panel on most compact disc players is too small to display at once all of the user information provided by the player.

The Display Mode switch selects between current track, remaining tracks, elapsed time, remaining time, and other user information.

Pitch. A Pitch control is found on only a few CD player models (it was more popular in the early CD days, but it has fallen into disuse). It allows you to alter the pitch, usually without effecting the speed of the playback.

Headphone Volume. The Headphone Volume knob lets you adjust the listening level when headphones are connected to the headphone jack. Not all players have headphone jacks, and only a portion of these have headphone volume controls.

REAR PANEL CONNECTORS

Unlike your stereo amplifier or cassette deck, the back of the typical compact disc player is almost devoid of special connectors and switches. As shown in Fig. 2-24, most CDs have just one set of output terminals, for direct connection to the CD, TAPE, or AUX inputs of your amplifier.

A few specialty models have additional outlets, for graphics subcode output (video still pictures from subcode data), and direct digital data output. Some models also have an "anti-shock" switch, which can help prevent excessive mistracking when the player is subjected to light vibration. You should normally keep the anti-shock switch off, as it can cause greater-than-normal skipping when playing a moderately scratched disc.

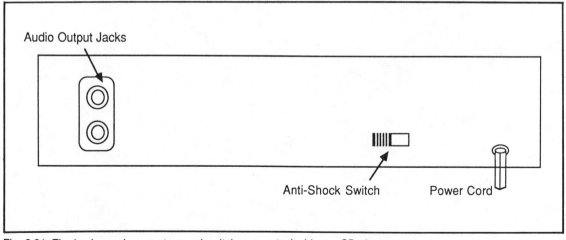

Fig. 2-24. The back panel connectors and switches on a typical home CD player.

REMOTE CONTROL

An increasing number of CD players come with wired or wireless remote controls. The control transmitters duplicate some or all of the player front panel operations. Players vary widely in the number of functions found on the remote control transmitters. The majority of remote controllers have about seven functions: Play, Stop, Pause, Track Up, Track Down, Skip Up, and Skip Down. Other controllers duplicate every function on the front panel of the player (even those used for track programming). A recent trend is to use one remote control for both CD and amplifier/receiver.

Chapter 3

Compact Disc
Player Specifications

Compact disc players have been touted as the "perfect" music source, and manufacturers are quick to point out their flawless technical specifications. But what exactly do these specifications mean, and are they indeed flawless? How can you interpret performance tests done by independent reviewers so that you know when a machine is good or bad? Do specifications really have a bearing on how good a certain compact disc player sounds? The following is an explanation of compact disc player specifications and the performance you can reasonably expect from a typical model.

FREQUENCY RESPONSE

Basically speaking, frequency response is the sonic range that the player can evenly and accurately reproduce. Frequency response is specified in Hertz (Hz), and with compact disc players, extends theoretically from 5 Hz to 20 kHz. This sonic range is effectively the range of human hearing, although most people can't hear extremely low or high sounds. A more reasonable hearing range for most adults is 100 Hz to 13 kHz.

In the first sentence of the paragraph above, note the words *evenly* and *accurately*. When a series of test tones are played through the CD, every frequency in the 5-20,000 Hz range must have the same level as the others. When this happens, the frequency response is said to be flat, and is expressed in specifications literature as 5 Hz to 20 kHz, ±0 dB.

Of course, the tones in real music are seldom even; nevertheless the CD player should be able to accurately reproduce those tones as they were originally performed. It's a simple matter of what goes in must come out.

Frequency response is a two-prong specification. You can get a clearer view of this by referring to Fig. 3-1. On one hand it's the sonic range that the player can reproduce, and on the other, it's the accuracy at which the frequencies can be reproduced relative to the original recording. In reality, no CD player has a perfectly flat frequency response of 5 Hz to 20 kHz. Most get up to about

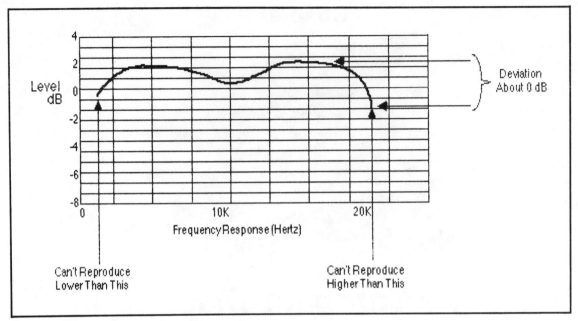

Fig. 3-1. A visual representation of frequency response.

18 kHz, where the amplitude of the high frequencies starts to diminish. By the time 20 kHz comes around, the tones have decreased in power level by 0.25 to 2 dB. The two stereo channels are most often tested separately, but not always.

A CD player that has a greater deviation from 0 dB at high frequencies isn't necessarily worse than any other player. It's a rare amplifier and speaker that can recreate frequencies beyond 17 kHz, so a little drop or increase at the very high end is hardly noticeable. Compare the frequency response of the compact disc player to that of a cas-

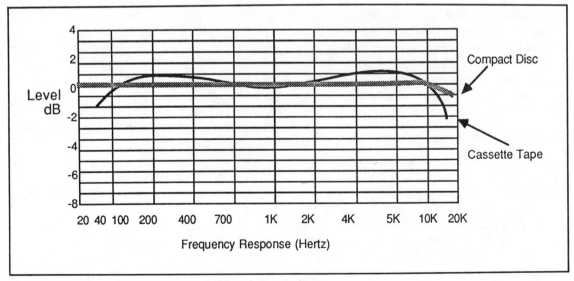

Fig. 3-2. An unfair comparison of compact disc and cassette tape.

sette deck, as shown in Fig. 3-2. Cassette tape, like all analog recording methods, has a narrower frequency response, and can't accurately reproduce sounds under 100 Hz or above 10 to 12 kHz.

SIGNAL-TO-NOISE RATIO

The signal-to-noise (or S/N) ratio refers to the ratio of music you want versus the extraneous sounds you don't want. The noise usually appears as hiss. Refer to Fig. 3-3. The idea is that the more noise there is, the less space there is for the music, so S/N actually measures the amount of amplitude space available for playback. It should be noted that S/N is not a measurement of the playback medium (in this case the disc itself), but specifies the amount of analog noise, in relation to the desired signal, that is introduced by the player's electronics.

In a CD player, some analog noise is created in the digital processing circuits, and a little more is generated by the D/A converter, the analog filter (if any), and preamplifier circuits. Because of this, CD players have a very low S/N ratio compared to other hi-fi gear, like cassette decks.

In specifications sheets, S/N appears as a ratio between a 0 dB signal and the background noise. A specification of 80 dB means that there is 80 dB of signal strength between the main signal and the noise. Theoretically, CD players have a S/N ratio of 97.5 dB, but in real life, the figure is a more reasonable 90 dB or so. The higher the dB, the better.

S/N measurements can be made in a variety of different ways, and you'll see a wide variation between what a manufacturer claims for his machine

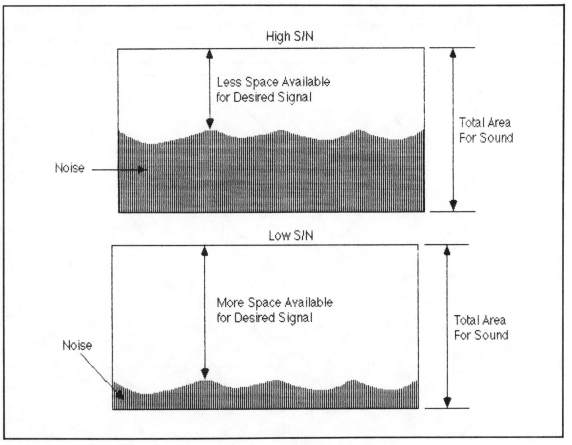

Fig. 3-3. Signal-to-noise, and how it affects the quality of the signal.

and what an independent reviewer may test.

Most manufacturers insert a band-pass filter between the player and the test rig that cuts off frequencies under 4 Hz and over 20 kHz, supposedly to block out-of-band (inaudible) noise components. The reasoning is that the noise components can't be heard, but they are picked up by test gear and can give erroneous (usually lowered) test results. Some critics say this isn't an accurate assessment, because the harmonics of some of the out-of-band components can actually cause some audible noise, and this would be present during normal listening. When comparing S/N specifications try to ascertain whether the measurement was made with or without a filter.

S/N tests made with and without a so-called weighting network can vary greatly. A weighting network puts more emphasis on certain frequencies than others. The network used with most CD player tests is *A-weighted*, where the lower frequencies are reduced, or attenuated. That makes the overall S/N figure appear better.

CHANNEL SEPARATION

Figure 3-4 demonstrates channel separation, measuring the leakage of signals that can occur between the right and left stereo channels. When signals from the two channels bleed into one another, there is said to be crosstalk. As you may have guessed, channel separation with compact disc is extremely high, because the music is digitally processed.

Channel separation is expressed as an amplitude in dB, like signal-to-noise. The figure is usually a negative number, such as -90 dB, or at lest assumed to be a negative number even when it is expressed without the minus sign. The -90 dB specification means that signals from the opposite channel are 90 dB *less* in intensity than signals from the present channel. Channel separation changes at various frequencies, so the test is usually made across the band, but the specification may indicate

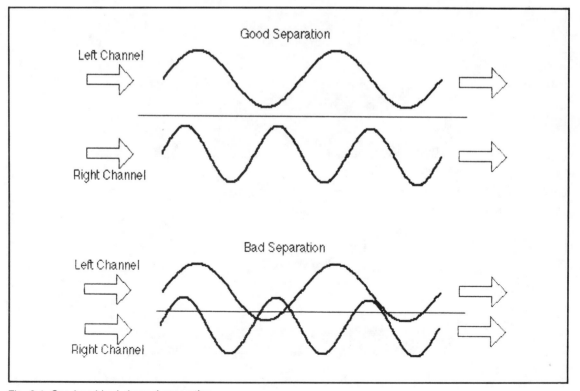

Fig. 3-4. Good and bad channel separation.

a specific frequency, usually 1 kHz. Most CD players have a channel separation of –85 dB or greater. The higher the number, the greater the separation, and of course, the better the sound.

INTERMODULATION DISTORTION

Intermodulation distortion, or IM for short, is what happens when analog circuits create brand new frequencies out of the ones being processed. If two frequencies are input into the player, a series of sum and difference frequencies might be generated by the analog circuits (digital circuits do not create IM).

As an example 100 Hz and 1000 Hz signals go into the player circuits, intermodulation distortion would be created if the circuits generated a difference frequency of 900 Hz and a sum frequency of 1100 Hz. In reality, many other less intense frequencies are created out of these new ones, and the effect goes on for as long as the circuit allows.

Because CD players have little analog circuitry, IM is kept to a respectable minimum. The amount of IM present is expressed as a percentage of the original signal. A measurement of 0.0025% or less would be very good. With such a low measurement, many manufacturers and independent labs don't even bother with listing IM.

PHASE LINEARITY

Analog audio signals are sine waves. The crests and valleys undulate with time. The timing of the wave, in relation to some reference point, is called *phase*, and is expressed in degrees. A wave that's properly timed with its reference point has a phase of 0 degrees.

Phase linearity measures the ability of the compact disc player to reproduce frequencies without creating what is known as frequency dependent time delays. Imagine a speaker system, like the one in Fig. 3-5, where the woofer (the bass part) is right in front of you, but the tweeter (the high frequency part) is 1,000 feet behind it. Put a sound through the speaker system and you hear the woofer immediately; the tweeter is delayed over a second, that's a frequency dependent time delay.

Delays of this nature do not occur with such severity in CD players, but there is some measurable delay—in all CD players—of high frequency sounds in relation to their low frequency counterparts. The problem is worst when the player has a poorly designed analog output filter. The high frequencies can be 10 to 90 degrees (or more) out of phase, and although it may not be immediately noticeable to you when you listen to a disc, some music passages may sound strange. Players with the latest digital filters tend to exhibit less phase linearity distortion—usually five degrees or less.

INTERCHANNEL PHASE RESPONSE

Phase linearity deals with sounds going through

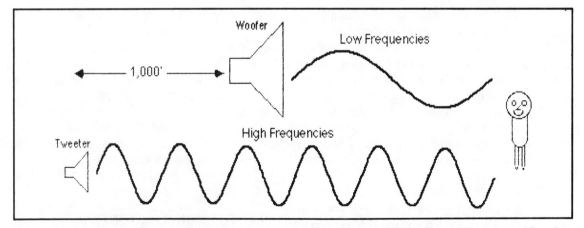

Fig. 3-5. Frequency dependent phase distortion (or delay) is similar to placing a woofer and tweeter apart, and listening to the music. The high frequencies reach the listener after the low frequencies.

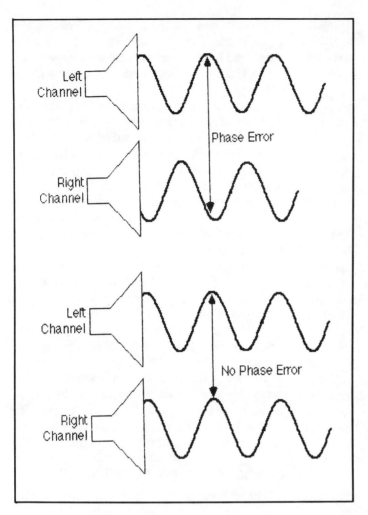

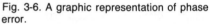

Fig. 3-6. A graphic representation of phase error.

one channel of the CD player; interchannel phase response deals with the sounds as they come out of the right and left stereo channels. More specifically, interchannel phase response is the measure of phase difference between the two channels, as shown in Fig. 3-6. If you play a disc with a single tone that's evenly balanced in both channels, the peaks and valleys of the sound wave coming out of the player should match up for the right and left sides. Deviations from this are expressed as phase error, in degrees.

Most CD players don't exhibit any measurable interchannel phase response at the very low frequencies, but there is often a marked phase error with higher tones. This is especially true if the player incorporates a single D/A converter. With this type of player, phase error of 90 degrees or more is not uncommon with frequencies above about 15 kHz. This phase error affects the quality of the music, but since few discs actually have sounds in this region, it's not generally noticeable to the ear.

A good player should have minimal phase error at all frequencies, and most higher quality CDs—especially those with dual D/A converters—are being manufactured these days with this in mind.

TOTAL HARMONIC DISTORTION

Total harmonic distortion, abbreviated THD,

is considered one of the most important specifications for any piece of audio gear. With compact disc players, THD is extremely low, so low in fact, that the limiting factor of the quality of your hi-fi is your amplifier, speaker, and cables. With CD, THD is really not an important consideration, although you may want to keep it in the back of your mind when evaluating a player.

THD measures the ability of the CD player to reproduce a signal without contributing additional frequency components—harmonics—of its own. Harmonics are sub-frequencies that are mathematically related to the main *fundamental* tone. For example, concert A note on the piano is considered to be 440 Hz in frequency. In actuality, the note is comprised of additional harmonics that are even and odd multiples of this frequency.

THD is measured as a percentage of newly created distortion in relation to the original signal. It varies in respect to both the amplitude of the sound and its frequency, so tests are made with specific tones and certain pre-determined levels. A typical test specification of THD for a CD player might read "0.05% at 1 kHz," meaning there is 0.05% or less THD when tested at 1 kHz. Some testers also tell you the signal level, which should be 0 dB. The 0 dB figure corresponds to the maximum amplitude possible without "overriding" the sound into distortion.

Manufacturers and independent labs employ a variety of THD tests, and there is a great debate over which is the right way (audiophiles have been debating test procedures practically ever since the phonograph was invented; it'll likely remain that way for some time to come). Since there is no standard way to test THD, figures may differ greatly between manufacturer and independent lab. In actuality, however, the disparity between the figures means very little, because THD is so low in compact disc players that it takes sophisticated electronics to uncover it. Even if the various claims of THD are several times off base, you'll probably not hear the difference.

DYNAMIC RANGE

In basic terms, dynamic range is the difference between the softest and loudest portions in a music selection. CD players have a theoretical dynamic range of 96 dB, which means there is a 96 dB difference between the most quiet and most loud passages in the music. In practice, the dynamic range is more like 85 dB to 90 dB, which is more than acceptable. These figures are really applicable for laboratory tests; it's unlikely you'll ever find a piece of music with this kind of range—the 1812 Overture included. Dynamic range is not as important as the other specifications we've discussed, unless the CD player is very poorly designed.

WOW AND FLUTTER

Wow and flutter are speed changes during playback that affect the pitch of the sound. Imagine playing a 1000 Hz tone through the CD player. Wow would cause the tone to glide slowly from, perhaps, 1050 Hz to 950 Hz. Flutter causes the same frequency (pitch) changes, but the affect is fast, like the warble of a European police siren.

The playback of a compact disc is carefully regulated by a microprocessor running under a highly accurate quartz crystal. During playback, data from the disc is temporarily stored in random access memory (RAM), which acts as a kind of reservoir. The RAM is filled to half capacity, and maintained there. Changes in the rotational speed of the disc are compensated for by the data in the RAM. If the disc goes too slow for a time, the microprocessor speeds up the disc to compensate. But the rate of data coming from the RAM, and trickled to the EFM demodulator, remains the same.

This means that wow and flutter are virtually non-existent in CD players. In fact, most test specifications leave wow and flutter off, or label it "immeasurable" or "below measurable limits." Though wow and flutter are extremely low in CD players, it does exist, and some testers go to great pains to measure it. Rest assured, however, that the measurement is meaningless since you'll never hear it.

ERROR CORRECTION

Error correction is not a test that manufacturers

regularly perform and list in their specifications, but it's an important one for compact disc players. Most independent labs have some test for error correction, although most are quaint and unscientific. It's not unusual to "test" error correction of a given CD player by whacking it on its side or top. If the player can take a heavy jolt without skipping, it's considered to have either good shock absorbers on the optical pickup, good error correction, or both.

Philips, co-inventor of the compact disc, sells a test disc labeled TS4A. This disc, which is available at some hi-fi dealers and larger record stores, is designed with deliberate flaws for testing error correction circuitry in a CD player. You can use the disc to test your player (as either a preventive or corrective maintenance procedure), or any player that you may be evaluating.

The disc has simulated fingerprints, scratches, and dust particles. By listening closely to the playback, you can tell if the player has poor, average, or above average error correction. Additional information on this disc, and how to make your own, can be found in Chapter 5.

Compact Disc Errors

The compact disc system is protected from the audible effects of all but the most gross data errors by a completely digital error correction system. There are actually two separate digital error correction schemes used in CDs: parity data (or redundant data) and Cross-Interleave Read-Solomon Code, or CIRC (interleaving for short).

The design of the compact disc player optics compensates for many of the effects caused by dust, dirt, and scratches, because the laser beam focuses past these surface obstructions.

There are four degrees of severity of compact disc errors, and each degree determines the type of correction the player employs. One player may handle a particular type of error better than another, so it is important to break them down.

☐ Fully Correctible Errors. As stated before, light scratches and small dust particles are usually not even noticed by the CD player optics. A speck of dust 0.5mm in size on the surface of the disc is out of focus to the laser; reduced to one millionth its original size.

However, a heavier scratch or larger dust particle, say one that's 2mm or so in size, will not entirely escape the laser beam. Such an obstacle would block several tens or hundreds of pits and the player would recognize the loss of data as dropouts. These dropouts are corrected by the parity data inserted with each frame or audio. Such minor dropouts are fully correctible and are not audible.

☐ Concealed or Interpolated Errors. Sometimes, an obstruction may block too many pits, and the parity data will not be able to reconstruct it. Because the data on the disc was encoded using a CIRC interleaving technique, the player can, in many cases, reconstruct the missing pieces by using interpolation (Fig. 3-7).

With some players, especially the early models, interpolations are sometimes noticeable as clicks or low-level distortion. But most interpolations on present day players are inaudible.

☐ Muting Errors. Let's say you've really gouged a disc and a large portion of it is damaged. It still plays but there is a long string of unconcealable data. There is no usable parity data and there is insufficient data to reconstruct the audio using interpolation. The player has one recourse left: mute the audio. The analog muting process involves turning down the volume of the music until the error has gone by. The volume is then turned back up. This happens very fast, and the muting circuits are damped—they turn the volume up and down gradually—so the error is not as noticeable as you may think.

☐ Detracking Errors. A tracking or focusing error is when pits on the disc are blocked or damped so completely that the laser goes off course. Detracking errors can also be caused by external vibration knocking the pickup out of place. In either case, the result is skipping, like on an LP record. You can test the resistance a player has to serious disc damage, and its immunity to focus and tracking error, by using the TS4A test disc, or one of your own design.

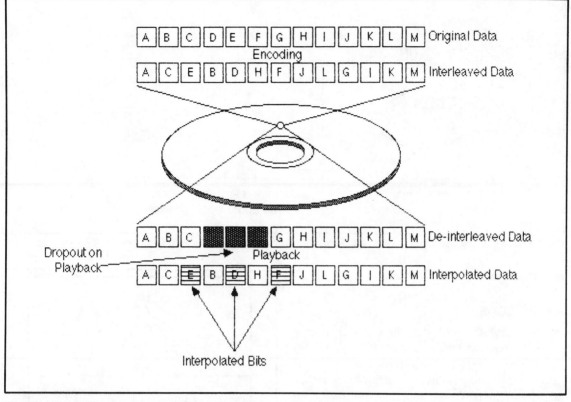

Fig. 3-7. Interleaving attempts to replace missing data by interpolation—examining the data on either side of the absent information and approximating a new value.

OUTPUT VOLTAGE

This specification measures the voltage of the audio output terminals located on the back of the CD player (and sometimes the level of the headphone jack). Compact disc players are supposed to have a 2 rms volt level (when measured with a 0 dB signal), but few are this exact. You'll find models that vary from a little over 1 volt to well over 10 volts.

How does the output voltage affect CD player performance? In most cases, it does not, but it does have a bearing on how well the player interfaces to your hi-fi system. The higher the output voltage, the higher the sound level will be at any given volume on the amplifier. So if you are switching from a cassette deck with a normal output voltage, to a CD with an abnormally high output voltage, you must remember to turn down the volume on the amplifier.

Some of the better compact disc players have a variable output control, so you can tailor the voltage to better match your system. With a voltmeter connected to the output terminals (Fig. 3-8), and dialed to the ac volts functions, you can more accurately set the output voltage to the 2 volt standard. You need a test disc with a constant 0 dB tone for this. The Philips TS4A has such a tone track, as do similar test discs from Denon, Sony, Technics, and others.

The output level on the headphone jack is not standard on CD players, and also varies widely. Again, the better players have a level control so you can turn up the headphone volume to suit your taste. If your player lacks a variable headphone control, and the sound is too loud, use headphones equipped with a volume control, or use a headphone

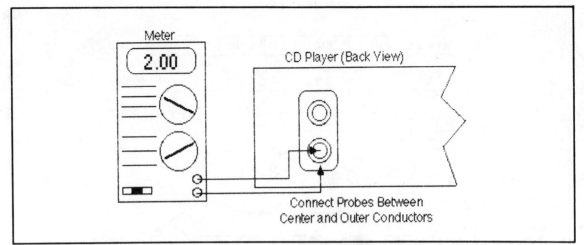

Fig. 3-8. A way to test the output level of a CD player. You must play a test disc with a constant 0 dB tone.

attenuator, available at electronics stores.

SPARS CODE

The SPARS Code describes the recording process used in making a compact disc. The three letter code considers the original, mixing, and mastering recorders, any of which can be either analog or digital. The best results are usually obtained when all three recorders are the digital variety (Fig. 3-9).

Keep in mind that the SPARS Code considers only the *recording format* used in the music making process. Audio special effects, reverberation, Ambisonic processing, and other elements are generally added in analog form. In the case of a fully digital recording, these effects are created by first converting the digital audio to analog form at the mixing console. After processing, the signal is reconverted to digital form, then recorded.

It should be noted that even a fully digital (DDD) disc may not be sonically perfect. The sound quality of a disc is no better than the engineering that put it there. Poorly placed microphones, faulty equipment, and amateur mixing techniques may make a completely digital disc aurally intolerable. When shopping for discs, don't be lulled into buying every Triple-D disc you find (which are currently rare). Choose your CDs as you would records

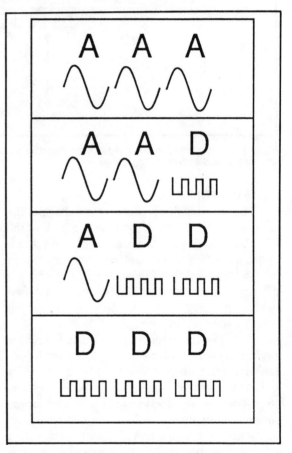

Fig. 3-9. The SPARS Code, and how to interpret it.

or tapes: by listening to new songs on the radio, gathering personal recommendations from friends and associates, and reading disc reviews in magazines.

The SPARS Code was designed to remove the marketing fluff that can confuse buyers; yet not all disc publishers use it. Some CD publishers insist on using ridiculous catch phrases to promote their product. You'll often find discs labeled "digitally mastered," which is like a bottled water company claiming their water is "wet." By definition all CDs must be digitally mastered, as explained in Chapter 1. A better description for the so-called digitally mastered disc is the AAD SPARS Code.

(AAA). A fully analog recording, from the original session to mastering. Since at least the mastering recorder must be digital to make a compact disc, this code is not applicable to CDs.

(AAD). Analog tape recorder used during session recording and subsequent mixing and/or editing. A digital recorder was used to make the master. Currently, most discs are AAD.

(ADD). Analog tape recorder used during session recording. Digital recorders used during mixing (or editing) and mastering.

(DDD). A fully digital recording.

Chapter 4

The CD Environment

Success with your compact disc player depends on how well it is integrated with the rest of your hi-fi system. A haphazard arrangement will yield inferior results, and you won't be able to enjoy the full capabilities of the player. Many potential problems can be completely avoided by proper placement and hookup of your CD.

If your player is giving you problems, check this chapter first. It provides details on how to properly install, adjust, and use a compact disc player. CD isn't necessarily a difficult technology to use; on the contrary, it's quite simple. Nevertheless, a compact disc player is different than any other piece of hi-fi gear you've ever owned, and there are some special considerations to keep in mind.

UNPACKING

If you have yet to buy or unpack your CD player, here are some quick tips to keep in mind.

Concealed Damage

When unpacking your CD player from its box,

be on the lookout for concealed damage. This is breakage that you can't see on the outside of the box but becomes apparent when you take the player out of its shipping container. If the player has been damaged, return it immediately to the dealer. Exterior damage is a good indication that internal components are damaged, too.

Save the box and all packing material, at least until you've had the player a month or so. Most mechanical and electrical problems will arise in this time, and you'll need the box to return the player for warranty repair.

Transit Screws

This next point is important, nearly all CD players are equipped with one or more transit screws which are located on the baseplate (bottom) of the unit (Fig. 4-1). These screws anchor the pickup and other internal moving parts during transit. If the transit screws are not removed prior to installing the player, the machine won't work.

Compact disc repair technicians claim that fail-

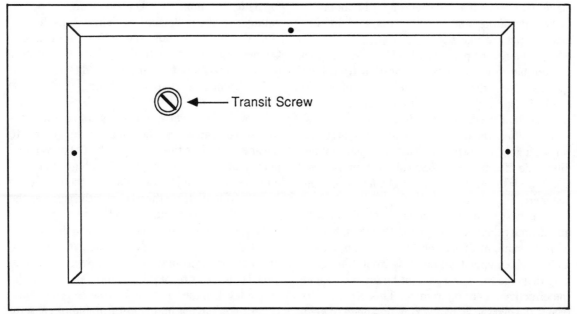

Fig. 4-1. Most home players are equipped with one or more transit screws. Be sure to remove or loosen them before using the player.

ure to remove the transit screws account for the majority—over 60 percent—of the service calls they get. Most service centers don't charge for this kind of mistake, but you can avoid the hassles of returning the machine by following the directions packed with the player. On many machines, the instructions for the transit screws are duplicated on a sticker placed on the rear or underside of the player.

The transit screws on some CD players are designed so that they can be loosened, but cannot be removed, (these are called captive transit screws) with others, you must take out the screws entirely. If the player doesn't provide a receptacle for the screws, save them in a place where they won't be lost. You will need to reinsert the transit screws should you transport or ship the player at some future time.

INSTALLATION

Keep these installing tips in mind when adding your compact disc player in your audio system.

Ventilation

Unlike your hi-fi amplifier, compact disc players do not generate a lot of internal heat, but it is still important to avoid obstructing the player's ventilation slots. A player that gets too hot will perform erratically.

The laser diode is designed to operate over a very limited temperature range, and is extremely susceptible to operating temperatures over 100 degrees or so. If the laser gets too hot, its light output becomes uneven, which can cause mistracking and excessive unconcealed errors. If this happens, check to see if the player has become overly warm. Turn it off for an hour or two and test it again. It should return to normal after cooling.

Placement

The optical pickup used in CD players for the home generally do not use damping or shock absorbing materials. This makes them much more prone to mistracking caused by external jolts than car and portable players, which are specifically designed to withstand this kind of treatment. You should always place a home CD player on a level shelf or platform that's free of vibration and shock. Be sure that the shelf can adequately support the player. If it looks like the shelf might break under the weight of the unit, by all means, find another place to put the player.

Unlike record players, CD players are not as susceptible to the effects of vibration from loud speakers. Nevertheless, the sound quality of the CD can be impaired if you place it too close to a set of speakers that are driven at high volume. The vibration can effect the digital and analog circuitry and cause ringing, distortion, and other unpleasant audible side effects. As a good rule of thumb, position the player at least six to eight feet from any speaker.

It is best to locate a compact disc player with an infrared remote control out in the open, but out of direct sunlight. If possible, avoid placing it in an audio rack equipped with a glass front. The glass may disperse the infrared light beam and reduce the effectiveness of the remote. This is especially true if the glass is smoked. You may need to keep the glass front open when operating the player with the remote.

Be sure that the player is within range of the remote (usually 20 feet or less), and that you can aim the remote control transmitter in a direct line— more or less—to the player. The remote may not work if it is used at angles greater than 30 degrees off to either side of the front panel of the player (Fig. 4-2).

Hookup

CD players are relatively easy to connect to audio amplifiers. Just stretch a stereo cable from the AUDIO OUT connectors of the player to the CD, AUX, or TAPE inputs of the amplifier (Fig. 4-3). There are some important points to remember to avoid problems.

☐ Always turn the amplifier off before attaching any cables to it. Turn everything in your hi-fi system off. During installation, you may ground out an input to the amplifier simply by touching the end of one of the cables. If the volume on the amp is set too high, you run the risk of overloading and damaging the amplifier's electronics.

☐ Never connect a CD player to the PHONO inputs of the amplifier. CD players have an output voltage of about 2 volts, which is considerably higher than the output voltage from a turntable. Connecting the player to the PHONO input may overload the amplifier, and cause damage to the amp's circuits or to your speakers.

Some CD players have a variable output control, so you can adjust the voltage level going into the amplifier. Use this control if the CD player supplies a signal that's too low or too high. For optimum results, you'll want to adjust the control so that the volume from the player is the same as the volume from the turntable and cassette player.

After the CD player is connected to the system, insert a disc and play it. Next, place an LP on the turntable or a tape in the cassette. Switch between the CD player or turntable/cassette and adjust the output level on the CD until the volume is the same. Unless you have a high-end turntable or cassette player, you'll quickly note how good the CD player sounds!

☐ If the TAPE and AUX inputs on your amp are already taken, you can still use the CD player by adding a selector switch. These are available at many electronics stores. They let you select from several inputs and route the signal to one output. You could connect the CD player and the tape player, for example, to the switch, then route the switch to the LINE input of your amplifier (Fig. 4-4). Be sure the selector you use is intended for audio use, and has adequate internal shielding.

Cables

Use only shielded cable designed for audio applications. The cables should be the highest quality you can afford. If the player comes with its own cables, inspect them carefully. If they feel or seem cheap, purchase a new set. The few extra dollars are well worth it.

Avoid the use of adapters on the cable ends as they can pick up extraneous hum caused by nearby alternating currents. A number of CD players use gold-plated audio plugs. We personally feel the gold-plating does little to improve the overall sonic

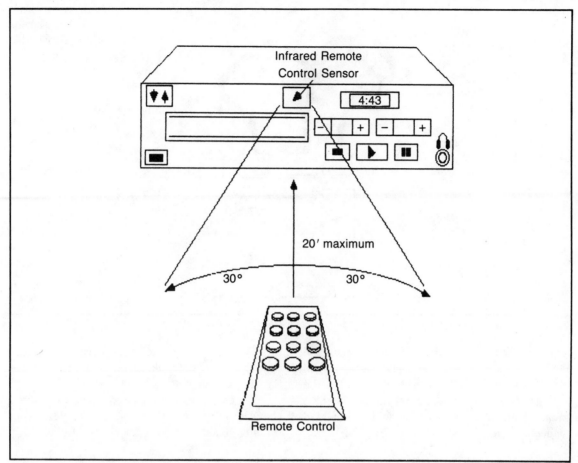

Fig. 4-2. Effective use of the remote control requires you to be within 20 feet of the player and no more than 30 degrees off to either side of the remote control sensor.

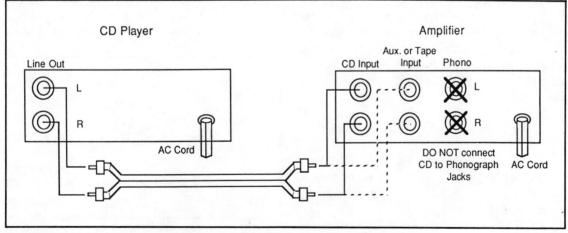

Fig. 4-3. Recommended connection diagram between CD player and amplifier/receiver.

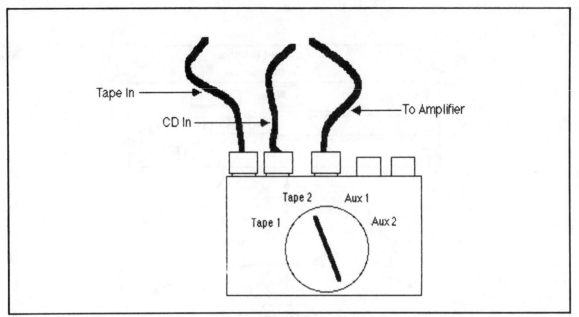

Fig. 4-4. Use a selector if you run out of inputs on your amplifier.

quality of the average player. However, many audiophiles swear by them, and say that the small added expense is well worth it. Supposedly, the plating provides better sound and you get the maximum benefit from using cables with gold-plated connectors. Decide for yourself.

Cable Routing

If you're like most hi-fi enthusiasts, you probably have a tangle of wires behind your stereo system. For better sound spend a few moments to "dress" the cables so that they are neater. This not only makes troubleshooting problems easier, it reduces the chance of ac-induced hum entering signal cables and amplified by the system. Keep these points in mind.

☐ Use cables that are just long enough to do the job.

☐ If the cable is a bit long, loop it gently and wrap it together using masking tape or, better yet, a plastic tie wrap (available at hardware and electronics stores).

☐ Whenever possible, keep signal cables and ac cords away from each other.

☐ Avoid looping ac cords, because this sets up an inductive field, like an electromagnet or motor, that can increase hum.

☐ If signal cables and ac cords must be routed near each other, cross the two at right angles. Avoid running signal cables and ac cords parallel.

Checkout

After installation is complete, plug the CD player in a wall socket. (Note, as illustrated in Fig. 4-5, the polarization of the plug and socket.) Most

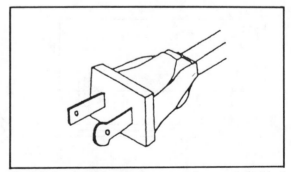

Fig. 4-5. A polarized ac cord, now used on most electrical devices sold in the U.S.

60

electrical devices sold these days have polarized plugs—one prong is slightly larger than the other. They are designed to fit only one way into the wall socket. If the electrical outlets in your home are not equipped with polarized outlets, be sure to orient the power cable from the CD in the same direction as the power cable from the amplifier (Fig. 4-6). By retaining the proper polarization for the two components, you eliminate the possibility of a ground loop and you won't be bothered by the effects of ac induced hum.

Turn down the volume on the amplifier, then apply power to the amp and CD. Select the CD on the amplifier, insert a disc, and play it. Slowly turn the volume up to a comfortable listening level. It will take a few seconds for the disc play to start, so be patient.

Unlike cassette decks and turntables, you won't

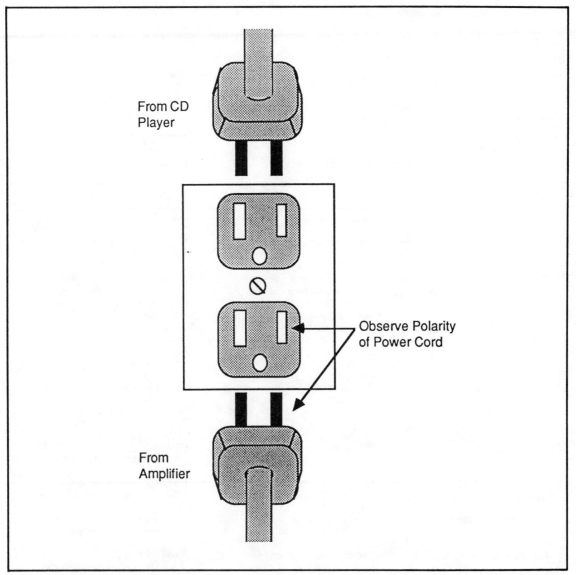

From CD Player

Observe Polarity of Power Cord

From Amplifier

Fig. 4-6. To help reduce hum, be sure to orient the plugs from your CD and amplifier the same way in the wall socket.

hear much (if any) background noise before the song plays. Don't be tempted to adjust the volume to the proper listening level by judging the amount of hiss you hear through the speakers. If your amp has any power at all, when the music finally starts you'll be jolted out of your chair! Wait until the music begins, THEN turn up the volume.

Check all of the front panel controls. Skip through the selections to make sure the pickup in the player can access the entire width of the disc. If your player stops or skips after playing only the first few minutes of the first selection, suspect the transit screws. Perhaps they are not out all the way, or a screw is still in place (remember, many machines have more than one screw, so make sure you get them all).

IF SOMETHING GOES WRONG

You've connected your CD player to your amplifier, did everything that you thought you should do, but it doesn't seem to work. Table 4-1 is a quick troubleshooting guide you can use to help right the mistake. These problems assume a simple cause. For a diagnosis of more serious problems, see the troubleshooting flowcharts in Chapter 9.

ACHIEVING OPTIMUM SOUND

Nothing beats the sound of a compact disc player. Yet there are a number of ways you can im-

Table 4-1. Basic Troubleshooting Guide: CD Installation.

1	2	3
BASIC TROUBLESHOOTING GUIDE -- CD INSTALLATION		
PROBLEM	CAUSE	REMEDY
Won't turn on.	Not plugged in.	Plug into good electrical socket.
	Switched outlet.	Switch on outlet.
	Blown fuse.	Replace fuse (usu. internal).
Load drawer or door won't open.	Transit screw in place.	Loosen all transit screws.
	Microprocessor problem.	Turn unit off and on again.
No sound.	CD not selected on amp.	Select proper input on amplifier.
	Bad or incomplete connection.	Check or replace cables.
	Volume turned down.	Adjust volume.
	Speaker switch off.	Turn speakers on.
	Level control too low.	Adjust output level on CD.
Will not play disc.	Disc loaded upside down.	Load it label side up.
	Transit screw in place.	Loosen all transit screws.
	Disc dirty.	Clean disc.
	Disc scratched.	Repair or discard disc.
	Warped disc.	Discard disc.
	Condensation on disc or in player.	Wait 30 minutes to dry.
Portions of disc won't play.	Transit screw in place.	Loosen all transit screws.
	Disc dirty.	Clean disc.
	Disc scratched.	Repair or discard disc; skip track.
Sound is distorted.	Bad or incomplete connection.	Check or replace cables.
	Level control too high.	Adjust output level on CD.
Player does not respond to push buttons.	Disc not properly loaded.	Reload disc properly.
	Microprocessor problem.	Turn unit off and on again.
Remote does not work.	Bad or missing batteries.	Install fresh batteries.
	Infrared light path blocked.	Unblock path (including glass).

prove the sound to achieve maximum performance from the player.

System Quality

Invariably, the music you hear from your CD will interest you in upgrading your hi-fi system. Unless you have the ultimate stereo gear, you'll always feel there is some way you can improve the sound by replacing this speaker or that amplifier. Before you rush out and spend a few thousand dollars on an audiophile hi-fi system, consider these points.

The loudspeakers are the most important, but most often neglected, link in the hi-fi chain. If you make any improvements in the system, the speakers are the best place to start. You don't necessarily need the latest whiz-bang speaker design, but you should opt for quality components in a well-designed enclosure. And don't be fooled into spending extra for "digital ready" speakers. *Any* good pair of speakers are digital ready. There are no special designs or refinements that go into so-called digital ready speakers.

You can test your speakers by listening to the CD with a good pair of headphones. There will always be a difference in sonic quality, but if there is a marked variance—in favor of the headphones—the speakers are probably low in quality. If the speakers are good, you will prefer to listen to the music through them and not the headphones.

Whether or not the speakers are good quality, you should make sure they are rated to match your amplifier. Don't use speakers that are rated for a maximum of 50 watts on a 100 watt-per-channel amp. This is true even if you regularly listen to music at low volumes.

The amplifier should be good quality, with low total harmonic distortion (THD). The power of the amp is not as important as the clarity with which it reproduces music. There should be no noticeable hiss or hum during quiet sections when the volume is turned up to the regular listening level. Of course, a higher capacity amp will be able to deliver less distorted music at high volumes. The effect of high volume distortion is called clipping (Fig. 4-7). If you like your music loud, don't overdrive a small amp by cranking the volume up so high that the distortion level exceeds 50 percent!

The turntable, cassette deck, and other components that are out of the CD-amplifier-speaker link make no difference in the quality of sound from the compact disc player. If you are happy with your present cassette deck and turntable, keep them.

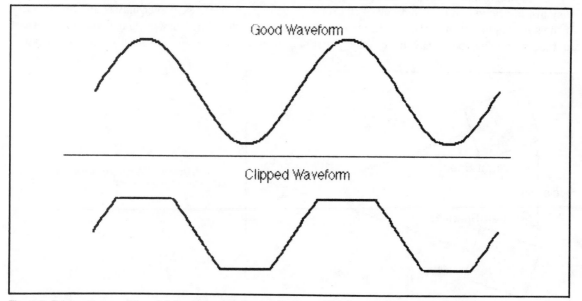

Fig. 4-7. Driving the amplifier at full volume can cause clipping, which is a severe form of distortion.

Speaker Placement

Almost as important as the quality of speakers in a hi-fi system is where they are located in the room. There are many do's and don'ts regarding proper speaker placement, and you can ruin the sound from even the best hi-fi's by carelessly tossing the speakers in the corners of the room.

It's best to consider the listening room as an extension of the loudspeaker cabinet. In fact, the rich, full sound you hear from a good set of speakers comes not from the speaker enclosure, but the sound reverberating throughout the room. Other considerations:

☐ Position the speakers so that they are directed to the central listening point in the room, this point shouldn't be any closer than about eight feet from the speakers. Any closer and the direct sound from the speakers will overpower the room acoustics. The spot where the sound from the two speakers meet is called the "sweet spot" (Fig. 4-8), and is where the illusion of the "stereo image" is the greatest.

☐ Position the right and left speakers evenly so that they are the same distance away from the sweet spot. This increases the stereo image.

☐ Speakers almost always sound better when they are positioned on the long wall of the room. If the sound is too boomy, the speaker placement in that particular room may be causing what's known as standing waves. Try a new location.

☐ Place speakers from six to eight feet away from each other. Placing them closer together diminishes the stereo effect; further apart creates a sonic "hole" in the stereo effect.

☐ Avoid placing the speakers in the corner of the room. This greatly diminishes smooth frequency response.

☐ Keep speakers off the floor, particularly if the floor is carpeted.

☐ It's best to position the speakers two to three feet from all walls. The closer a speaker is placed to a wall, the more bass it produces. This tip can't always be observed, but try to follow it as much as you can.

☐ If hanging speakers on the wall, use mounting brackets designed for the job, and be sure to use the proper anchoring hardware. Avoid placing the speaker too close to the ceiling, where it will unnaturally reproduce the bass range.

☐ If the stereo image is blurred or lacking depth, there may be excessive mid and high frequencies. Dampen these by placing a wall hanging or other soft, absorbing material on the wall between the two speakers.

☐ Some room sizes are better than others. Your compact disc player may sound much better in your den, but lousy in your living room. Apart from room acoustics caused by windows, drapes,

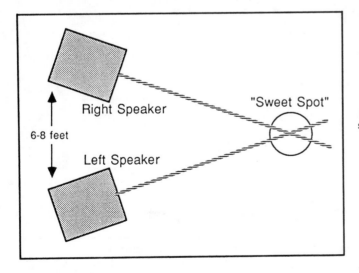

Fig. 4-8. Position the speakers to create a sweet spot in the listening area.

Table 4-2. Ideal Dimensions for Listening Rooms.

1	2	3	4
IDEAL DIMENSIONS FOR LISTENING ROOMS			
	Height	Width	Depth
Small Room			
Ratio	1	1.25	1.6
Dimensions	8'	10'	12'9"
Average Room			
Ratio	1	1.6	2.5
Dimensions	8'	12'9"	20'
Large Room			
Ratio	1	1.25	3.2
Dimensions	8'	10'	25'6"

carpeting, and the like, the room dimensions play an important role. (See Table 4-2 for dimensions for the ideal CD listening environment.)

Equalization

Basically speaking, equalization is electrically altering the music so that it sounds as much like the original recording as possible. Equalization is necessary to adjust for the frequency response of the amplifier and speakers, and to balance the room acoustics. Equalization is also used to tailor the sound to your personal tastes. You may prefer a more bassy sound, and you can use the equalizer to boost the low frequencies. Or, you may prefer the high range. Again, use the equalizer to increase the high frequencies and bring them out.

Equalizers are sometimes built into amplifiers, but they are generally separate components on the higher-end hi-fi gear. Equalizers consist of a series of slide potentiometers; each slide controls a certain frequency band. One slide may alter the frequencies between 1 kHz and 2.5 kHz, for example, while another alters the frequencies between 2.5 and 5 kHz. The better equalizers employ separate controls for the right and left stereo channels, so you can individually adjust the output of each speaker.

Equalization is particularly important to compact disc listeners. Unlike other stereo components, like a cassette deck or turntable, the frequency response of the CD player is reasonably flat over the entire audio range. You may not be used to this, and the sound from the CD may seem overly bright. Until you get accustomed to the new sound, you can use the equalizer to "tone down" the sound. Unfortunately, you'll have to reset the equalizer when you go from CD player and cassette deck or turntable, because they all have different response curves.

You might want to use the equalizer to balance the sound from your speakers to match the room acoustics. In fact, the better the speakers, the more you'll have to tailor the music with an equalizer. Good speakers have a greater range and flatter frequency response curve than cheaper ones. You'll want to bring these out with an equalizer.

DISC SCRATCHES, DIRT, AND DEFECTS

Here's a short quiz for you: compact discs can be scratched and they still deliver clean, sharp sound? True or false. If you said false, you're right. It's a common fallacy that CDs can be played after being brutalized by the family pet. While it's true that compact discs hide the effects of *minor* scratches far better than LP records, a large scratch, or even a series of small ones, can make a disc completely unplayable.

Chapter 5 discusses disc upkeep (and even repair), but you should know right off about the effects that scratches, dust, dirt, fingerprints, and warpage cause on CD sound quality. All can cause the player to fail, so if your CD is not working properly, suspect the disc first. Check your player against a known good disc. If the problem goes away, the disc is probably bad and should be repaired or replaced.

Scratches

Small scratches that occur radically along the bottom of the disc (that is, from center to edge), pose the least problem to the player. If the scratch is less than about 1mm wide, and doesn't dig too deeply into the plastic layer, the player will all but ignore it, and any error present will be completely concealed. Scratches that occur parallel to the edge of disc, (Fig. 4-9) trace the same path as the pits encoded on the disc. This means more successive pits may be obstructed. The error may not be completely concealed, and the audio output may pop or skip.

The deeper the scratch, the more chance that an audible error will occur. Scratches on the surface of the disc are pretty much out of focus to the photodetectors. But deep scratches are more in focus, so they appear larger to the laser. More data can be blocked, so an audible error may occur.

Scratches on the top (label) side of the disc,

even shallow ones, can ruin the disc. The plastic layer on the top is extremely thin, so it doesn't take much of a scratch to gouge into the aluminum stamping that contains the digital information. You should avoid all scratches on the top.

Dirt and Dust

A speck of dust on the bottom surface of the disc will appear one millionth its original size to the laser. This makes small dirt and dust particles practically invisible to the compact disc player. Although a small accumulation of dust and dirt won't noticeably affect your discs, they can eventually create scratches, which cause more damage, and hence more unconcealed errors. Keep your discs clean by wiping them with a dry, untreated cloth (Fig. 4-11). Always wipe from the inside of the disc to the outside, not along the circumference of the disc. A lintless cloth works better than a cotton rag, because it won't leave behind small bits of fabric. (See Chapter 6 for more information on routine disc care.)

Fingerprints

Fingerprints are really pools of skin oil, and they greatly affect the playability of a compact disc

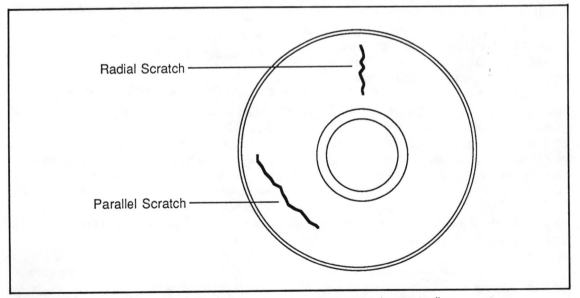

Fig. 4-9. Radial and parallel scratches. Parallel scratches cause the greatest damage to discs.

Fig. 4-10. Before use, wipe the disc with a clean, lintless cloth.

player. As you know, the compact disc system works by reflecting laser light from an aluminum stamping sealed in the disc to a series of photodetectors. Skin oil is partially reflective, and it acts to bounce some of the laser light back into the photodetectors before it ever gets to the aluminum stamping. The result: Lost data or a weak signal. Both can cause mistracking, loss of sound quality, and unconcealed errors.

A light coating of skin oil acts to diffuse the laser light. The return on and off beam reflected from the aluminum stamping is diffused, so the light is considerably weaker than it should be. The player will try to correct this by boosting the light output of the laser. This makes the laser diode work harder than it should, which could conceivably shorten its life span.

For maximum sound quality, your discs should be absolutely free of fingerprints. Clean them regularly with a recommended compact disc cleaner.

Warpage

LP records can be played with even a great amount of warpage. The needle simply rides up and down the waves of the warp. The sound may not be all that great, but playback is possible.

Not so with compact discs. Any warpage beyond the small amount introduced in the manufacturing process will cause the disc to fail. If the disc is visibly warped—it was left out in the open sun for a few hours—it is permanently ruined. Even when you can't see the warpage, it may be enough to cause mistracking. To test for warpage, lay the disc on a mirror and check for gaps. You might be able to repair minor warpage.

Manufactured Defects

So far, we've discussed disc faults that are caused by improper handling (the proper way to treat discs follows in this chapter). Although quality control in the manufacture of compact discs is presently high, all discs have several hundred permanent defects in them. These are manufactured defects, and they range from mistakes in the aluminum stamping to air bubbles in the plastic coating to off-center discs (see Fig. 4-11).

If there is a consistent error on a disc, and close inspection does not reveal a scratch or a piece of dust, suspect a defect in the disc. Most record stores have a refund policy where they will replace a defective disc free of charge.

You can see some manufactured defects simply by looking at the disc. Shine a light at the disc at a 45 degree angle, and closely examine the bottom side. Air bubbles will appear as small dark spots in the plastic. If the aluminum stamping is off center with respect to the plastic shell of the disc, you'll see a marked variance in the distance between the edge of the stamping and the outer edge of the disc (Fig. 4-11). Errors in the disc stamping are generally not visible, because they are too small to be seen with the naked eye (even high powered microscopes don't always reveal gross stamping errors).

PROPER DISC HANDLING

Your compact discs will last the lifetime they were designed for if you follow these rules:

☐ Always return the disc to the jewel storage box after playing.

☐ Never stack two or more discs on top of one another. If the discs slide around, the silk screened

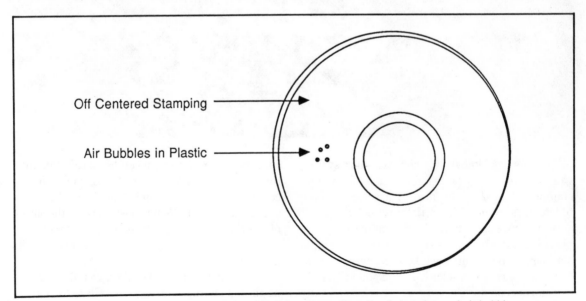

Fig. 4-11. Two not-so-common but usual defects in compact discs: off centered stamping and air bubbles.

Off Centered Stamping

Air Bubbles in Plastic

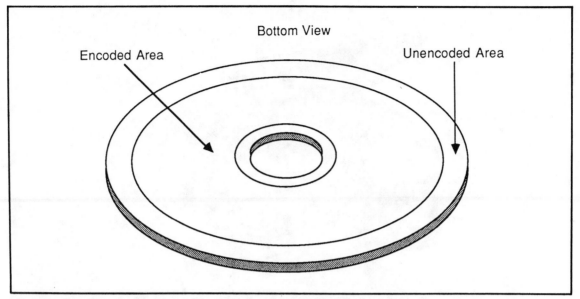

Bottom View

Encoded Area

Unencoded Area

Fig. 4-12. The unencoded area appears as a distinct band on the outer bottom edge of the disc.

label on one disc may scratch the bottom of the disc above it.

   ☐ Some CD enthusiasts stack two discs in the player. The extra thickness from the disc on top is supposed to ensure better clamping inside the player. We don't recommend this. The discs slide over one another, and the silk screened label from the lower disc will invariably scratch the bottom of the other disc. The extra weight of the two discs can also cause premature failure of the disc spindle motor.

   ☐ Handle the discs by the inside hub and edges only.

   ☐ If you look closely at the bottom of the disc, you'll generally see a pronounced band towards the outside edge. As the data on a compact disc is recorded from the inside to the outside, this band represents the blank, unencoded portion of the disc (Fig. 4-12). If you must touch the disc by the surface, limit it to this band only.

   ☐ Clean your discs regularly following the instructions provided in Chapter 6. If a disc becomes scratched, and no longer plays properly, see the section on disc repair in Chapter 6.

Chapter 5

Tools and Supplies
for CD Player Maintenance

The tools and supplies necessary for proper compact disc player maintenance are not extensive or expensive. Apart from common household tools, you need only a few speciality items to maintain your CD player in good operating condition, and to diagnose minor problems. The chapter details these tools and supplies, and how to use them.

WORKSPACE AREA

Regular CD upkeep does not require removal of the player from its comfortable nest in your hi-fi system. As long as you dust the cabinet of the player regularly, and provide adequate ventilation for keeping the power supply cool, you need only remove the player for repair or a preventative maintenance interval.

For minor repair and preventative maintenance, you need a work area that's reasonably free from dust, well lit, and comfortable for you. Avoid taking your compact disc player out in the garage, where there is a greater chance for dust and airborne oil to contaminate its inner workings. A kitchen table or inside work area is ideal.

Before going to work on the player, lay out a small piece of clean carpeting or heavy fabric over the work table. This will protect the table as well as the player from scratches and dents. Collect all the tools you'll be using and have them on hand, preferably in a tool box. Special tools and supplies can be stored in an inexpensive fishing tackle box. The tackle box has lots of small compartments for placing the screws and other parts that you remove. If you don't use a box, borrow a cup or bowl from the kitchen to temporarily store parts you remove from the player.

For best results, your workspace should be an area where the CD player will not be disturbed if you have to leave it for several hours or several days. The work table should also be one that is off limits or inaccessible to young children, or at least an area that can be easily supervised. Some of the chemicals used to clean players and discs are highly toxic, so you should keep them out of reach of children.

There is a risk of electric shock and exposure of infrared laser light when the top of the player is removed. Take every precaution to avoid injury and never leave the player unattended where curious fingers can touch high voltage wires.

BASIC TOOLS

You'll need a screwdriver and a few other common tools to disassemble the player. Most CD players use Philips screws, so be sure you have a Philips screwdriver handy. Others use flathead or allen screws. Determine which tools you need ahead of time and obtain the proper ones. Don't try to make do with the wrong tool. Using a small flathead screwdriver to loosen an allen screw only strips the head of the screw.

Be sure to save all the screws you remove; they are not as easily replaced as you think. The majority of compact disc players are made in Japan, and use screws with Japanese metric threads. You can't easily find them at hardware stores and they can be expensive if purchased at specialty outlets.

A pair of pliers and a soft rubber mallet are also handy tools to have, although you may not need them. The pliers are used to loosen or tighten nuts, grommets, and plastic standoffs; the mallet is used to tap the cover back on after you've finished. Both of these tools can be misused and can cause serious damage if used carelessly. So go easy.

Tweezers or a pair of small long-nosed pliers help you grasp small parts—like screws that have fallen inside the player! A pair of regular manicuring tweezers is fine, but try to get the kind with the flat, blunt end. Tweezers with a pointed end aren't as useful.

VOLT-OHM METER

A volt-ohm meter is used to test voltage levels and the impedance of circuits. This moderately priced electronic tool is the basic requirement for intermediate compact disc maintenance and repair, and is necessary for anything beyond routine cleaning. If you don't already own a volt-ohm meter you should seriously consider buying one. The cost is rather minimal considering the usefulness of the device.

There are many volt-ohm meters (or VOMs) on the market today. For work on compact disc players, you don't want a cheap model and you don't need an expensive one. A meter of intermediate quality is sufficient and does the job admirably. The price for such a meter is between $30 and $75 (it tends to be on the low side of this range). Meters and available at Radio Shack and most electronics outlets. Shop around and compare features and prices.

Digital or Analog

There are two general types of VOMs available today: digital and analog. The difference is not that one meter is used on digital circuits and the other on analog circuits. Rather, digital meters employ a numeric display not unlike a digital clock or watch. Analog VOMs use the older fashioned—but still useful—mechanical movement with a needle that points to a set of graduated scales.

Digital VOMs used to cost a great deal more than the analog variety, but the price difference has evened out recently. Digital VOMs, (Fig. 5-1) are fast becoming the standard; in fact, it's hard to find a decent analog meter anymore.

Analog VOMs are traditionally harder to use, because you must select the type and range of voltage you are testing, find the proper scale on the meter face, then estimate the voltage as the needle swings into action. Digital VOMs, on the other

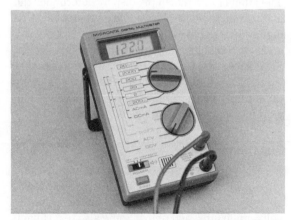

Fig. 5-1. A digital volt-ohm meter, suitable for use with CD players.

hand, display the voltage in clear numerals, and with a greater precision than most analog meters. Because of their increased popularity and ease of use, this chapter will concentrate on digital VOMs exclusively.

Automatic Ranging

As with analog meters, some digital meters require you to select the range before it can make an accurate measurement. For example, if you are measuring the voltage of a 9-volt transistor battery, you set the range to the setting closest to, but *above*, 9 volts (with most meters it is the 25 or 50 volt range). Auto-ranging meters don't require you to do this, so they are inherently easier to use. When you want to measure voltage, you set the meter to volts (either ac or dc) and take the measurement. The meter displays the results in the readout panel.

Accuracy

Little of the work you'll do with compact disc players require a meter that's super accurate. A VOM with average accuracy is more than enough. The accuracy of a meter is the minimum amount of error that can occur when making a specific measurement. For example, the meter may be accurate to 2000 volts, ± 0.8 percent. A 0.8 percent error at the kinds of voltages used in CD players—typically 6 to 12 volts dc—is only 0.096 volts.

Digital meters have another kind of accuracy. The number of digits in the display determines the maximum resolution of the measurements. Most digital meters have 3-1/2 digits, so it can display a value as small as .001 (the half digit is a "1" on the left side of the display). Anything less than that is not accurately represented; then again, there's little cause for accuracy higher than this when working a compact disc player.

Functions

Digital VOMs vary greatly in the number and type of functions they provide. At the very least, all standard VOMs let you measure ac volts, dc volts, milliamps, and ohms. Some also test capacitance and opens or shorts in discrete components like diodes and transistors.

For our purposes, these additional functions are not necessary, and you need not spend the extra money on a meter that includes them. To make effective measurements, you need to take diodes and transistors out of the circuit to accurately test them. The design of most compact disc players makes this difficult and inadvisable, even for a seasoned repair technician. (Component failures are usually repaired by service techs by swapping the entire circuit board and not replacing components.)

The maximum range of the meters when measuring volts, milliamps, and resistance also various. For most applications, including compact disc troubleshooting, the following maximum ratings are more than adequate:

dc Volts	1,000 volts
ac Volts	500 volts
dc Current	200 milliamps
Resistance	2 megohms

Meter Supplies

Most meters come with a pair of test leads—one black and one red—each equipped with a needle-like metal probe. The quality of the test leads is usually minimal, so you may want to purchase a better set. The kind with coiled leads are handy. They stretch out to several feet yet recoil to a manageable length when not in use.

Standard leads are fine for most routine testing, but some measurements may require the use of a clip lead. These have a spring loaded clip on the end; you can clip the lead in place so your hands are free to do other things. The clips are insulated to prevent short circuits, and you can get clips that attach onto regular test leads.

Meter Safety and Use

Most applications of the meter involve testing low voltages and resistance, both of which are relatively harmless to humans. Sometimes, however, you may need to test high voltages—like the input to a power supply—and careless use of the meter can cause serious bodily harm. Even when you're not actively testing a high voltage circuit, it may be exposed when you remove the cover of the CD player.

If the player is plugged in while the cover is off (which it will be if you're testing for proper operation), and you're not measuring voltages at the power supply, cover the power supply terminals, (if exposed) with a piece of cardboard or insulating plastic.

Proper procedure for meter use involves setting the meter beside the unit under test, making sure it is close enough so that the leads reach the test points inside the player. Plug in the leads and test the meter operation by first selecting the resistance function setting (use the smallest scale if the meter is not auto-ranging). Touch the leads together: the meter should read 0 ohms. If the meter does not respond, check the leads and internal battery and try again. If the display does not read 0 ohms, double-check the range and function settings, and adjust the meter to read 0 ohms (not all digital meters have a 0 adjust, but most analog meters do).

Once the meter has checked out, select the desired function and range, and apply the leads to the player circuits. Usually, the black lead will be connected to ground, and the red lead will be connected to the various test points in the player. Figure 5-2 shows a continuity test of the Power switch on a CD player. The black (ground) lead is clipped to one terminal of the switch; the red lead is touched to the other terminal.

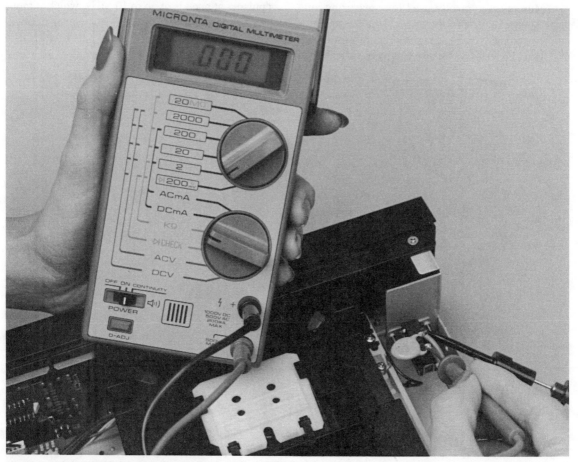

Fig. 5-2. Using the VOM to test the continuity of a switch.

NEVER blindly poke around the inside of a compact disc player in an attempt to get some kind of reading. Apply the test leads only to those portions of the player that you are familiar with—switch contacts, power contacts, and so forth. If you have a schematic diagram for the player, refer to it for the location of the test points.

One safe way to use the meter is to attach a clip on the ground lead and connect it to the chassis or circuit ground. Use one hand to apply the red lead to the various test points; stick the other hand safely in your pocket. With one hand "out of commission," you are less likely to receive a shock because you weren't watching what you were doing.

LOGIC PROBE

Meters are typically used for measuring analog signals. Logic probes test for the presence or absence of low voltage dc signals that represent digital data. The 0's and 1's are usually electrically de-

fined as 0 and 5 volts, respectively (although the actually voltages of the 0 and 1 bits depends entirely on the circuit). You can use a meter to test a logic circuit, but the results aren't always predictable. Further, many logic circuits change states quickly (pulse) and meters cannot track the voltage switches fast enough.

Logic probes (Fig. 5-3) are designed to give a visual and (usually) aural signal of the logic state of a particular circuit line. One LED on the probe lights up if the logic is 0 (or low), another LED lights up if the logic is 1 (or high). Most probes have a built in buzzer, which has a different tone for the two logic levels. That way, you don't need to keep glancing at the probe to see the logic level.

A third LED or tone may indicate a pulsing signal. A good logic probe can detect that a circuit line is pulsing at speeds of up to 10 MHz, which is more than fast enough for compact disc player applications. The minimum detectable pulse width (the time the pulse remains at one level) is 50 nano-

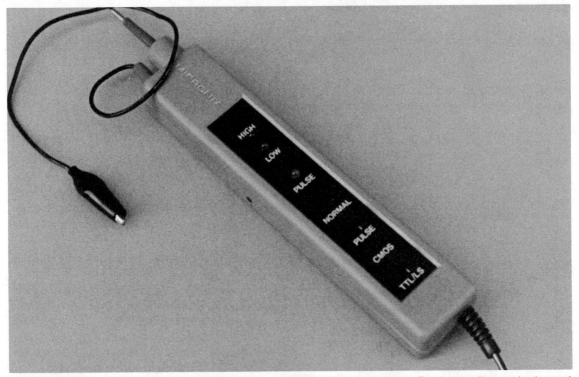

Fig. 5-3. A digital logic probe, sometimes helpful in diagnosing CD player faults. For intermediate and advanced troubleshooting.

seconds, again more than sufficient for testing CD players.

Although logic probes may sound complex, they are really simple devices, and their cost reflects this. You can buy a reasonably good logic probe for under $20. Most probes are not battery operated; rather, they obtain operating voltage by the circuit under test.

Unless you plan in-depth troubleshooting and repair of your compact disc player, a logic probe is not as important as a VOM. It is a handy tool to have should the need ever arise, but routine maintenance does not require it.

Using a Logic Probe

The same safety precautions apply when using a logic probe as they do when using a meter. When the cover of the player is removed, potentially dangerous high voltages may be exposed. If you are working close to these voltages, cover them to pre-

vent accidental shock. Logic probes cannot operate with voltages exceeding about 15 volts dc, so if you are unsure of the voltage level of a particular circuit, test it with a meter first to be sure it is safe.

Successful use of the logic probe really requires you to have the circuit schematic to refer to. It's nearly impossible to blindly use the logic probe on a circuit without knowing what you are testing. And since the probe receives its power from the circuit under test, you need to know where to pick off suitable power. You can easily damage the probe—and possibly the circuit under test—if you connect the power leads incorrectly.

To use the probe, connect the probe's power leads to a voltage source on the board, clip the black ground wire to circuit ground, and touch the tip of the probe against a pin of an integrated circuit or the lead of some other component (Fig. 5-4).

Please note: CD players often use negative

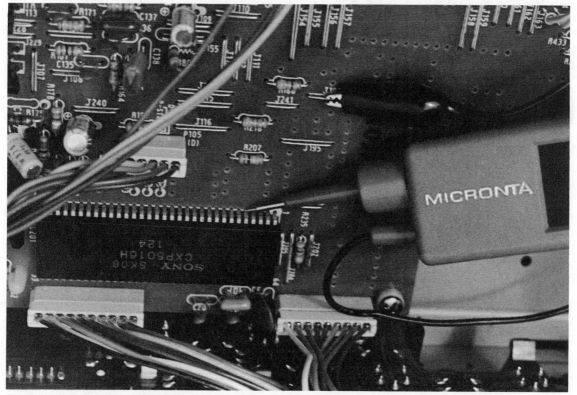

Fig. 5-4. Using the probe to test the logic level at an IC pin.

voltages with respect to ground. To the logic probe, there is little difference between connecting the power leads to a positive and ground rail, or connecting the power leads to a negative and ground rail. However, avoid connecting the power leads to a positive *and* negative rail, because the voltage differential might exceed the maximum supply voltage of the probe. For instance, connecting the lead between the +9 and −9 rails will feed 18 volts to the probe, which is higher than its rated operating voltage.

LASER DETECTOR

Video disc players use a laser that emits a visible beam that's easy to spot. You can tell that the laser is working just by looking at it. The laser diode used in compact disc players, however, operates at 780 nanometers, which is in the infrared region of the light spectrum. Despite the colorful advertising art that manufacturers often use to depict the operation of the CD player, the beam is not a bright red streak of light, like the light sabers in a Star Wars movie.

Because you can't see the laser light, you need to use a special infrared light sensor to determine that the laser is indeed working. Such sensors are not readily available at any reasonable cost, but

they are easy to make. This section describes the circuit and construction details of an inexpensive but versatile laser light sensor. You can also use the sensor to test other sources of infrared light, including the wireless remote control for your CD player.

Bear in mind that you need not construct the sensor unless you are actively involved in the repair of compact disc players, or unless you firmly suspect that the laser in your player has gone awry. The laser diode used in CD players is a long-lasting solid-state device, with an average operating life of 5,000 or more hours, and should long outlast most of the mechanical components of the machine. Still, laser diodes are known to break down after only a short period of time. It's not impossible for a laser diode in a compact disc player to go on the fritz after only one or two years of use.

Circuit Description

The laser light sensor is a simple circuit that employs only three parts: an infrared phototransistor, an LED, and a resistor. The schematic is shown in Fig. 5-5. All the parts are commonly available at Radio Shack and most other electronic part stores. You need some sort of battery supply to operate the circuit. We've built the circuit with four

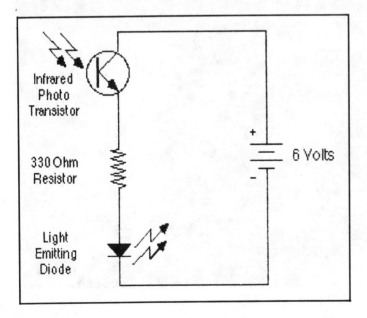

Fig. 5-5. Schematic of the laser light sensor.

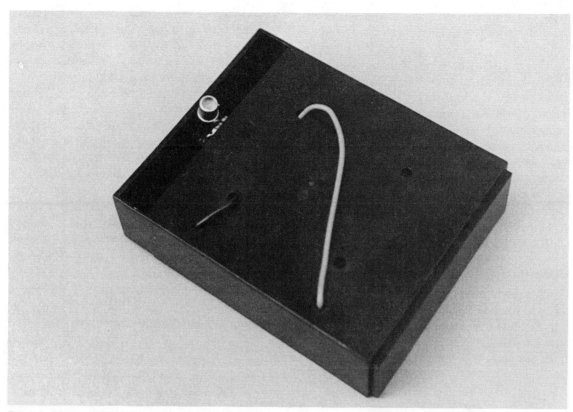

Fig. 5-6. An assembled laser light sensor.

"AA" batteries enclosed in a self-contained battery compartment. The compartment also serves as the case for the sensor electronics.

Alternatively, you can use a 9-volt transistor battery mounted in a simple clip holder. The resistor limits the current flowing through the LED, but the 330 ohm value selected is safe for use with supply voltages up to 9 volts. If you use a higher supply voltage, increase the value of the resistor, using *Ohm's Law*. Failure to do this may cause the visible LED in the circuit to burn out.

You can determine the value of the resistor by taking the supply/voltage and subtracting the voltage drop through the LED (usually 1.2 volts). Divide the result by the current you want flowing through the LED (usually about 20 milliamps). For example, with a supply voltage of 9 volts, subtracting the drop in the LED makes 7.8 volts. Divide that by .02 (20 milliamps) and you get 390. The ex-

act value of resistor to use, then, is 390 ohms. There is a lot of slack built into this, because LEDs can take higher currents without risk of damage. On a practical level, don't exceed 30 to 40 milliamps.

For best results, solder the components on a small perforated board, or use an 8-pin IC socket. The components fit in the contacts of the socket without soldering, but you may wish to solder the leads in place to prevent them from coming out. Soldering into the socket is a little tricky, because the plastic can melt. An easy way is to fit the component leads into the contacts of the socket, and briefly touch the leads with the tip of the soldering iron. Before the plastic of the socket melts, apply the solder. The electrical contract has already been made inside the socket by the contacts; the solder simply serves to anchor the leads in place. Place the assembly in a box, (Fig. 5-6) to prevent damage during storage and use. The LED is mounted on the other side of the socket, so that it can be seen when the sensor is pointed towards the optical pickup.

Orientation of both the phototransistor and LED are critical. Installing them backwards will cause the circuit to not work. The phototransistor is marked with a tab or indentation so that you can easily identify the emitter and collector. Refer to the specifications sheets that came with the transistor, or consult a transistor guidebook. The plastic rim on the cathode side of the LED is almost always marked with a small indentation. You can install the resistor in any direction. Be sure to connect the power leads in the proper way too. Reversing the leads could destroy the phototransistor.

Using the Sensor

You can test the sensor by connecting the battery and pointing the phototransistor directly into a bright light (the sun and regular light bulbs all have infrared light content). The LED should glow. If it does not, check your work to make sure the

Fig. 5-7. Using the sensor to test the operation of the laser in a portable player.

components have been wired correctly (of course, be sure the battery is good; test it with your VOM).

Once you're sure the sensor works, you can test the laser diode in your compact disc player. You must get the phototransistor within one to three inches from the objective lens of the optical pickup for the phototransistor to pick up any light. Figure 5-7 shows the sensor being used on a portable CD player (the LED can be seen at the tip of the index finger). Note the metal clips inserted into the latching mechanism of the player. These clips defeat the safety interlock switches in the player, so the laser will turn on when the top is open.

This brings us to an important point. The light from the laser diode, though invisible, can cause eye damage if you stare directly into it. When testing the laser diode, keep your eyes out of the direct optical path of the light. Avoid getting closer than 12 inches from the objective lens.

Defeating Laser Safety Interlocks

You must activate the laser to test it, which means you must put the player into Play mode. Obviously, you also need to remove the top cover of the machine to access the pickup and operate it without a disc. Most drawer-type or door-type players will go into play mode with no disc installed, but only for a moment. During the initial playback stage, the pickup attempts to read the disc. But because there is no disc, the player will soon stop.

Some players, particularly ones that are top loading (including the portables, have a variety of safety interlock features that prevents the laser from turning on unless a disc has been inserted, and the door or cover has been closed. To get the laser to turn on with these, you must locate the interlock switches and defeat them.

Figure 5-8 shows inserting the pieces of a bent paper clip into the interlock switches of a common portable CD. You can use toothpicks, paper, or other objects to push the switches closed, to simulate that a disc has been properly loaded. Some interlocks, however, depend on electrical contract made by a pin in the top cover, so you may need to use metallic objects to complete the circuit.

You'll know that the switches have been defeated when you push the play button and the

Fig. 5-8. Using bent paper clips to defeat the safety interlock switches, for testing the laser.

disc spindle starts to spin. With all CD players, the objective lens will pop up and down one to three times during the initial startup time. The pickup is trying to focus on a disc. During this time, the laser is on and you can test it.

Even some drawer and door loading CD players have internal interlock switches. If the disc spindle does not spin, look for an interlock switch and defeat it. Most interlock switches are located along the side and the back of the loading drawer, as shown in Fig. 5-9, and a few machines have interlock switches attached to the cabinet. The laser is defeated when the top cover is removed.

Depending on the design of the player, some switches must be closed (depressed) for the laser to work, while others must be open. You might encounter electronic switches; these are optical and

sense when a disc is present, light from a small infrared LED is blocked off to a phototransistor. You can easily defeat this type of electronic switch by placing a stiff piece of paper between the LED and photodetector.

If the pickup is tucked too deeply within the player to closely position the phototransistor, you may need to attach longer leads to the transistor. Use any insulating wire but keep the lead lengths under six inches if at all possible. Twist the two lead wires together in a braid. You can use shielded wire, the same kind used in audio applications, if the lead length must be longer than six inches.

AMPLIFIER AND SPEAKERS

A small portable amplifier and speakers are invaluable when troubleshooting and repairing a bro-

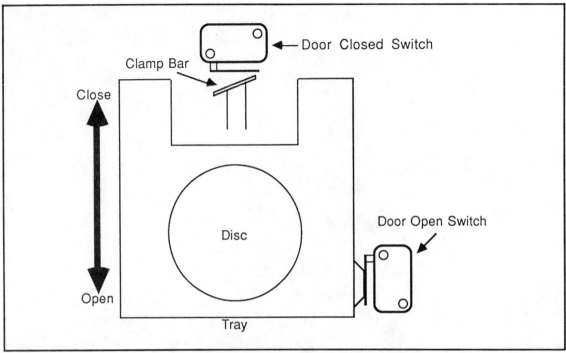

Fig. 5-9. Typical locations of interlock switches in and around the disc loading mechanism.

ken compact disc player. You can keep the CD connected to the amp and test the player as you go through the various troubleshooting procedures. It's a lot easier than hooking the player back up to your hi-fi whenever you want to test something.

The amplifier need not be special, but it should be stereo, especially if you're having trouble with the audio output stages of the player. You can use any small speakers that are rated for use with the amplifier. Alternatively, if the amp has a headphone jack, you can use headphones to listen to the audio output. Use caution, however, because unexpected sound coming through the player can be deafening if the volume is turned up. When not needed, you should take the headphones off.

ASSORTED SUPPLIES

Unlike the family automobile, the compact disc player requires little in the way of oiling and lubing—if at all. Some cleaning and lubrication supplies may be necessary, however, and any well-equipped maintenance kit will have a little of both.

Spray Cleaner

The cabinet of the player can be cleaned with a damp sponge. If dirt and grime are a problem, use a mild spray household cleaner, such as Fantastik or 409. Apply the spray to the sponge or cloth, not directly onto the cabinet. Excess can run inside and possibly cause damage.

Cleaner/Degreaser

Freon, the stuff used as a coolant in air conditioners, is also a solvent. Unlike most petroleum-based solvents, Freon doesn't melt plastics, and the kind of Freon that you can readily buy is non-toxic and non-flammable. It does have a distinctive odor, but it is harmless.

Freon by itself can be used as a basic degreaser and cleaner. You can use it to remove things like grime and dirt in hard to reach places. Freon is available at most any industrial supply house, or if such a business is not nearby, purchase a can of compressed air at a photographic store. Using the can upside down expels the pure Freon propellant.

Fig. 5-10. Three commonly available non-residue cleaners.

Freon is often mixed with alcohol to make a more potent cleaner. Use caution with this stuff: it is flammable and toxic. The Freon and alcohol mixture can be used as a general cleaner, a degreaser, even as a lens cleaner for the objective lens mounted in the pickup. Chapter 6 shows you how to use the mixture to clean the lens.

The Freon/alcohol mixture is available as an all-purpose cleaner/degreaser that you can buy in a spray can. The cleaner is available at Radio Shack and most any electronics supplies store. Figure 5-10 shows three cans that use Freon and alcohol in various mixtures, but they all pretty much do the same thing. The cleaners leave no residue, so you can spray it on and it'll dry with no trace.

The cleaner/degreaser can be used on all the internal components of the compact disc player, including the printed circuit board, optical pickup, and disc loading mechanism. Always remember to turn the player off and let it cool down before spray-

ing. Otherwise, you run the risk of a short circuit. Spraying the cold liquid on warm parts can crack some components.

Lens Cleaning Material

In addition to Freon and alcohol, you can clean the objective lens on the optical pickup with most any lens cleaner that's recommended for photographic use. Never use lens cleaners or polishers designed for eyeglasses on the optical pickup of a compact disc player. These usually incorporate silicone, which can adversely react with the coating on the objective, and permanently ruin it.

Keep in mind that cleaning the objective with a fluid is not generally necessary, unless the lens has a thick coating of dust or nicotine, or has been tainted by a greasy fingerprint. All you'll probably need is a packet of non-treated lens tissues (again, available at photographic stores), or a swab made of cotton or chamois. Moisten the objective lens with a "huff" of breath. Avoid rubbing the lens with a dry swab.

Grease and Oil

The mechanical components of a CD player are few and far between, and most do not require any special lubrication. Some lubrication is especially recommended if the player has been used in adverse environments (a portable or auto CD player would fall into this category) or is more than two or three years old.

Just about any light machine oil can be used for the components that need oiling. The oil should not have anti-rust ingredients. Good candidates are 3-in-1 Oil or most any oil designed for sewing machines. Another good oil is that kind designed for musical instruments. The high grade oil comes in a handy applicator bottle. Some bottles come with a syringe-type needle for applying the oil in hard to reach places.

The best oil to use is the kind designed for small machined parts. This oil, which is packed in a small bottle with a syringe applicator, has special penetrating lubricants that ordinary oils lack. You can buy this oil at most industrial supply houses, and some camera and electronics stores.

The "grease" should be a non petroleum-based product. There are a variety of greaseless lubricants from which to choose. A light-grade lubricant, such as that used in 35mm cameras, is suitable. You can obtain it from most industrial supply stores and camera repair shops. A small tube goes a long way.

Refer to Chapter 6 for more details on common CD components that require oiling and lubrication. Note that some mechanical components do not require oil or lubrication, and in fact can be harmed by them. Motors fall into this category. It's a safe bet that if there is no sign that oil or lubricant has ever been present on a mechanical part, it does not need it!

Miscellaneous Cleaning Supplies

There are a variety of other supplies that may

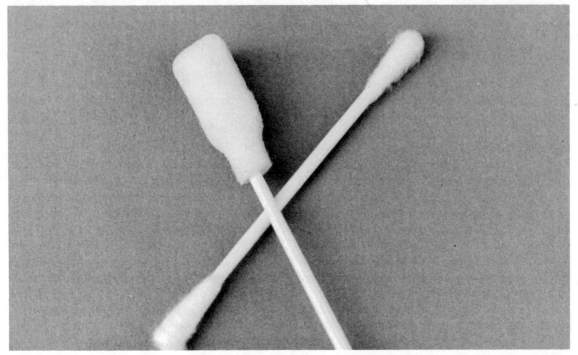

Fig. 5-11. Cotton swabs can leave behind lint; sponge swabs leave no fabric that can interfere with the proper operation of the player.

come in handy when repairing and maintaining a CD player.

□ Brushes let you dust out dirt.

□ Contact cleaner enables you to clean the electrical contacts in the player.

□ Cotton swabs help you soak up excess oil, lubricant and cleaner.

□ Sponge-tipped swabs are like cotton swabs, but leave no little pieces of lint behind (see Fig. 5-11).

□ Orange sticks (from a manicure set) and nail files let you scrape junk off circuit boards and electrical contacts.

□ The eraser on a pencil goes a long way to rub electrical contacts clean, especially ones that have been contaminated by the acid from a leaking battery.

□ Modeling putty (for plastic models) can be used to mend cracks and chips on the plastic exterior of the CD player cabinet.

□ Contact cement, white glue, and other common adhesives are excellent for repairing broken plastic and metal parts.

□ A small magnet makes it easier to pick up screws and ferrous metallic objects that have been accidentally dropped into the player.

□ Non-slip cleaner removes oily build-up from rubber parts like rollers and belts. Alcohol should not be used to clean rubber parts, as it can dry them out.

USING TEST DISCS

Test discs enable you to put your CD through a series of diagnostic procedures that examine the player's ability to successfully reproduce music on a damaged disc. This may seem rather daff, but test discs can be used not only to determine whether a player is well designed, but if its tracking, focusing, and electronic error correction circuits are working properly. If you test your CD with a disc when you first buy it, then again a year later—and the player doesn't fare as well—it's a good indication that the player needs preventative maintenance.

Commercial Test Discs

You can buy a commercial test disc from any of several CD player manufacturers. The discs contain carefully recorded audio signals that are designed for use in adjusting the player after servicing. As such, the discs aren't much to listen to, unless you are a fan of single-note tones that go on for minutes. Most test discs also include simulated damage—dust particles, scratches, even fingerprints. The damage is carefully controlled, so that during playback, you know the extent of disc damage a player can tolerate before it is thrown off course.

The premier test disc is offered by Philips and goes by stock number TS4A. The TS4A disc contains some short music selections that are obstructed by a variety of simulated and deliberate damage. The first type of damage on the TS4A disc is a wedge-shaped area on the aluminum signal surface. The wedge was created by scratching the master-disc mold.

The minimum width of the wedge, as seen by the laser, is 400 μm. This inner surface wedge is meant to simulate either pinholes in the disc's aluminum stamping, or scratches on the outside of the disc. Philips says that all players should be able to navigate through the 400 μm wedge with no audible errors. The wedge enlarges to 500 μm and 600 μm. Many players can handle these with no problem, as well.

The TS4A disc also includes a series of opaque black dots 300, 500, 600, and 800 μm in diameter. These are painted on the outside of the disc, so the laser actually sees them as much smaller obstructions when it focuses on the signal surface. The dots are supposed to simulate bubbles in the plastic protective layer. Philips says that all players should be able to handle the 300 μm dot, but most late-model players can play through most without any problem.

A rectangular grid of tiny dots represent a real greasy fingerprint. Because the rectangle is oriented so that it is longest in the direction of disc rotation, the fingerprint test is the toughest one of all. Though it is a difficult test, your player should be able to pass through the fingerprint with little or no error.

Making Your Own Test Discs

The Philips TS4A test disc was engineered at a time when compact disc players were still in their infancy. Player design has improved greatly, and the vast majority of CDs can play through the TS4A disc with no problem. The disc is good to have as a benchmark, but you can put your player through a much more rigorous ordeal by making a test disc yourself. Your own test disc is also cheaper.

You can make a test disc using any CD you already own. The disc will not be damaged, but you should use one that, if accidentally hurt, would pose no great loss. To make the disc, purchase a roll of graphics arts tape, the kind used to make thin lines for charting and graphing purposes. You can get the tape at any art supply store and the cost is minimal—under $2.50 for one roll. The tape comes in a variety of colors and widths. Black matte tape that is 1/32-inch wide is a good candidate for test discs. Thinner tape is harder to work with and

doesn't really stretch the error correction circuitry in the player. You can really test a player's tracking ability by using 1/16-inch wide tape.

Place a strip of the tape radially along the bottom (play) surface of the disc, like a spoke on a wheel (Fig. 5-12). Make sure it adheres to the disc and that the tape is trimmed neatly at the edge. Don't worry about the tape damaging the player. It won't. The worst thing that can happen is the tape will come off inside the player. Should this happen, and the tape can't be extracted when you open the drawer, remove the top cover to gain direct access to the pickup area. In any case, if you press the tape onto the disc well enough in the first place, it is unlikely that it will come off.

To the player, the black strip acts as a thick scratch. The 1/32″ width at the bottom of the disc corresponds to roughly 1 or 2 μm at the data surface, which still means that at most, only a few dozen pits will be totally blocked off by the player.

Fig. 5-12. Placing a thin strip of matte black graphics arts tape on the bottom (play) side of the disc, in order to test the error correction systems in a player.

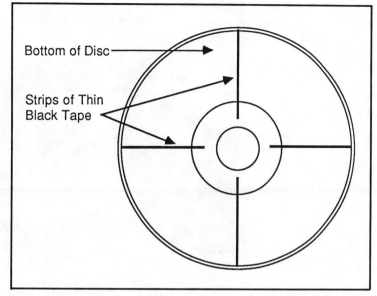

Bottom of Disc

Strips of Thin
Black Tape

Fig. 5-13. Add more strips on the disc until unconcealed errors occur. Place the strips opposite each other, like the spokes on a wheel.

All but the very worst players will track through the single piece of tape. You can test the threshhold of your player by adding more strips. Place a second strip opposite to the first, and try the disc. Add two more strips 90 degrees away from the other two (Fig. 5-13). Try the disc again. A good player will be able to play with up to six to eight strips on the disc before errors are heard.

You can use your test disc to evaluate a player before you buy it. If the player doesn't seem to be able to handle the disc with any more than three or four strips, you may want to look at another machine. You can also use the test disc as a bench-

mark. Try the test disc when your machine is new. Note it's upper threshhold, the maximum number of black strips it can accommodate before audible errors occur.

At regular intervals—say every six to 12 months—recheck the operation of the player with the same disc. If the player can't accommodate as many strips, it's a good indication that it is in need of a checkup. The objective lens in the optical pickup might be dirty, or the slide rails used in the transport may be sticking due to an accumulation of dust or nicotine. See Chapter 6 for more information on preventative maintenance procedures.

Chapter 6

General Preventative Maintenance

"An ounce of prevention is worth a pound of cure." The saying applies in many walks of life, and it definitely goes for compact disc players. A few well-spent moments keeping your CD player in top-notch condition goes a long way. You'll save money in the long run and enjoy your CD player investment more.

In this chapter, you'll learn how to give your compact disc player a routine preventative maintenance checkup. This includes the player, the player's remote control, and your collection of discs. You'll also learn how to test the player for proper operation, and how to repair moderately damaged discs.

FREQUENCY OF CHECKUP

The preventative maintenance (PM) interval for your CD player varies depending on many factors. Under normal use, you'll want to give the player a PM checkup every 6 to 12 months. By normal use, we mean a player operated in an average household environment, not on a factory floor or

at the beach. You may need to perform the PM checkup on a more timely basis if your player is subjected to environmental extremes, or is exposed to heavy doses of dust, dirt, water spray (especially salt water), airborne oil, and sand. A chart of suggested PM intervals for machines that receive light, medium, and heavy use appears at the end of this chapter.

How do you know if your CD player needs a preventative maintenance checkup? Experience is your only guide, but if you have not yet gained the experience in how often the player needs routine maintenance, you can't judge if the service interval is required. As you become acquainted with your compact disc player, you will get to know when it needs a checkup. In the meantime, here are some clues that can point you in the right direction:

☐ The outside of the player is covered with caked-on dirt, dust, or other grime. If the outside is dirty, so is the inside.

☐ The summer has come and gone and you feel the player has seen all the good times with you.

Was your portable player buried in the sand at the all-night beach party? It might still play, but this doesn't mean that it's clean.

☐ There are more disc errors, including gross mistracking, than there used to be. Something is amiss inside the CD, but not serious enough to impair playback entirely.

☐ The player makes unusual sounds during disc loading and playback.

☐ None of your CDs skip, they just don't sound as good as they used to. The music is weak or is missing its normal full body.

A WORD OF CAUTION

It's important to remember that unless you are an authorized repair technician for the brand of player you own, taking it apart to perform the preventive maintenance procedures outlined in this chapter will probably VOID THE WARRANTY. Most compact disc players have a warranty period of a year or so (some more; some less), and you might as well take advantage of it. There is usually no reason to perform a PM checkup within the warranty period.

One exception to this is if the player has been accidentally damaged by water, dirt, or sand, and although it still plays, you'd feel better if it were cleaned. Factory warranty service does not cover this type of cleaning, and you'd pay handsomely for it. The cleaning and "repair" cost may well exceed the price you paid for the machine. In this case, there's nothing stopping you from doing the work yourself. If your CD is subjected to heavy abuse, check the procedures in Chapter 7.

PERSONAL SAFETY

If your CD is an ac operated home model, removing the cover exposes 117 volts of alternating current. Given the right circumstances, this current can kill you. Remember to unplug the unit at all times when you are not actually testing its operating. Even with the power switch off, but the player still plugged in, the electricity is still present at the terminals near the unit's power supply.

Warning signs that appear on the back of ac operated CD players, and in their manuals, say there is potential dangerous voltages inside. When you see the triangle and lightning bolt sign, as shown in Fig. 6-1, heed them. The other warning sign, the triangle and exclamation point, also shown in the figure, says that you should refer to the owner's manual before operating the equipment. Few people actually do this, but, it's still a good idea.

The laser used in compact disc players is low power, but its pencil thin, focused beam can cause eye damage if you look directly into the objective lens when the machine is on and working. The laser emits a beam in the infrared light spectrum and is invisible. To paraphrase an old saying, "what you

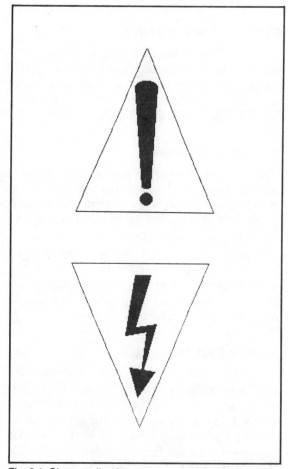

Fig. 6-1. Observe all safety warnings outside and inside the compact disc player.

can't see won't hurt you," does NOT apply to the laser diode in a compact disc player.

For safety's sake, turn the player off and unplug it when performing the routine maintenance procedures outlined in this chapter. If the CD must be plugged in and switched on for a particular test, always assume that the laser is functioning, even when a disc is not in the player. Therefore, cover the objective lens with a piece of stiff paper to block the beam. Don't use tape as the sticky adhesive can gum up the surface of the lens, and cause you additional trouble. Remember to take the paper off when you insert a disc for playback.

WARNING: Do not perform the steps in this chapter unless you feel confident in your ability and have observed all safety precautions.

GENERAL MAINTENANCE

Before you go poking around inside the compact disc player, first take a close look outside. You can perform these preventative maintenance steps on a more regular basis, because they do not entail removing the cover of the player.

Manuals of Operation

An important measure in your efforts to minimize CD player troubles is to read the instruction manuals that came with your equipment. This may sound a bit obvious, but you'd be surprised how many hi-fi enthusiasts never take the time to thoroughly read the operating manuals. The manufacturers of the equipment include the manuals so you can get the most out of your expensive purchase. Keep them at hand, and refer to them whenever you have a question.

Exterior Dust and Dirt

On the top of your hi-fi system maintenance list should be routine external cleaning. Every few days, take a dry cloth and wipe each component of your video system. Don't use dusting sprays; these actually attract dust, luring dirt back onto your equipment. Use a soft, sable painter's brush for those hard to reach places. Be sure to clean the ven-

tilation slots as these are favorite hiding places for dust.

If you need to get rid of stubborn grime, apply a light spray of regular household cleaner onto a clean rag, then wipe with the rag. Never apply the spray directly onto the player, as the excess can run inside. Never apply a petroleum-based solvent cleaner as it might remove paint and melt the exterior plastic parts. Some plastics, when in contact with a petroleum-based solvent, let off highly toxic fumes.

Cables

The cables and connectors hooking the compact disc player to the amplifier must be in good shape. Be sure the cables are on tight and that none of them are damaged. Many hi-fi enthusiasts have a tangle of cables behind their stereo gear, and just one bad wire or connector in the bunch can cause grief.

If you suspect that a cable may be bad, or causing interference and hum try a replacement to see if the problem is solved.

Alternatively, you can use a volt-ohm meter, as shown in Fig. 6-2, to test the continuity of the cable. Attach the test leads to the center conductor of both ends, and take a reading. The meter should read 0 ohms. Do the same for the outer conductor.

Check also that the cable has not shorted by applying the test leads to the inner and outer conductors on one end of the cable (be sure not to hold onto the metal probes of the test leads you might get false readings). The measurement should read infinite ohms (open circuit).

INTERNAL PREVENTATIVE MAINTENANCE

To gain access inside the player, it should be removed from its location in your hi-fi system. Disassemble the player only in an open, well illuminated work area.

Disassembly

Disassembly of most compact disc players is

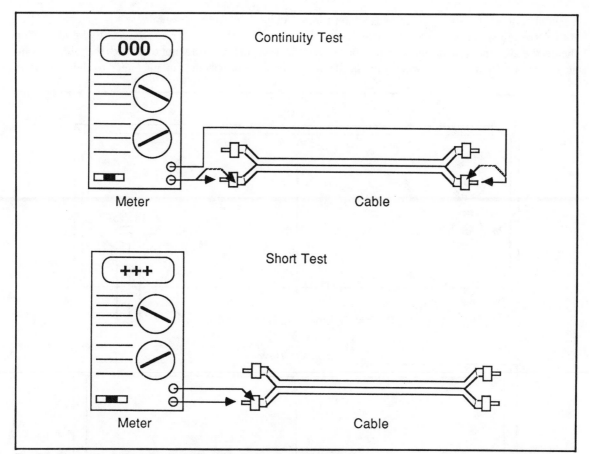

Fig. 6-2. The method of testing an audio cable for continuity and shorts.

simple and straightforward. The typical ac operated home unit is composed of a top and bottom piece; you loosen two or more screws and remove the top portion of the cabinet. The screws are usually located at the rear and bottom edges of the player, as shown in Fig. 6-3.

You should not loosen every screw you see, especially those on the bottom center portion of the cabinet, because they may anchor the internal components to the base plate. Be particularly wary of screws located immediately under the disc loading door (other than transit screws), as they may very well hold the delicate transport and pickup mechanisms in place. Loosen one screw at a time and attempt to remove the top cover (or at least see if it is coming loose). If a screw seems to hold an inter-

nal component in place, retighten it and try another. Basic disassembly instructions for many ac operated home compact disc players appear in Chapter 10.

Save the screws in a cup or container. If the screws are different sizes, note where they came from for easier reassembly. Keep washers, grommets, spacers, and other hardware with their related screws. The additional hardware has been used for a reason, and should not be omitted when the player is reassembled.

If necessary, write a list of the parts you remove, and the order in which they were removed. If a certain screw has a rubber washer, a metal washer, and a locking washer on it, write down the order in which they are assembled on the screw.

Carefully inspect the parts you remove to determine if they are aligned or oriented in a certain way. Indicate the alignment or orientation on your sheet so you are sure to duplicate it when you put the machine back together again.

With the screws removed, gently lift off the top cover, being careful not to disturb the internal components or wiring. You may need to slide the cover

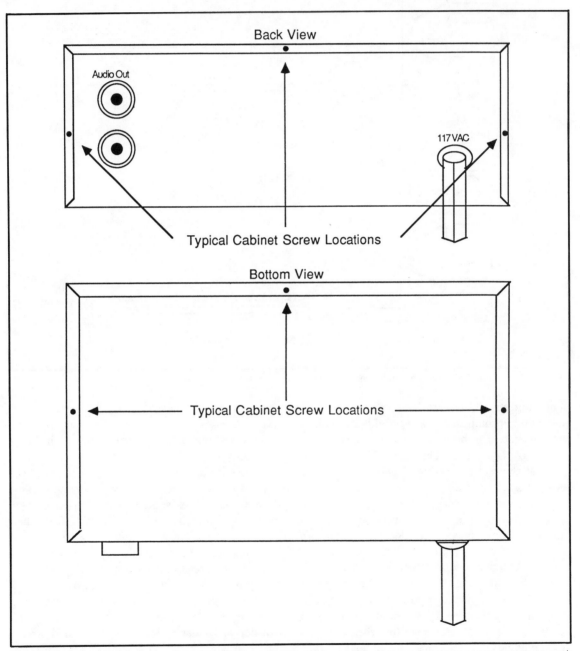

Fig. 6-3. Typical cabinet screw locations on an ac operated home player. Other players have one or two screws on each side of the cabinet.

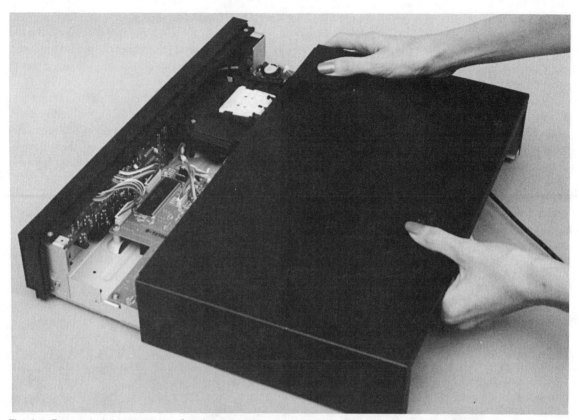

Fig. 6-4. Removal of the top cover. Carefully slide the cover off, being sure you do not disturb the components inside the player.

back before taking it off, if the cover tucks under a lip in the front panel (Fig. 6-4).

With most players, the interior will be sparse and unimpressive—that's both the beauty and mystique of compact disc! They are simple and complex at the same time. The relative emptiness of the cabinet makes working on them that much easier. Portable and automotive compact disc players, because of the close proximity of parts, are somewhat harder to work on.

Once the cover is off, you should not attempt to disassemble anything else inside the machine, except where noted below. This is especially true of the drawer disc loading mechanism and the pickup, which are aligned at the factory with special tools. Loosening the wrong screws can skew the orientation and position of critical components. This may require a service technician (which is ex-

pensive) and a special alignment jig (which you cannot easily get for yourself) to correct the mistake.

About Static Electricity

Static electricity build-up in your body may harm the integrated circuits and other components on the main circuit board. Do not touch any part unless you have first drained the static electricity from your body. If you plan to handle the circuit boards, use a grounding strap around your wrist. The strap is available at most electronics supply stores. Follow the instructions supplied with it for proper use.

Preliminary Inspection

Take a few moments to acquaint yourself with the inside of the player. Note the position of the optical pickup, the main circuit board, the auxiliary boards for the front panel, indicator, and headphone (if any), the routing of the cables, and the incoming power supply lines. Figures 6-5 through 6-9 show the innards of a typical late-model CD. Be particularly wary of the power supply board or power supply section on the main PCB. The filtering capacitors (which usually look like tall cans) retain some current even when the player is turned off and unplugged. Avoid touching the leads of the capacitors and make sure that you do not short the leads together. You may damage the capacitor and components on the board.

Front loading disc players—those with drawers or doors—obviously have more complex loading mechanisms than their top-load cousins. There is more to look at in a front-load machine and consequently more points that may need preventative care.

Note the type of pickup mechanism—slide or swing arm. Slide mechanisms often need a light dab of lubricant to keep the pickup moving smoothly back and forth along the length of the rails. Swing arm pickups generally do not require any type of lubrication.

There is little, if any, adjustment or calibration that you can—or should—do once inside the compact disc player. Potentiometers on the main circuit board are factory set and require an oscilloscope or special test circuitry for proper adjustment.

Rollers and Belts

Visually check the rollers and belts used in the disc turntable mechanism and (sometimes) disc loading mechanism. If worn or cracked, they should be replaced. You can replace the belts yourself. Obtain the service literature for your player from the manufacturer, identify the part by its part number,

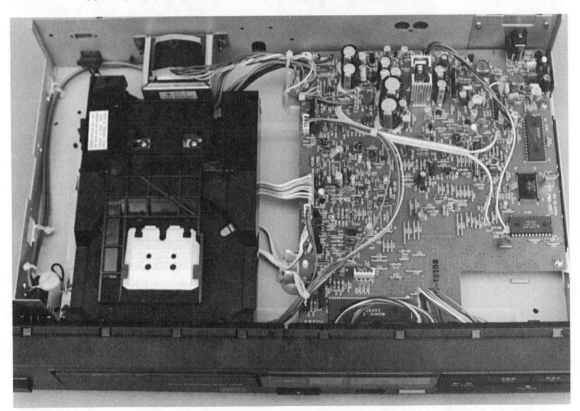

Fig. 6-5. The inside of a typical compact disc player. Not much, right?! Many players have even less inside them.

Fig. 6-6. The main PCB. This board also contains the power supply circuits. Note the two heat sinks supporting the voltage regulators (back center of picture).

Fig. 6-7. The disc loading mechanism. On the top is the flapper (also called the clamper or chucker).

Fig. 6-8. The optical pickup, nestled under the loading mechanism. Nothing in the pickup is serviceable; the entire module must be replaced if bad. Note the slide rails on the front and the back of the pickup.

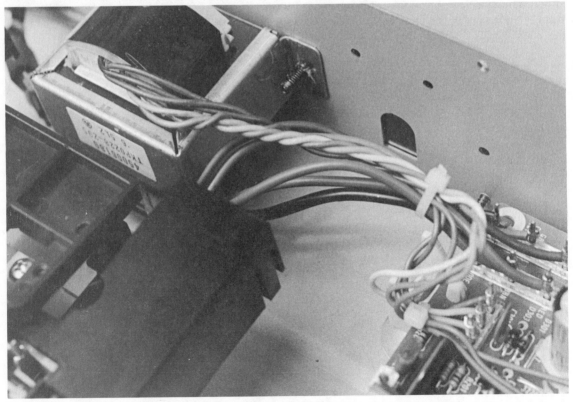

Fig. 6-9. The transformer and power connections to the main PCB.

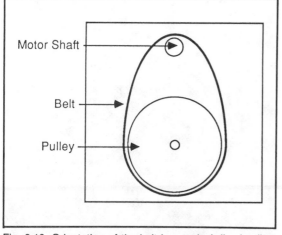

Fig. 6-10. Orientation of the belt in a typical disc loading mechanism. The belt is easy to replace, but you must get to it first. Avoid disassembly of the internal parts of the player; use dentist's picks or other small tools to replace the belt.

and order it from the manufacturer. Dentist's picks, which you can buy at most electronics and surplus outlets, let you more easily remove and install belts that are hard to reach. Figure 6-10 shows a typical belt configuration as used in the disc spindle mechanism.

Rubber rollers and belts that are slipping can be cleaned with a special cleaner. The non-slip cleaner is available at Radio Shack and most electronics stores. Apply it to the belt or roller with a cotton swab or sponge applicator, as shown in Fig. 6-11. The cleaner takes a few moments to dry, so wait two or three minutes before operating the machine.

Avoid the use of solvent-based cleaners on rubber parts, as these chemicals can prematurely dry up the rubber, or worse, melt it. Never apply a lubricant of any kind to a roller or belt, as this will

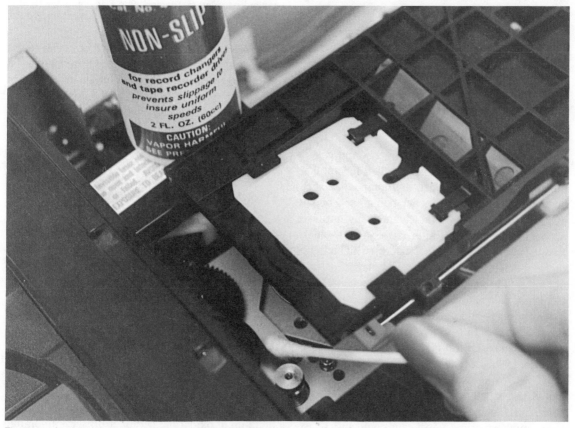

Fig. 6-11. Applying non-slip cleaner to the disc loading belt.

defeat their purpose. If the rubber squeaks, it's an indication that something is not properly aligned, or that the roller or belt needs replacement.

Topical Cleaning

Dust, dirt, and nicotine from cigarette smoke can accumulate in the interior of the CD player and should be removed. Use a soft brush to wipe away excess dust and dirt. If there is a lot of sediment, use a small hobby vacuum cleaner.

Remaining dust and other junk may be blown out of the insides of the player. Purchase a small can of compressed air at a photographic shop (about $3) and liberally squirt it inside the machine. That should free just about everything that shouldn't be there. Remember to keep the can upright, as the propellant might drip out. As much as possible, position the air flow so that debris is blown *out* of the player, not deeper inside!

The use of household cleaning sprays should be avoided, as these not only can leave a residue that impairs the proper operation of the player, but are water based, and might short out the circuitry. Do not use a cleaner that contains a solvent of any kind, and DO NOT clean the machine with an oil-less lubricant such as WD-40 or LPS. These sprays are non-conductive and will cause the player to fail completely.

You can clean nicotine sediments and caked-on dirt using a cleaner recommended for application on mechanical and electronic components. Figure 6-12 shows such a cleaner being used on the main PCB board (apply the cleaner only until the player has cooled down after use). Some cleaners have a built-in degreaser that disperses oil build-up; these are fine for use in your CD player, as long as they are designed for direct application onto electronic parts. Whatever cleaner you use, make sure it leaves no residue after drying (which usually takes less than 15 seconds). If the cleaner leaves a noticeable residue, it is unsuitable for use inside your compact disc player.

The cleaner is available at most electronics stores, and usually comes in spray form. The spray comes out fast, so you can use the pressure to dislodge stubborn grime. Most cans come with an ex-

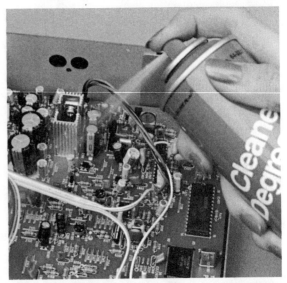

Fig. 6-12. Use a can of cleaner/degreaser spray to remove deposits of grime, nicotine, and other contaminants that have settled on the internal components. Use only a non-residue cleaner designed for use on electronic and mechanical parts.

tension spray nozzle tube. Attach the tube to the spray button, and squirt into hard to reach places.

Prior to cleaning, be absolutely sure the disc player is unplugged from the wall outlet. Never use the spray where there is live current. You could receive a shock or start a fire. After cleaning, wait at least three minutes for all the cleaner to evaporate before applying power to the player.

Electrical Contact Cleaning

It's rare that the electrical contacts inside the player will need cleaning. However, exposure to outside elements can quickly oxidize plated electrical contacts (now you know why you should never place your CD near an open window where it might be exposed to the damp outside air). The contacts can also be contaminated by an accumulation of cigarette smoke.

If you see a heavy amount of oxidation or nicotine, carefully disconnect the wire leading to the contact and clean the contact with a commercially available contact cleaner. Clean the exposed part of the wire in a similar fashion. If there is a heavy build-up of oxidation, scrape it off with an orange

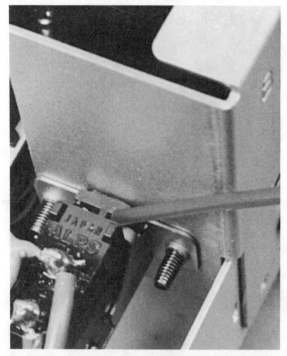

Fig. 6-13. Use the extension tube to spray the cleaner into hard to reach places, like the contacts of a switch.

stick or nail file, then use the cleaner.

Most contact cleaner is in spray form, and the spray may squirt the cleaner to an overly large area. If you don't want this, spray the cleaner into a cotton ball or swab, then use the cotton as an applicator. Be sure to leave no lint from the cotton on the contacts. If cotton threads are a problem, purchase some sponge-tipped applicators. Most electronics and many record stores sell them. For very hard to reach places, use the extension nozzle tube. Figure 6-13 shows spraying the contacts of a dirty power switch.

Lens Cleaning

If there is any measurable amount of dust, dirt, nicotine or other contaminants in the inside of the player, you can bet there is a coating on the objective lens of the optical pickup too. With top loaders and drawer-type front loaders, the lens points up, so dust and debris can settle on it easily (with door-type front loading players, the pickup is mounted on a vertical plane, and is not as susceptible to settling contaminants).

You must find the pickup first. With many drawer-type players, a disc flapper, also called the chucker or clamper, obstructs the pickup from view. You can usually gain access to the pickup simply by opening the drawer. Don't manually open the drawer as it is on a geared track and you may strip the gears if you force it. Plug in the player, turn it on, and open the drawer in the normal fashion with the open/close switch. Once the door is open, turn the machine off and unplug it for safety's sake.

The flapper pops up for disc insertion and is spring loaded. It pops back down when a disc is in place. So if the pickup is still partially covered by the clamping flapper, you can gently lift up the flapper from the front, as shown in Fig. 6-14.

The flapper *can* be removed if absolutely necessary, but you should use caution (unlike other components of the pickup mechanism, the flapper is not critically aligned). With most CD players, the flapper is attached to the main portion of the pickup mechanism by one or two screws. Slowly loosen the screws and carefully remove them from the player (don't drop them into the machine!). Remove the flapper. The spring will come loose, so grab it and keep it handy for reinstallation.

With the objective lens exposed, blow excess dust from it using a small bulb blower, available at photographic stores. If the lens is still dusty or dirty, apply lens cleaner to a small piece of lens tissue or to a cotton swab (Fig. 6-15). A small amount of the cleaner is more than sufficient; there is no need to drown the lens in cleaning fluid. NEVER use lens tissue or the swab without moistening it first with cleaner, and DO NOT apply cleaner directly to the lens. Wipe with a dry tissue or swab.

The objective lens in portable and top-loading CDs is typically accessible without removing the top cover of the player. This makes the lens more susceptible to dust, grime, and fingerprints, but it also makes cleaning it easier. If you own a portable or top-loading player where the objective lens is easy to reach, make it a point to clean the lens at least every 6 to 12 months.

Fig. 6-14. Lift the flapper gently to gain access to the pickup or disc spindle.

Oiling and Lubricating

Compact disc players generally do not require much in the way of lubrication, because it has so few moving parts. But the handful of mechanical parts in a CD player are either moving, spinning, or sliding. To keep the player in top working shape, you should lubricate these parts at every major PM interval; more if you use your player outdoors where it is subjected to extremes in temperature or excess dust and dirt. You should also lubricate the mechanical parts if you clean the machine with a spray cleaner/degreaser. The cleaner acts to strip any oil or grease off from the moving parts, and using the player without lubrication may wear it out prematurely.

Here's a good rule of thumb to remember when lubricating your compact disc player:

□ If it spins, oil it.

Fig. 6-15. Clean the objective lens of the optical pickup with a suitable swab and cleaner.

98

☐ If it slides or meshes, grease it.

Light machine oil is the best lubricant for spinning parts, such as the bearings of idlers and rollers. You should *never* use a spray-on lubricant, such as WD-40. Apply the oil only to the rotating part, not the entire shaft or roller. More is not necessarily better. Never apply oil directly to a motor. For small parts, apply the oil with a syringe applicator, as shown in Fig. 6-16.

A non-petroleum based grease is the best lubricant for sliding and meshing parts, the bulk of which are found in the pickup assembly and disc loading mechanism. This includes cams, bell cranks, gear surfaces, and levers. As with oiling, apply only a small dab of grease. Spread the grease by moving or sliding the part back and forth a few times.

If the part can't be easily moved, or is geared down and won't budge, power the player and insert a disc. To spread the grease, cycle the loading drawer or other mechanism by using the front panel controls of the player.

Swing arm pickups generally don't need any type of oiling or lubrication, but slide pickups do.

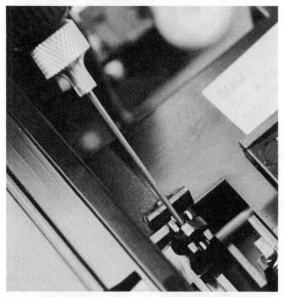

Fig. 6-16. Small parts may need occasional oiling. For best results, use an oil and applicator designed for small mechanical parts.

With slide pickups, the optical assembly slides along two metal rails, which should be kept lubricated to assure smooth travel.

With the pickup exposed (remove the flapper if necessary), apply a small amount of grease or oil to each rail. You can't manually slide the optical pickup back and forth. Insert a disc, turn the machine on, and advance the pickup along the rail by pushing the track buttons on the front panel of the player. Go back and forth several times to spread the grease evenly. Inspect that no grease has accumulated at the end of the rails. If so, remove it.

Some players have a mechanical interlock attached to the cabinet that disables the player electronics if the top cover is removed. If the top is off your player, and the disc won't turn when you push the Play button, check to see if there is an interlock switch on the cabinet. If the switch is the microsized leaf type, depress it to engage the Play mode. If the switch is magnetic, place a small magnet on the sensor, or place a wire jumper between the switch contacts.

Front Panel Controls

The front panel operating controls seldom need preventative care, unless the player has been subjected to heavy doses of dust, dirt, damp air, and cigarette smoke. You can clean the bulk of the control switches with a brush or compressed air. The control panel in most players use sealed membrane switches, so the internal switch contacts are not affected by dirt (the membrane switches are located behind the actual switch button, which you push when operating the player).

If the switches in your CD are the regular open contact type, you may need to apply a small amount of electrical contact cleaner to dispel the dirt. Again, you need not perform this procedure unless the player has been exposed to heavy amounts of contaminants or the controls are not working properly. The contact cleaner dries quickly, and without leaving a residue. You should wait several minutes after cleaning, nevertheless, before you turn the machine on and attempt to use it. Never clean the switch contacts when the machine is turned on or plugged into the wall socket.

Final Inspection

Before you replace the top cover, double-check your work. Like the bumbling surgeon who leaves objects inside people after an appendix operation, don't leave tools, hardware, used cotton swabs, or cleaning supplies inside the chassis of the player.

Check to make sure that you have properly replaced ALL parts. Failure to properly replace the loading flapper, for example, may cause considerable damage to the disc and player when a disc is loaded.

Reassembly

If all looks satisfactory, replace the top cover and reassemble the player with the screws you removed. Be sure the cover is aligned properly before tightening any of the screws. If the cover will not fit under the lip in the front panel, use a rubber mallet to gently pop it into place (never force it). When all the screws are in place, tighten them lightly. DO NOT over-tighten, or you might strip the threads of the screw and chassis.

Checkout

After every PM interval, check the player for proper operation. You should use one known good disc and a test disc (either a commercial disc or one you've made). Keep these operational points in mind during the checkout process:

☐ The disc loading door or drawer operates smoothly, and accepts the disc as it should. Similarly, the disc is properly ejected.

☐ The first selection cues up and plays properly from beginning to end.

☐ Pressing the track switches advances through all of the selections on the disc.

☐ All front panel indicators operate normally.

☐ All the function buttons on the front panel of the player and the remote-control work as they should.

☐ The audio output is normal, without any noticeable errors (except, perhaps, with the test disc).

MAINTENANCE LOG

You may wish to keep a log book of all the maintenance checks and cleaning you've performed on your compact disc player. Use the sample log form that appears in Appendix E, or make your own. In your log, be sure to note the exact checks and maintenance procedures you performed, and when you performed them. If you have replaced any parts (like rollers and belts), note their part numbers in the log, and troubles you may have had when installing them. By keeping a thorough log, you can better estimate the timing of the preventive maintenance intervals for your specific player.

REMOTE CLEANING

A number of compact disc players are equipped with wireless infrared remote control units. These allow you to change selections or skip through songs at high speed from the comfort of your easy chair. Because the remote control can be taken anywhere in the house, it's often subjected to a lot more abuse than the other components in your hi-fi system. You may pride yourself in a clean compact disc player, but the remote may be filled with dirt, grime, and sticky syrup from a spilled soda pop.

Exterior Cleaning

Cleaning the remote control is straightforward and easy. Start with applying a damp cloth to the outside and remove exterior dirt and grime.

Battery Compartment Cleaning

Remote controllers are battery operated. Given the right circumstances, all batteries can leak, and the spilled acid can corrode the electrical contacts and can impair proper operation of the controller. If your remote control is operating sporadically, this may be the problem.

If the batteries have leaked, or if the battery contacts have become only slightly dirty, clean them as follows. You can also use this procedure for cleaning the battery compartment in portable CDs.

Fig. 6-17. You can clean the battery contacts in a remote control (or portable player) with a pencil eraser. Blow out the eraser dust when you are through.

☐ Carefully remove the batteries and discard them. Immediately wash your hands to remove any acid residue. Battery acid burns.

☐ Wipe off the battery acid residue with a damp cloth, and remove as much of the excess from the contacts as you can.

☐ Remove the remaining residue by rubbing the contacts with the tip of a pencil eraser. Blow the eraser dust out of the battery compartment when you are through (Fig. 6-17).

Test the controller with new batteries. If the battery leakage is more extensive, you will have to take more drastic action. Refer to Chapter 7 for more details on how to clean heavy deposits of battery acid.

Interior Cleaning

To clean the inside of the controller, you must disassemble it by removing the screws holding the two halves of the controller together. The screws are small and you will need a set of jeweler's screwdrivers to properly remove them. Some screws may be insidiously hidden in the battery compartment,

under the manufacturers label, or even beneath the thin metal cover on the front of the unit.

When the screws have been removed, separate the two halves. Clean the inside of the controller with a soft brush or can of compressed air. If liquids have been spilled inside the controller, spray the inside of the controller with a suitable cleaner/degreaser.

With most remote controllers, the circuit board is attached to the front panel and must be removed if you want to access the front switches. With the controller resting on a flat surface, remove the circuit board screws carefully and gently lift off the control board. The plastic pushbuttons may be loose, so be sure not to knock them out of place when you remove the board (if so, putting them back isn't hard, but it can be time consuming). Clean the switches and front side of the circuit board with a spray from the can of cleaner/degreaser, as shown in Fig. 6-18.

Remote Control Testing

Let's say you've replaced the battery in the remote controller and you've cleaned it inside and out. It still doesn't seem to work. Since the infrared light from the controller is invisible, it's difficult to test whether the controller is indeed working or if the problem lies in the CD player itself.

Many remote controllers have visible LED indicators that flash when you push a button on the transmitter. The LED is typically connected along with the high-output infrared LEDs that send the remote control information to the player. You can be fairly certain that the controller is operating properly if the visible LED flashes.

The infrared LEDs in your remote controller will not last forever. It's possible (but not likely) that one or all of the high-output infrared LEDs have gone out. If only one of the several LEDs that are typically built into the controller is faulty, you should still be able to operate the controller, but you may have to get in close to the player.

The laser sensor described in Chapter 5 is one way to accurately test the controller. This sensor is sensitive to *any* infrared light source, and it will

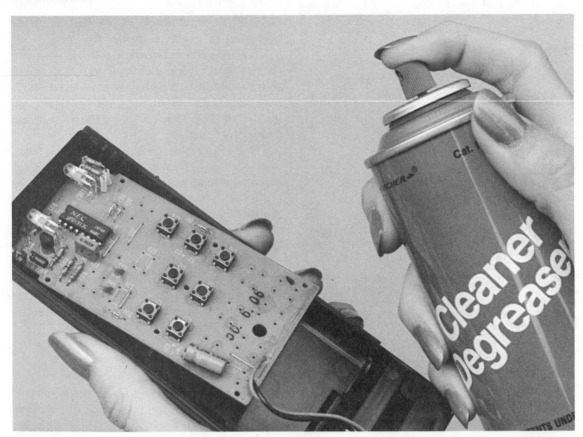

Fig. 6-18. The switches and printed circuit board of the remote can be cleaned using a suitable cleaner/degreaser.

register the light emitted by the remote controller as easily as it does to the light generated by the laser diode in your compact disc player.

To use the sensor, position it closely to the front of the controller and start pushing buttons. If the LED on the sensor lights up, the controller is good. The fault probably lies in the player. If it does not light up, double-check the operation of the sensor and try again. If the LED on the sensor still doesn't light up, it is fairly certain the remote control is at fault.

There are a variety of reasons why a remote control does not operate properly, and none of them have anything to do with a faulty controller or sensor in the CD player. If you are having trouble with your remote control, and have performed the routine cleaning outlined here, check the remote con-

trol troubleshooting charts in Chapter 9 for more information.

DISC MAINTENANCE

One of the greatest myths surrounding digital audio is that the compact discs can be scratched and marred, and still deliver clean, crisp sound. *Don't you believe it!*

Every scratch on the disc can conceivably contribute a little to diminished sound quality. The benefit of the compact disc medium is not that scratches can't harm the disc, but that small scratches do not create the crackly surface noise that's so annoying in LP records. To realize the full benefit of CD technology, the disc must be reasonably cared for.

Data dropouts caused by small scratches are

corrected automatically by the redundant information encoded on the disc. Larger scratches, or even small ones that run parallel to the edge of the disc, may cause larger dropouts that can't be entirely corrected by redundant data. The lost music must be artificially recreated by the player, and depending on the error, and the quality of the error correction circuits in the player, the effect of the scratch may indeed be audible.

Fingerprints pose an even greater problem, because the oil in the fingerprint is semi-reflective to laser light. The fingerprint can therefore reflect the beam, jumbling the data and causing very noticeable errors in the music. A fingerprint smudge can diffuse the laser light, which also causes errors. Dust, dirt, hair and other foreign objects, however small, can contribute to a decrease in sound quality, given the right circumstances.

A scratch on the top of the disc, even a relatively light one, can result in a completely unplayable disc. The top of the disc is coated only with a very thin layer of protective plastic. Immediately underneath this thin layer is an even thinner (0.11 μm) aluminum stamping that holds the disc data. A scratch of any size at all (even, 1mm in size) that extends into the aluminum stamping could very well permanently ruin the disc. Now do you see why it pays to treat your discs with care?

Proper Disc Care

We've mentioned this in earlier chapters, but it's worth stating again. Your best hedge against the effects of unpleasant compact disc errors is to keep all your discs in the jewel boxes they came in (you paid over 50 cents for the box in the cost of the disc, so use them!). When you finish with a disc, replace it immediately in the jewel box. Don't carelessly throw the disc on the table and don't pile them up on the player. If you lose a jewel box, you can buy a replacement at most any record store.

If you have a portable or automotive CD player, and you carry your discs with you, you may not want to lug the bulky jewel boxes with you. That's perfectly acceptable, but protect the discs in

sleeves. The sleeve, available at most any record store, is made of spun polyester, so it doesn't shed paper bits or fibers onto the disc.

Disc Cleaning

You can clean discs manually or with a specially designed mechanical disc cleaning device. Both methods yield the same results, although the mechanical cleaner is a little easier to use.

You should never use a mechanical cleaner device, cleaning solution, or cleaning cloth designed for vinyl LP records. Cleaning products for LP records have a different chemistry that can actually harm the plastic coating of compact discs. Mechanical cleaning devices for LPs clean parallel to the edge of the record—that is, with the grooves. Cleaning a compact disc in this manner increases the chance of a long scratch, one that goes in the same direction as the encoded pits. This can cause an audible error because more pits are affected, and the error correction circuits can't compensate for it. Radial scratches, those that occur at right angles to the direction of the pits, do not pose as serious a problem.

The best cleaning solution for compact discs is a mixture of isopropyl alcohol and trichlorofluorothene. The latter ingredient is best known as Freon TF. This mixture is commonly available, if not specifically packaged for compact discs, then as a cleaner for photographic lenses and computer disk drives. Read the contents to make sure.

Apply the cleaner with a chamois or soft, clean sponge material. Wipe from the inside to the outside of the disc—never around the circumference of the disc. Fingerprints and grime may require a few extra drops of cleaner. The cleaner does not harm the disc in any dose, so don't be afraid to use too much. For most applications, however, a little cleaner goes a long way.

Mechanical cleaners for compact discs work in a variety of ways, most involve applying cleaning solution to the disc, as illustrated in Fig. 6-19, and turning a crank, which spins a cleaning wheel over the disc. Be sure to follow the directions included with the cleaning device. Misuse can damage the

Fig. 6-19. Applying an alcohol/Freon solution on a disc prior to cleaning.

disc. The cleaning solution dries quickly, but if you've used too much, it may pool up on the surface of the disc. Be sure the disc is dry before you put it back into its jewel box or insert it into the CD for playing.

Because of the type of plastic used to manufacture compact discs, they actively attract dust and other particles. Yet you should NEVER use an anti-static spray on a CD. Use of an anti-static spray, or a cleaner with anti-static chemicals in it, may damage the disc. If you are plagued by dust contaminating your discs, wipe them with a soft, dry, lintless cloth immediately prior to play (Fig. 6-20). Wipe the disc from the center to the edge. You can purchase a lintless cloth at most photographic stores. Be sure you get the kind that is NOT

treated. Some lintless clothes are treated with anti-static solution—you want to stay away from them.

Disc Repair

Despite even the most careful handling practices, compact discs can and do become seriously damaged. If one of your discs has been scratched to a point where it cannot be played on the CD without error, there is a chance that you can repair it and make it playable again.

Inspect the scratch, and decide if it's on the top (label) or bottom (play) side of the disc. If the scratch is on the top of the disc, and it's deep, there's really nothing you can do. The scratch has obviously gouged into the aluminum stamping and has destroyed the data tracks.

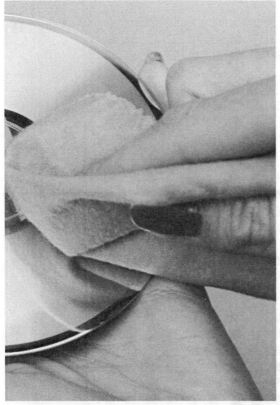

Fig. 6-20. Use a clean, lintless cloth to gently wipe dust from your compact discs. Wipe from the center of the disc to the outside, never along the circumference as you would with an LP.

If the scratch is on the play side, and does not extend to the signal layer, you can smooth it out using a rubbing compound designed for car paint. This method is not foolproof, and should only be used on a disc that's otherwise unsalvageable.

Apply a very small amount of rubbing compound to a clean, damp cloth, then slowly rub the scratch with a back and forth motion with the cloth or your fingers, as shown in Fig. 6-21. For best results, rub at right angles to the disc edge, to minimize scratches that occur parallel to the data tracks. Go over the spot several times in light, gentle coats. When you think you've reduced the scratch (you probably won't eliminate it altogether), clean the disc as usual and play it in your machine. If mistracking still occurs, try using the rubbing compound once again.

Warpage

A warped compact disc is a sad thing. Unlike conventional LPs, a warped CD can't be played because of the close focus tolerance of the optical pickup. A very small amount of warpage is common in all CDs, introduced in the manufacturing process, but the amount is extremely small in human standards. You can't see it with the naked eye.

Slight warpage can be repaired under certain circumstances, and make an unplayable disc playable again. You can test for warpage by laying the disc on a mirror or piece of window glass. Gently rock it back and forth to see if you can feel any movement. When pressed against the mirror, you can often see where the disc deviates from the surface of the glass.

In some instances, you can reduce or eliminate warpage by warming the disc and applying pressure to it for a period of time. A number of CD en-

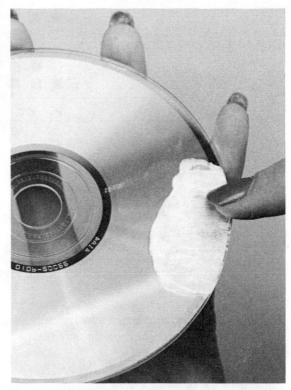

Fig. 6-21. Scratches in the plastic layer can sometimes be reduced by gently rubbing the disc with a rubbing compound designed to remove oxidized paint from car finishes.

Light Use

PM (Months)	3	6	9	12	15	18	21	24	27	30	33	36
Interior Dusting/Cleaning	□	□	■	□	□	■	□	□	■	□	□	■
Lens Cleaning	□	■	□	■	□	■	□	■	□	■	□	■
Lubricate Pickup Slide	□	□	□	□	□	■	□	□	□	□	□	■
Lubricate Drawer/Door Ass'y	□	□	□	□	□	■	□	□	□	□	□	■
Remote Battery Terminals	□	□	□	■	□	□	□	■	□	□	□	■
Discs	□	□	■	□	□	■	□	□	■	□	□	■

Medium Use

PM (Months)	3	6	9	12	15	18	21	24	27	30	33	36
Interior Dusting/Cleaning	□	■	□	■	□	■	□	■	□	■	□	■
Lens Cleaning	□	■	□	■	□	■	□	■	□	■	□	■
Lubricate Pickup Slide	□	□	□	■	□	□	□	■	□	□	□	■
Lubricate Drawer/Door Ass'y	□	□	□	■	□	□	□	■	□	□	□	■
Remote Battery Terminals	□	□	■	□	□	■	□	□	■	□	□	■
Discs	□	■	□	■	□	■	□	■	□	■	□	■

Heavy Use

PM (Months)	3	6	9	12	15	18	21	24	27	30	33	36
Interior Dusting/Cleaning	□	■	□	■	□	■	□	■	□	■	□	■
Lens Cleaning	■	■	■	■	■	■	■	■	■	■	■	■
Lubricate Pickup Slide	□	□	□	■	□	■	□	■	□	■	□	■
Lubricate Drawer/Door Ass'y	□	□	□	■	□	■	□	■	□	■	□	■
Remote Battery Terminals	□	■	□	■	□	■	□	■	□	■	□	■
Discs	■	■	■	■	■	■	■	■	■	■	■	■

Your Machine

PM (Months)	3	6	9	12	15	18	21	24	27	30	33	36
Interior Dusting/Cleaning	□	□	□	□	□	□	□	□	□	□	□	□
Lens Cleaning	□	□	□	□	□	□	□	□	□	□	□	□
Lubricate Pickup Slide	□	□	□	□	□	□	□	□	□	□	□	□
Lubricate Drawer/Door Ass'y	□	□	□	□	□	□	□	□	□	□	□	□
Remote Battery Terminals	□	□	□	□	□	□	□	□	□	□	□	□
Discs	□	□	□	□	□	□	□	□	□	□	□	□

Chart 6-1. Recommended preventative maintenance intervals for a CD player receiving light, medium, and heavy use. Use the chart on the bottom to mark the PM intervals for your machine.

thusiasts have had some luck with the process, and although it's not guaranteed that it will work in all cases, it's at least worth the try if the only alternative is to throw the disc out.

Start by warming the disc in the heat of the summer sun or by using a blow dryer set on low heat. The plastic won't even begin to melt at temperatures below the 100 to 150 degrees that we're talking about, but it will make it a little more pliable. Don't put the disc in the kitchen oven or you might accidentally melt it. When the disc is sufficiently warm to the touch, sandwich it between two pieces of wax paper and lay it on a flat surface. Place something heavy on top, like a few large books. Keep the disc there for a few hours. You may need to repeat the process a few times.

Chapter 7

CD Player First Aid

If an accident happens to your compact disc player—you spill your cup of coffee into it, for example—there is no need to panic. By following some simple cleaning and checkout procedures, you can reduce or eliminate potentially costly repairs.

This chapter discusses first aid treatment for a number of accidents, and how you can repair all or nearly all of the damage yourself. Even if your CD player is presently working fine, read through this chapter to acquaint yourself with the recommended procedures. You never know when they'll come in handy.

TOOLS AND SAFETY

Most of the repair procedures require disassembly of the player. If you haven't done so already, please read Chapters 5 and 6 for more information on how to take your CD apart, and what tools you need to do the job right. Pay particular attention to the safety points in Chapter 6. Failure to treat the power supply and laser diode built into

your CD player with respect may cause bodily harm.

The steps outlined in this chapter are designed to help you minimize the damage of accidents, not make them worse. If you are not confident in your ability to perform some of the repair procedures, or lack the proper tools and cleaning supplies, then by all means don't do them. When in doubt, refer to a qualified technician.

DROPPED PLAYER

Compact disc players are not meant to be dropped off bookshelves, stereo racks, tables, or car seats, but it happens. A drop onto soft carpeting may only shake up the player a bit, but not cause serious internal injury. A harder impact, however, may break or bend the cabinet, or chip off a piece of the front panel.

A cracked cabinet or other broken piece on the exterior of the player can usually be mended with a strong adhesive. If the part is plastic, just about any clear glue recommended for use on plastic will suffice. After gluing, hold the pieces together with your fingers until the adhesive sets, or tape the pieces together like a surgical suture until the glue is completely dried.

Checking for Internal Damage

After a player has been dropped, even if there is no visible damage, inspect is carefully. Don't test it by plugging it in and playing a disc. You may cause additional damage.

You can quickly check if parts have come loose inside the player by unplugging the unit from the wall socket and gently shaking it. If you hear rattles, you can bet something is bouncing around that shouldn't. Even if you don't hear loose parts, it's a good idea to disassemble the player before attempting to use it. Follow the disassembly instructions provided in Chapter 6.

When the top cover of the cabinet is removed, look for the loose parts and ascertain where they came from. If the broken piece is plastic, glue it back on with a suitable cement. Broken metal parts are harder to mend, but there are a number of adhesives for metal that might do the job. The alignment of internal parts is often critical to the operation of the compact disc player, so make sure you glue the repaired piece on straight.

While the top is off, visually inspect the interior of the player for hidden damage—things other than completely broken pieces. Pay particular attention to circuit board(s), the disc loading mechanism, and the pickup mechanism. If any part of the pickup mechanism looks broken, bent, or out of place, you should return the player to a qualified repair center. If the broken pickup cannot be serviced, it must be replaced, and replacement requires exact alignment using special tools.

Check the printed circuit boards inside the player. If you see any hairline cracks, it's a bad sign. A broken printed circuit board must be replaced. Using the player as it is may cause more damage, because components may be shorted. You could conceivably burn out the laser diode, power supply, motors, and other costly parts by attempting to operate the player with a faulty circuit board.

Fortunately, however, it takes a very healthy jolt to break a circuit board, so it is not a common occurrence.

Broken Wires

A strong enough impact may cause electrical wires and connectors to break or come off. Sometimes, the connector, like the one in Fig. 7-1, is just jostled in its socket. Look very carefully at these, because some connectors may look fine from the outside, but electrical contact inside has been broken. Press all the connectors firmly into their sockets just in case. If the connector has come out all the way, you can plug it back in to its respective socket. Broken wires leading to connectors and boards must be resoldered. If the solder joint is accessible, and does not require precision work, you can do the work yourself. If you are unfamiliar with proper soldering techniques, refer to Appendix G for a quick lesson.

If more than two wires have come undone, and it is not obvious where they go, consult the schematic diagram for your player, if available, or

Fig. 7-1. After a fall or heavy jolt, press down all connectors to make sure they are properly seated.

return the player to a service shop. Don't take chances. If two wires are loose, you have a 50 percent chance of soldering them back properly. You also have a 50 percent chance of soldering them back in the wrong place. Not particularly great odds, considering what is at stake.

Leakage Current Test

Prior to turning on your CD player, even if you do not take it apart to inspect for internal damage, be sure to check for possible leakage current. This test determines if any part of the ac line has come in contact with the metal cabinet or base. It is a safety check to prevent a potential shock hazard. You'll need a volt-ohm meter to perform the test.

With the CD player unplugged, short the two flat prongs on the end of the ac cord, as illustrated in Fig. 7-2. On the meter, select the kOhm function and a range of no less than 1,000 kOhms. Connect one test lead from the meter to the jumper on the ac cord. Connect the other test lead to any and all bare (not painted) metal parts of the player. For

a typical CD player, the meter will read about 500 to 1,000 kOhms—if you get any reading at all.

A reading substantially lower than this is a good indication that the power supply has come into contact with the metal parts of the player. If this happens, inspect the power cord as it leads into the player, as well as the on/off switch, the transformer (usually bolted onto the back of the machine), and the wires leading from the transformer to the printed circuit board. If the wires are broken, or are shorted to the cabinet, repair the fault before using the player.

Not all exposed metal parts of the CD will return a high value. Touching the center conductor of one of the audio output connectors could yield a very low resistance, of 40 or 50 kOhms. This is normal with some machines.

FIRE DAMAGE

Fire damage includes the effects of both the heat and the smoke of fire. Intense heat can totally destroy the CD player, of course, but even moder-

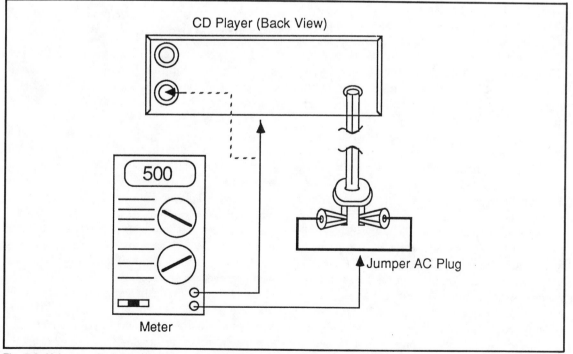

Fig. 7-2. Using a volt-ohm meter to test for possible leakage current.

ate heat (150 to 175 degrees) for even a short period of time can cause considerable damage to the player's electrical and mechanical components. After a fire, check for obvious damage to plastic parts. If a disc was in the player, remove it and inspect it for warpage or other damage. If it is warped, then there is a good indication that the other plastic parts inside the player are warped as well. Disassemble the machine and inspect it thoroughly.

Minor warpage of plastic parts, as well as expansion of metal parts, during the heat of a fire can throw components out of alignment. You can test this by playing a disc from beginning to end (you can skip through the selections to save time). If the pickup is out of alignment, playback will be impaired for at least some portions of the disc. Perform this test only after thoroughly inspecting the player and being certain that powering it up won't cause additional damage.

Smoke Damage

Many people erroneously think that heat from a fire causes the greatest damage. Insurance companies will tell you that smoke, not heat, is worse. Why? The smoke gets everywhere, even rooms that were not touched by the fire itself. The black soot of smoke cakes everywhere, and has an acid-like effect that can eat through finishes and protective layers. If the CD works at all after a fire, failure to remove the layer of soot in its interior might cause considerable damage later.

If you are the victim of a fire, you should promptly clean your CD player (and other electronic gadgets for that matter) as quickly as possible. This minimizes smoke damage to the exterior cabinet. Thoroughly wipe the outside of the player using a damp sponge. This will pick up the bulk of the soot.

Matters are a little different on the inside of the player. Using a household cleaning spray on the mechanical and electronic parts of a CD player is not recommended, partly because the cleaner is water-based, and poses a potential short circuit hazard, and partly because it is not really effective in cleaning hard to reach places.

A cleaner/degreaser spray can be used to thoroughly clean the inside of the player. Spray the cleaner heavily to remove the soot. Use the extension spray tube (usually included with the can) to get hard to reach places. The cleaner evaporates after five or 10 seconds. If soot remains, spray again. If the smoke build-up is heavy, spray the cleaner on and brush it off with a small painter's brush.

The cleaner/degreaser leaves no residue, but it may remove the lubrication on some of the mechanical parts in the player. After using the cleaner/degreaser, lubricate the player, if necessary, following the instructions provided in Chapter 6.

If you're not sure if a part needs oiling or greasing, try using the player for a while. Watch its operation carefully to see if lubrication is called for. You'll have to leave the top cover of the player off to do this. Some CDs have an interlock switch that cuts power to the machine when the top cover is off. If your unit has an interlock switch, it must be defeated before you can play a disc.

The objective lens in the optical pickup will need a complete cleansing as well, following the lens cleaning procedure discussed in Chapter 6.

WATER DAMAGE

Each year, water does more damage to personal property than fire. Even if you don't live in a flood basin, there is always a chance that your compact disc player may be subjected to milk, or some other liquid. Something may spill into it, like water, coffee, or soda pop. If you have a portable player, you may drop it into the water while lounging near the pool. It's happened before, and it'll happen again.

If your CD player is ac operated, and it becomes wet, *immediately* unplug it. If it is unsafe to reach the plug, turn the power off at the circuit breaker of fuse box. Do not touch a wet CD player; you may receive a bad shock. If the player shorts out when water spreads inside its cabinet, there is a very good chance that it is seriously damaged, and should be taken to a repair shop for proper service. If there is no sign of immediate short circuit damage, you can minimize any further problems by following the steps below.

Removal of Excess Liquid

Of first importance is to soak up the excess liquid. Use paper towels to blot up the extra. If you feel any liquid has seeped into the player, you must disassemble it and remove the standing water from the inside as well.

If the player was dunked into fresh water, you need only to wait until the remaining moisture evaporates. Some water may be trapped under components, so even if the surface of the circuit board and internal parts are dry, there still might be water lurking underneath. You may use a hair dryer—on low or no heat—to help speed up the drying process. Do not dry with high heat, as you may warp some parts. Even after the water is gone, some moisture may still be present, particularly on smooth metal parts and around the optical pickup area. Allow another two to three hours for condensation to evaporate.

You can test for remaining moisture by placing the player in a plastic garbage bag. Seal the end and place the bag overnight in a warm but dry place. If there is moisture remaining in the player, condensation will form inside the bag. It's a clue to let the player dry out some more.

Some players have a built-in dew-circuit that prevents playback if there is condensation in the unit. If your player still doesn't work after drying, this may be the problem. Pay particular attention to the optical pickup. Condensation on the outside of the lens, or even inside the pickup (they are not always sealed or waterproof) may be the fault. If the player turns on but won't play a disc, keep it on for a while to help evaporate the moisture.

Removing Sticky or Staining Liquids

If the player was subjected to sticky or staining liquids—which include salt water, coffee, sugary soda pop, and milk—you need to thoroughly clean the player inside and out. This prevents residue from the liquid from interfering with the proper operation of the unit (salt water will corrode the metal parts, for example). If the liquid is thick, use a damp sponge to wipe up as much as possible.

Thoroughly spray the player with a cleaner/degreaser. Apply the cleaner/degreaser

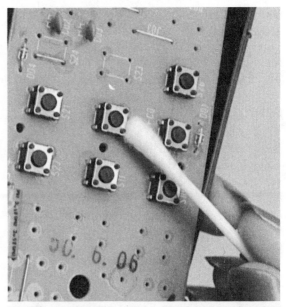

Fig. 7-3. Use a swab to clean caked-on grime or dirt from around the switches and other components on the remote control PCB.

heavily until all signs of the residue are gone.

Because the cleaner/degreaser is non water-based, you can also use it to remove any water that may remain in the player. The cleaner/degreaser will act to displace the water, removing it from even hard to reach places.

The remote control transmitter is often subjected to heavy abuse, because it can be placed on tables along with food and drink. Crumbs, liquids, and other matter can easily fall in the cracks and gum up the switch contacts inside, or short out wire terminals and connections. Disassemble the remote, and thoroughly clean the switches. You can spray the cleaner on, or use a damp cotton swab, as shown in Fig. 7-3.

After cleaning, moving parts may require lubrication. See Chapter 6 for more details on lubricating CD players. Clean the objective lens in the optical pickup prior to use.

After Cleaning Test

When you are satisfied that all the moisture has been removed, and that the player has been properly lubricated and cleaned, perform a leakage current test. If the leakage test proves negative, plug in the unit and turn it on. Test the player completely for proper operation. If the test proves positive, some moisture is still present inside the player, and it should be allowed to dry out more.

SAND, DIRT, AND DUST

The optical pickup in a compact disc player is sensitive to even a small amount of dirt. Players used outside in dusty or sandy environments are susceptible to premature failure, especially if they are accidentally dropped in the sand at the beach or carried on a long distance desert hike, where the dust from the great outdoors permeates everywhere.

Removal of every last speck of sand, dirt, and dust is critical to ensure proper operation of the player, and to prevent possible damage to the optical pickup and discs. This is particularly true if the player is filled with gritty sand. A soft brush can be used to wipe away the bulk of the sand, or if there is lots of it, you can use a vacuum cleaner with a brush attachment. Remaining sand, dirt, and dust can be removed from the cabinet, chassis, and interior with a tac cloth, designed for wiping away sawdust from woodworking projects. Tac cloths are available at any hardware store.

Even though the visible dirt and sand may be gone, there still may be an accumulation of micro-sized particles of dust. You can clean the entire inside of the player by liberally squirting it with your trusty can of cleaner/degreaser. The fluid cleans quickly, leaving no residue. The cleaner/degreaser is a solvent, but it is not petroleum based, so it will not harm metal or rubber parts.

Sand and dirt have a way of getting into the most unusual places. Be sure to inspect the headphone and audio output jacks on the player. Grit inside will prevent proper electrical contact, and you may not get any sound from your player. You can clean the jacks with a swab soaked in alcohol (see Fig. 7-4). Clean both the inside and outside.

You may need to oil and lubricate the spinning and sliding parts in the player after cleaning. Follow the directions outlined in Chapters 5 and 6.

Fig. 7-4. Sand and grit can be removed from around and inside the output terminals (and headphone jack) with a swab dipped in cleaner.

FOREIGN OBJECTS

Just about any service technician of audio and video equipment will tell you that a good portion of machine repairs are caused by people inserting "foreign objects" into the mechanism. Horror stories of this sort abound, and most are innocent mistakes caused by children. How about the one where a five year old boy stuck a peanut butter sandwich into the disc drawer, because he wanted to know what kind of sound it would make? Or the time when a young girl used her father's compact disc player as a piggy bank? She put all her extra pennies, nickels, dimes, and quarters into the ventilation slots of the player. She had amassed quite a savings until the player suddenly went on the fritz.

This kind of accident is best avoided by warning young children that the compact disc player is not a toy. You can make your own rules in your home, but if you allow your children to use or even touch the CD player, spend a few moments instructing them on the right and wrong way to play discs.

Children are naturally curious about things, especially something new like a CD player, and you'll greatly reduce the chance of a serious accident if you provide adequate do's and don'ts ahead of time.

Despite the best efforts, warnings, and rules on your part, foreign objects may still get lodged inside the player. Some might even be your fault. When this happens, immediately turn off the player and unplug it. If the object cannot be completely retrieved, disassemble the player and remove it.

Sandwiches, cookies, candy, and other objects often leave their mark even after you have removed them. You can use a brush or vacuum to remove the crumbs. Heavier or stickier sediments will require removal with a squirt from the cleaner/degreaser.

LEAKED BATTERIES

Portable compact disc players, when used outside, as well as remote controls for home players, run off battery power. Given the right set of circumstances, even the best made battery may leak. The acid from the battery oozes everywhere, and not only blocks electric current, causing failure, but corrodes the inside of the battery compartment and the battery terminals.

Your best defense against leaking batteries is to remove them if your player or remote is not used for a long time. Batteries tend to leak the most when they fail to conduct electricity, so a battery that sits, unused, in a portable or remote has a very good chance of leaking. If the batteries are still good when you take them out (you can test them with a battery tester or volt-ohm meter), use them in something else.

If storing batteries—new or used—keep them in a cool dry place. You can greatly prolong the shelf life of batteries by storing them in the refrigerator (not freezer). Again, batteries can leak just about everywhere for any reason, so to prevent contaminating your food with battery acid, wrap them up in a sealed food storage bag.

Removing Battery Acid

Should the batteries leak in your portable or remote, remove them immediately and throw them away. Avoid excessive contact with the battery acid as it can burn skin. Use a lightly dampened cloth to remove the excess battery acid deposits from the battery compartment. If the batteries leaked only a little bit, there may not be any deposits in the compartment or on the terminals. If the terminals look clean and bright, install a new set of batteries and test the unit.

If there is excessive battery acid deposits, clean the entire compartment with isopropyl alcohol or a can of cleaner/degreaser. Use a cotton swab to scrub the cleaner on the terminals. You can remove any remaining battery acid deposits by rubbing the surface of the contacts with a pencil eraser.

Chapter 8

Troubleshooting Techniques and Procedures

The word "troubleshooting" means aiming at trouble and firing away until you hit the bullseye. In a more practical sense, troubleshooting means locating and eliminating sources of problems, but doing so in a logical and predescribed manner.

Troubleshooting is the basis of electronic and mechanical repair, and a thorough grasp of its techniques and procedures is important. Just as you can't hope to shoot at a target with a blindfold around your head, you cannot wildly attack a problem in your compact disc and pray that you luck onto the solution. Troubleshooting lets you approach the problem from all angles, and zero in on the cause, with the least amount of wasted time, energy—and most of all—money.

This chapter details the concepts behind CD player troubleshooting techniques, and how to apply them to actual hands-on procedures. If you are already familiar with electronic and electro-mechanical troubleshooting, the information in this chapter may seem old hat to you. If so, skip to the next chapter. It contains troubleshooting flowcharts that you can use to pinpoint common problems with

your compact disc player. If you are not already familiar with basic troubleshooting techniques and procedures, be sure to read this chapter, as it contains useful information you won't want to miss.

THE ESSENCE OF TROUBLESHOOTING

You can better understand the role that troubleshooting plays in the repair of compact disc player ailments by using a more familiar concept: figuring out what's wrong with the family car. Let's say you go out to your car one morning, turn the key, and the car won't start. The battery turns the engine, but even after 10 or 15 tries, the car simply won't start, and every minute you spend cranking the engine is every minute you are late for work.

You could open the hood, tear out the engine and rebuild it, or you could replace random parts, thinking that it's got to be one of them that's causing the problem. You know better of course, and you stop and think for a minute: why won't the car start? The engine turns over, so you can rule out a bad battery. But the problem could be in the ignition system, the fuel lines, or a number of other sub-systems. In fact, there are several possible causes:

☐ The engine is flooded.
☐ The spark plugs are fouled.
☐ The engine isn't getting gas.
☐ The engine timing is off.
☐ The spark isn't strong enough.
☐ There is no spark.
☐ The engine isn't getting enough air because the choke is closed.

Once you have identified the possible causes, you can take corrective steps on a one-by-one basis. Start with the most common or probable cause, then work your way down. In most cases, failure to start the engine is caused by flooding. To remedy this, you open the hood and remove the air filter and perhaps a couple of spark plugs. The gas evaporates and you start your car. If the problem still persists, you go to step two, and so forth.

We've just outlined the basic three step process to troubleshooting, and it applies to compact disc players just as it does to hard-starting cars.

Step 1. Analyze the symptom ("car won't start but engine turns over") and develop a list of possible causes.

Step 2. Arrange the causes in order, from the most likely to the least likely.

Step 3. Start at the top of the list (most likely cause), and by a process of elimination, inspect, test, or otherwise rule out each possibility until the problem is located.

Once the problem has been found, you can clean or repair the faulty component.

TROUBLESHOOTING FLOWCHARTS

It's sometimes easier to visualize the troubleshooting process by using flowcharts. These are graphic representations of the possible causes and their solutions. The exact form of the flowchart can vary, but the basic information they contain is the same.

One example of a troubleshooting flowchart is shown in Chart 8-1. The chart is labeled with the

problem (or symptom), which in this case is, "Engine Turns Over But Won't Start." Below the title is a set of boxes. The boxes are stacked vertically, and each box on the left hand side contains a possible cause for the malfunction, usually a bad or dirty part or sub-system. The boxes are organized from the most likely to the least likely, so you won't waste your time with an unusual fault when the actual cause is really quite common.

In each level are two or three boxes. These boxes contain the suggested remedy, and in some cases, the procedure for testing the suspected part or sub-system.

Arrows connect the boxes in such a way that by thinking of the boxes as questions, you can answer them simply with a Yes or No response, and navigate yourself around the chart. Each No answer to a possible cause brings you down to the next level. Answer Yes to a cause, and you move laterally as you make tests and repairs.

In actual practice, however, you don't really know where the problem originates until you test each possible cause. At each level you initially answer with a Yes response, until you have the opportunity to test it out. If the test proves negative (not the cause), you move down to the next level.

USING THE TROUBLESHOOTING CHARTS IN CHAPTER 9

The troubleshooting flowcharts in Chapter 9 follow the same form and logic as our example above. If your player isn't working properly, find the chart that most closely matches the symptoms of the player. Some players may exhibit multiple symptoms, and you may need to consult several charts as you attempt to pinpoint the cause.

Once you've identified the proper chart to use, start at the top level, and work your way down, eliminating those causes that you're sure are not the source of the problem. Double-check your work, to make sure you haven't missed something, and don't forget the obvious. By far, the majority of problems with compact disc players are caused by seemingly innocent things, like a scratched disc, a dirty switch, or a selector on the player or amplifier that's not set correctly.

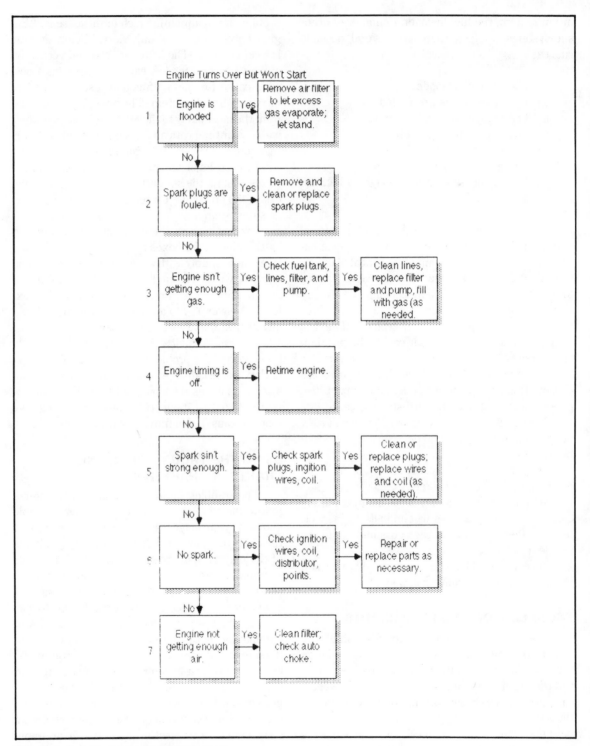

Chart 8-1. Sample of a troubleshooting chart.

Whatever you do, avoid the temptation to tear your CD player apart before you adequately identify the cause. Disassembly and removal of any part, even the top cover, should only be done until after you've eliminated the other causes. Remember that some of the components in CD players cannot be repaired or replaced without special tools and techniques, so make it a point to not remove any parts unless you absolutely have to.

WHAT YOU CAN AND CAN'T FIX

You can try to fix anything in your CD player. It's yours, you own it, and you're free to do anything you like with it. Many problems are easily handled by the home technician, and there is no reason why you should not diagnose and repair them yourself. However, there are a number of malfunctions that are best left to a repair technician, who has access to the service literature and special alignment and test jigs for your player.

Here is a general list of the components and assemblies you can fix in your CD yourself, and those that should be referred to a qualified technician. This list is not absolute by any means. Your level of expertise, and the amount of service material and tools you have or can obtain, greatly influence the types of repairs you can perform.

What You Can Do:

□ Clean and inspect the lens and optical pickup assembly.

□ Clean the exterior and interior to remove dust, nicotine, and other contaminants.

□ Clean and replace belts and rubber rollers.

□ Inspect and replace springs.

□ Lubricate gears, shafts, and other moving parts to prevent them from grinding.

□ Replace or resolder broken wires.

□ Clean or replace dirty or broken switches, including front panel switches.

□ Test for proper operation of the drive spindle and loading mechanism motors, and replace them if necessary (these usually do not require critical alignment).

□ Replace the main printed circuit board (PCB) and ancillary boards (special handling of the boards required).

□ Replace common electronic components (resistors, capacitors, diodes) on the PCBs, but only if original value is known.

What You Should Not Do

□ Disassemble the optical pickup.

□ Adjust the optical components inside the pickup.

□ Align or replace the optical pickup assembly (always a critical adjustment).

□ Adjust trimmer potentiometers on the main PCB, without the use of a schematic and an oscilloscope.

□ Remove, replace, or align the disc loading mechanism (usually a critical adjustment).

□ Replace integrated circuits, transistors, or any other component where an exact replacement or substitute cannot be guaranteed.

WHAT TO DO IF YOU CAN'T FIX IT

Should you find that repairing your CD player is beyond your technical expertise and resources, don't fret. Make a note of the problem and the suspected cause, reassemble the player, and take it to be serviced. By performing the basic troubleshooting procedures ahead of time yourself, you make the repair tech's job that much easier.

You may not get a reduction in the labor charge, but you may find the problem is fixed properly the first time around, with no costs added because of "additional work" the technician found was necessary after the machine was opened. A player that must be returned to the service shop time and again is often the result of a communications problem between you and the repair technician.

Some repair techs and service centers frown on consumers repairing their own CD players. But if you've followed the directions in this book and in the manufacturer's literature, and used the right tools and cleaning supplies, you've done nothing that the service shop would not have done—and charged you handsomely in the process. When performed properly, routine maintenance and troubleshooting procedures do not harm the compact disc player.

Avoid a repair shop that adds an additional service fee simply because you've opened the top cover and made some preliminary tests. Unless you have broken the player even more, the service fee is completely unnecessary, *and probably illegal*. After all, an automotive garage would not add $50 to their price of a tune-up because you changed the oil 1,000 miles ago.

If you are sure that the fault lies in a component that cannot be repaired, and replacement does not require critical adjustment, contact the manufacturer and ask for a parts list (if you don't already have it). Identify the faulty component and order a replacement. Most manufacturers that sell replacement parts to the public ask for payment in advance, and the easiest way to do it is by credit card. Few will ship COD.

If the manufacturer proves uncooperative, what then? Try to obtain the part from a repair center authorized to work on your brand of player (in this case, "authorized" simply means that the repair center has an open channel for replacement parts). The shop may tack on a small service fee, which is understandable.

Receiving the replacement parts from the manufacturer or a repair center may take as little as a week or as long as several months. At the worst, the broken part must be ordered from some warehouse in Japan, and it seems as if they ship it to the U.S. by sailboat. You've heard of the slow boat to China; in the case of replacement parts for CD players, it's the *very* slow boat from Japan. Owning an American-made or European-made player is not a guarantee that parts will arrive any sooner, however.

Keep records of when you ordered the part, and if you've written any follow-up letters or phoned the manufacturer directly. Ask for the names of everyone you speak with, and write them down. You never know when this additional information will come in handy.

TROUBLESHOOTING TECHNIQUES

Effective troubleshooting depends mostly on common sense, but here are some tips you'll want to remember.

Write Notes

Write copious notes. Write everything down, including how you removed the top cover, volt-ohm meter readings you made, visual observations, parts you replaced—in short anything and everything. By keeping notes, you will not only be able to retrace your steps should you get hung up on a particular fault, but you'll be able to better deal with recurring problems. The maintenance log in Appendix E provides blanks for notes; use additional sheets of blank paper if necessary.

Use the Proper Tools

Refer to Chapter 5 for more information on the proper tools to maintain and service your CD player. Don't make do with a tool that was not designed for the job. If you don't have the required tools and supplies already, spend a little extra on them. The maintenance and troubleshooting procedures outlined in this book require only the most basic hand tools and test equipment. Expensive items like oscilloscopes, function generators, and frequency counters are not required unless you opt for more detailed troubleshooting of your own.

Use Your Volt-Ohm Meter Correctly

A number of troubleshooting procedures require you to test the suspected component or assembly with a volt-ohm meter. Be sure to use this piece of equipment correctly, or you may wind up missing a potential fault, or replacing components that are perfectly good.

To test continuity, select the resistance function on the meter. If the meter is not auto-ranging, choose an initially high resistance range, on the order of 10,000 ohms or more. Attach the two meter leads (or probes) to either side of the switch, wire circuit, or connector you are testing, such as that

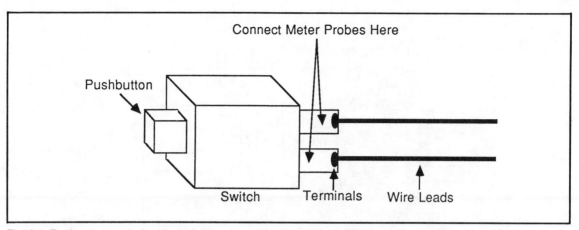

Fig. 8-1. Testing the continuity of a switch by connecting the probes of the meter to the switch terminals.

shown in Figs. 8-1 and 8-2.

Generally, continuity is a "go/no-go" test. You will either get a reading of 0 ohms, which means that the circuit or connection between the two test leads is complete; or infinite ohms, which means that the circuit is broken, or that the connection between the two test leads is open.

A reading of 0 ohms is exactly what you want sometimes, like when you are testing the closure of a switch or a length of wire to make sure it is not broken inside. Other times, 0 resistance means that something is shorted out, which is an unhappy situation. Likewise, a reading of infinite ohms (which meters display in a variety of ways), may

be correct for a given test; 0 ohms for another test. The troubleshooting charts in Chapter 9 provide more details on the typical readings you should get for any given instance.

When using the meter, make sure that you do not touch the metal part of the probes. Your body has a natural resistance, however high, and you will add or subtract it to the measurement you're trying to take. Always take your readings by grasping the test leads by the plastic insulator.

Volt-ohm meters test more than continuity, of course. For example, you will want to use the ac and dc voltage functions to test for proper voltage levels going into and out of the player's power sup-

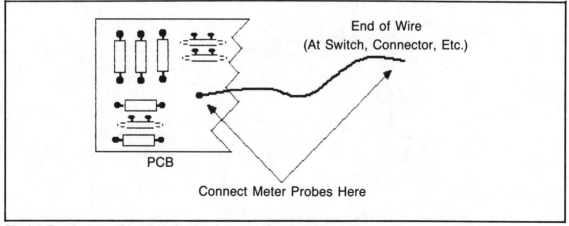

Fig. 8-2. Test for internal breakage in wires by connecting the VOM to either end.

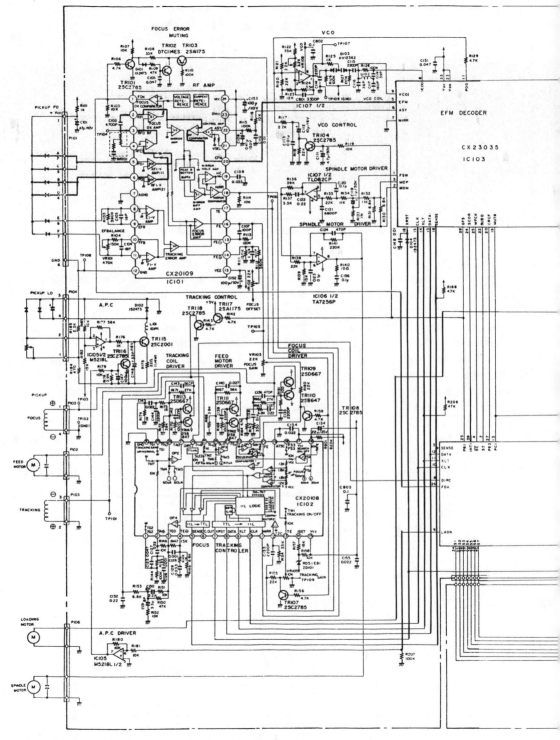

Fig. 8-3. Schematic diagram for a typical home CD player. Courtesy JCPenny.

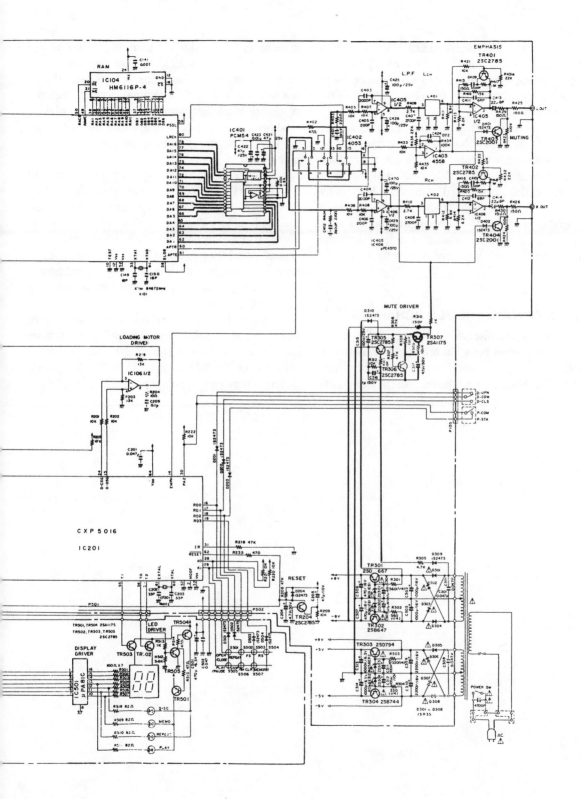

ply. Be sure to select the correct function *before* you connect the test leads to the live circuit. With many meters, connecting the leads to a dc voltage when the unit is dialed to ac may burn out a fuse or cause internal damage.

If the meter is not the auto-ranging type, always choose a range higher than the input voltage. If you are not sure of the voltage level, choose the highest one first, then work down. Most digital meters have built-in overload protection to prevent damage by choosing a too-low range. However, the needle in an analog meter can be permanently bent or broken if you accidentally choose a range that's too low, and the meter violently swings to the end of the scale.

GOING BEYOND THE FLOWCHARTS

Few compact disc players are designed exactly alike. Differences between brands, even between models of the same brand, require slightly different troubleshooting procedures. Use the flowcharts in Chapter 9 as a starting point only. The design and construction of your CD player may require additional troubleshooting steps. If possible, refer to the schematic or service manual to your machine. A sample schematic, for a basic 3-beam CD player, is shown in Fig. 8-3. It will often detail testing points or procedures that are unique to the particular model.

In other cases, the design of your player may not require that you perform some troubleshooting procedure. For instance, if your player is a top loader, it lacks a disc drawer/door loading mechanism, so problems with this assembly are of no concern to you. Likewise, car CD players will lack any type of power transformer, so it is not necessary to test it if you are having trouble with powering your unit.

To keep the charts as simple as possible, we've limited them to reflect problems inherent in front loading ac operated home models. If you own a portable or car CD player, allow for the design difference in your troubleshooting procedures.

Chapter 9

Troubleshooting
CD Player Malfunctions

Compact disc players are complex electronic and mechanical devices. Their reliance on special proprietary integrated circuits and zero-tolerance mechanical alignment leave the average consumer or electronics hobbyist reduced opportunity for complete home repair.

This does not mean, that doctoring the ills that beset the CD player is entirely out of your hands. On the contrary, the simplicity and modularity of CD player design make mechanical and electronic faults very rare—assuming that the machine was well manufactured in the first place.

In this chapter, you'll learn what you can do when your CD player goes on the fritz, and how to go about fixing it. The emphasis is on troubleshooting the mechanical sections of the player, and plenty of flowcharts are provided to graphically show the step-by-step process of the cure for a given ailment.

FIX IT YOURSELF

Service shops for CDs report that the follow-

ing causes represent by far the greatest majority—over 80 percent—of warranty and non-warranty repair. The causes are listed from most common to least common.

☐ Failure to loosen or remove the transit screw.

☐ Disc problems (includes improper disc handling or loading, warped disc, scratched or dirty disc).

☐ System connection (cable from CD to amp, speaker wires, etc.).

☐ Physical abuse or accidental damage.

☐ Dirty objective lens on the optical pickup.

You can save yourself the cost of a service call, not to mention headaches and frustration, by not only following manufacturers' instructions for operating your hi-fi gear, but by caring for your discs and your player.

SERVICE POLITICS

Ordinary mechanical and electronic breakdown

do occur, you can repair a number of these break-downs yourself. Most dysfunctions can be corrected by cleaning dirty electronic contacts and switches, oiling or greasing the moving parts, repairing the occasional broken or frayed wire, and replacing worn parts like rollers, belts, and plastic gears.

Unless you have specific training and experience in working with both high speed digital and analog circuits, and have the proper servicing tools, problems with the optical system (alignment, laser output, and so forth), as well as failed integrated circuits and other components on the circuit boards should be referred to a repair technician. More complex problems require a schematic or service manual, an oscilloscope, and a variety of specially made alignment and test jigs. They also require additional troubleshooting and repair techniques, which are beyond the scope of this book. If you are interested in learning more on this subject, see Appendix D for a selected list of general and specific electronic troubleshooting and repair guides.

Many manufacturers will sell you a copy of the schematic or service manual, but be prepared to spend up to $30 for it. The wait can take up to eight weeks. We provide the names and addresses of most CD player manufacturers in Appendix B.

Most CD manufacturers will not sell the test jigs and alignment tools directly to consumers. In fact, many player manufacturers won't even sell the tools to independent authorized service centers! Other than routine cleaning and checkout, along with replacement of some mechanical parts (most or all of which you can do yourself), service centers are directed to send defective players back to the manufacturer for repair.

One exception to this rule is defects in the main printed circuit board (PCB), which holds most or all of the circuitry for processing and converting the disc data into an analog signal. These problems can often be handled in the repair shop, but they almost always entail completely exchanging the old board for a new one. In the service trade, a technician who repairs electronic products simply by exchanging a PCB is euphemistically called a "board swapper." Technicians don't much like it (the implications in the phrase as well as the inability to get parts), but individual components and ICs are not available from the manufacturer, and they must take what they can get.

If you suspect a problem with the main PCB in your player, you may be able to get a replacement directly from the manufacturer and change the board yourself. This could save you $75 or more in labor costs. CD makers sell the boards on an exchange basis. You send in the old, defective board—along with a check or money order to cover the service fee—and they send you a good, tested board in return.

USING THE TROUBLESHOOTING CHARTS

The remainder of this chapter is devoted to a series of troubleshooting charts that detail the possible causes and suggested solutions for a series of common and not so common CD player ailments. The charts are not meant to be definitive, but they should go a long way in helping you pinpoint a problem in your player. See Chapter 8 for an explanation on how to use and interpret the charts. You are also referred to Chapters 5 and 6 on the tools and supplies of CD maintenance and repair, and how to use them. To avoid repetitive solutions sections and paragraphs have been numbered. The flowcharts will refer back to solutions rather than restating them in the section paragraphs.

To prevent overcomplicating the charts, they have been designed to apply specifically to ac operated home players. Many of the same problems, causes, and solutions will apply to all three types of players—home, portable, and car—but troubleshooting techniques may differ in certain situations.

You can still use the troubleshooting charts to diagnose most problems in portable or car units, however, because the basic reasons behind the fault will be similar. For example, a car CD player does not have an ac cord, so you would not test its cord if you are having trouble in operating the unit. But you *would* test the power line supplying the 12 volts dc to the player, in a similar manner as you would an ac cord.

The reason for leaning toward the home ac

operated units is that they are considerably easier to maintain and repair than the portable and car versions.

Look to the Simple Things First

In using or looking over the charts, you may find that some of the possible causes may seem overly simplistic. The biggest mistake you can make in servicing your compact disc player is overlooking the obvious. If something doesn't work, odds are, it's a simple cause with an equally simple solution. Repairs are a lot less expensive and time consuming because of it.

List of Charts

Here are the troubleshooting charts, in their order of presentation. The charts are numbered for cross-reference. Within the charts, the steps (or levels) are numbered, which correspond to numbers in the text. Unless otherwise specified, all troubleshooting procedures and tests should be done with the player turned off, and unplugged or removed from the power source. Most manufacturers suggest you reinstall the transit screws before disassembly. Be sure to remove or loosen the screws again when testing or moving the player.

9.1. When a player does not turn on, the cause is almost always mechanically related. (This goes for all three main types of compact disc players.)

9.1A.1 The first logical step is to insure that it is getting power from the ac wall source. Make sure that the cord is plugged in, and that the polarized plug is inserted properly. Do not defeat the purpose of the polarized plug by filing or cutting the wide prong.

9.1A.2 In homes equipped with switched outlets, (you flick a wall switch to turn the outlet on and off), the switch controls both outlet receptacles, other times just one. If the player is plugged into a switched outlet, make sure that it is turned on.

To rule out the possibility that the problem originates in the wall outlet and not in the player, plug a lamp into the socket and see if the lamp works. If the lamp seems dim, check the voltage at the outlet with a volt-ohm meter. It should read between 108 and 125 volts ac (117 is average). Be absolutely sure that you follow all safety precautions when testing the ac voltage or you may receive a serious shock.

9.1A.3 If the power cord is plugged into an amplifier or receiver, check to see if the outlet you have chosen is switched. Some amplifiers have a built-in switched outlet. The outlet is activated when the amplifier is turned on. If the outlet is unswitched (and will usually be labeled as such), the outlet is active at all times as long as the amplifier is plugged in. If the CD player is plugged into the amp, be sure that the amplifier itself is plugged into the wall socket. Try the lamp or meter test if you are unsure of the power outlet at the amp.

9.1A.4 Most players incorporate a transit screw that locks the moving parts in the player into place, preventing them from being knocked out of alignment during shipment. With a few players, leaving the transit screw in place, or failure to loosen it all the way, will prevent the machine from turning on. Be sure the transit screw is loosened or removed according to the manufacturer's instructions. There may be two or more transit screws, each locking down a different internal part, so make sure you get them all.

9.1A.5 Players with timers will usually shut down when in timer mode (the timer plays a disc starting at a specific time of the day). Follow the manufacturers instructions on deactivating or resetting the timer.

9.1A.6 If your player is equipped with a fuse, remove it and visually inspect it. If you can't tell that the fuse has blown, use a meter to check continuity. Attach the leads to either side of the fuse. If the fuse is good, the meter will read 0 ohms. An infinite reading indicates a bad fuse.

Note: Some compact disc players use current-limiting fuses. These are like regular fuses, except they use an internal resistor to limit the current flowing through them. If the fuse has an internal resistor (which can be easily seen through the glass capsule), the meter reading will register the value of the resistor. In most cases, the value will be low, under 1,000 ohms.

9.1A.7 After checking the ac sources, transit

screw(s), timer, and fuse, inspect all power cords for cracks and other signs of wear. A badly worn or damaged cord can cause a number of problems. A short will blow fuses (either in the house or in the player); an open line will prevent the ac from reaching the player.

Check the power cord using a meter. A short will register 0 ohms (or a low reading) when the test leads are connected across the two prongs of the ac cord. An open will register infinite ohms (or a very high reading) when the test leads are connected to the prongs and internal wiring of the player, as shown in Fig. 9-1. Test both prongs.

9.1B.1 The power wiring inside your player may be faulty. Open the player and check the connections leading to the power switch. Check for shorts and open circuits using the meter. Normally, only one side of the incoming ac will be connected to the switch. The other side will connect directly to the power transformer.

9.1B.2 If the wiring to the switch tests okay, try the wiring leading from the switch and to the inputs of the power transformer (called the primary). Also test the wiring from the output of the transformer (called the secondary) to the power supply model or main PCB. A sample schematic diagram of the power supply circuits from a typical CD is shown in Fig. 9-2.

To test that the transformer is delivering power, plug in the machine (if it is safe) and turn it on. With the meter set to read ac volts, with a range of no less than 25 or 50 volts, connect the test leads to the *outputs* of the transformer. Without a schematic, it may be difficult to make sense of the readings, but generally, you should get a reading of 6 to 24 volts when connecting the leads to any of the wires.

The power transformers used in most CD players have different tapoffs, so applying the leads at different tapoffs will yield a wide variety of results. You can be fairly sure the transformer is working properly if you get some readings when the meter is connected to the most of the secondary wires. Be sure to avoid the primary wires, as they carry the full 117 Vac from the wall outlet.

9.1B.3 It's easy to forget that switches are

mechanical in nature, and they can get broken, dirty, and corroded. Test the Power switch to make sure that it works properly. Connect the test leads of the ohm-meter to either side of the switch terminals. The meter should read 0 ohms when the switch is in the on position, and infinite ohms when the switch is in the off position. If the switch is the double pole type—two sets of switch contacts inside instead of just one—test each set separately. (Fig. 9-3)

9.2. It is often harder to troubleshoot a CD player when the machine turns on but doesn't play; however, at least you can rule out problems in the power supply, fuses, on/off switch, and all that other stuff.

9.2.1 Taking a compact disc player from the cold damp outside air to the warm inside air can cause condensation to form on the internal components. A few CD home players (and many portable and car models) have a dew sensor that prevents the machine from operating when there is condensation present. If you suspect condensation, visually inspect for moisture and wait 30 to 60 minutes for it to evaporate. You can speed up the drying process somewhat by using a hair blow dryer. Keep the dryer on low or no heat.

9.2.2 Some players are built with a cabinet interlock switch, which may be broken or open. All or some of the player is shut off when the top cover is removed. If the cover is off, look for a switch. Manually depress it and see if the player turns on.

To test the switch, make sure the player is off and unplugged. Use the volt-ohm meter to test the continuity of the switch. With the leads of the meter connected to either terminal of the switch, the reading should be 0 ohms when the switch is closed, and infinite ohms when the switch is open.

9.2.3 You may not be able to control the operation of the player if one or more of the front panel switches are dirty or broken. If only one switch is affected, you may be able to cycle the player through its other operations. You can isolate that switch by finding its solder contacts or connecting wires on the switch panel PCB (the switch panel may be a part of the main PCB in some players). Use the volt-ohm meter to test the continuity of the

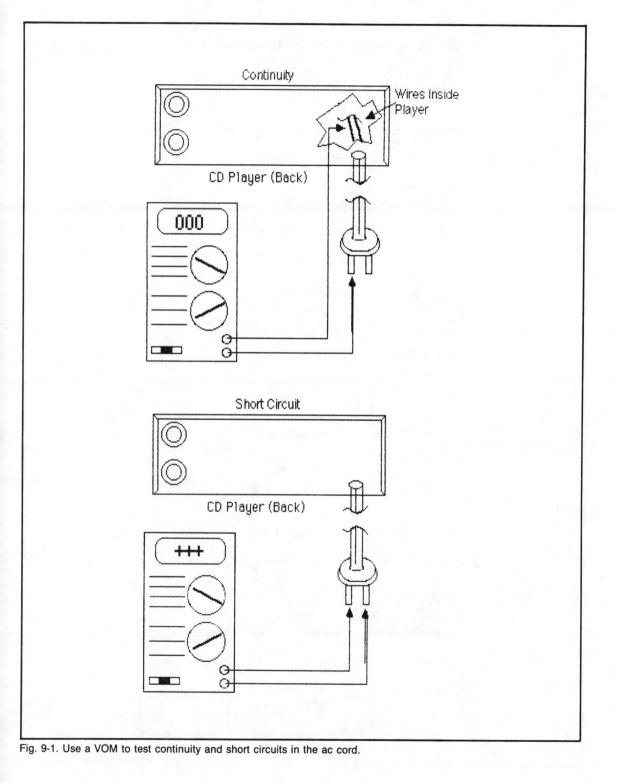

Fig. 9-1. Use a VOM to test continuity and short circuits in the ac cord.

127

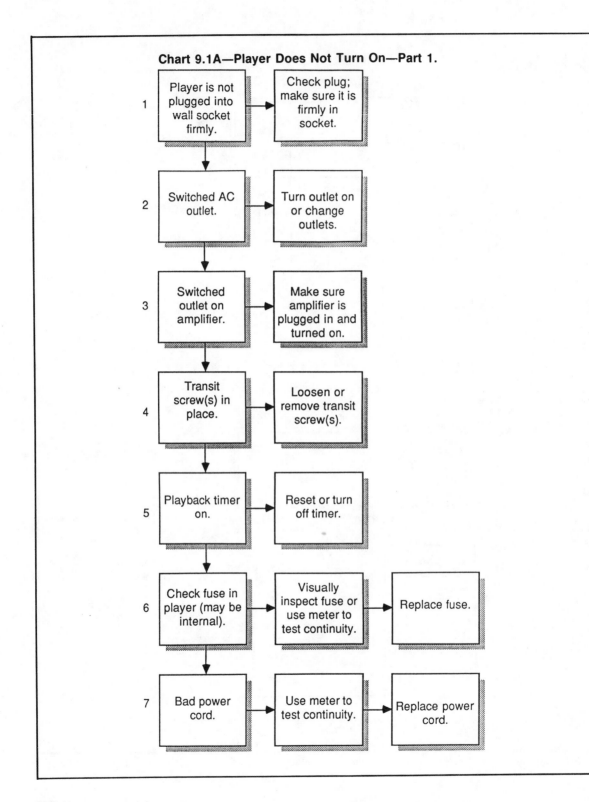

Chart 9.1A—Player Does Not Turn On—Part 1.

1. Player is not plugged into wall socket firmly. → Check plug; make sure it is firmly in socket.

2. Switched AC outlet. → Turn outlet on or change outlets.

3. Switched outlet on amplifier. → Make sure amplifier is plugged in and turned on.

4. Transit screw(s) in place. → Loosen or remove transit screw(s).

5. Playback timer on. → Reset or turn off timer.

6. Check fuse in player (may be internal). → Visually inspect fuse or use meter to test continuity. → Replace fuse.

7. Bad power cord. → Use meter to test continuity. → Replace power cord.

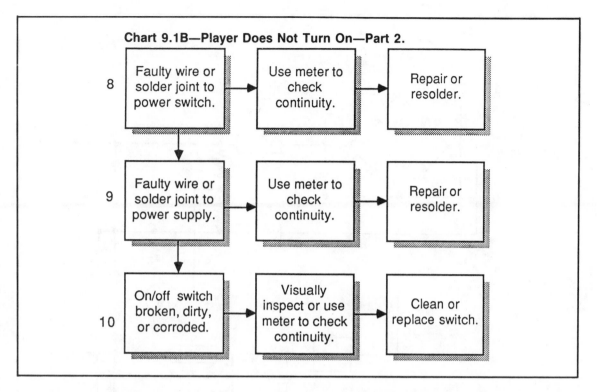

Chart 9.1B—Player Does Not Turn On—Part 2.

8 | Faulty wire or solder joint to power switch. → Use meter to check continuity. → Repair or resolder.

9 | Faulty wire or solder joint to power supply. → Use meter to check continuity. → Repair or resolder.

10 | On/off switch broken, dirty, or corroded. → Visually inspect or use meter to check continuity. → Clean or replace switch.

switch. Pushing the switch should change the reading from 0 to infinite ohms.

9.2.4 If all the front panel switches are inoperative, the problem may lie in the common connecting wire to the switches (if applicable) or to the front panel PCB. Test all the wires leading to the switch panel with the meter to make sure none are broken or loose. With the test leads connected to either side of the wire, a reading other than 0 ohms is an indication of an internal break in the wire. Inspect the solder points for signs of a cold or incomplete solder joint. Resolder the joint if necessary.

With many players, the front panel PCB is attached to the main PCB by connectors, as shown in Fig. 9-4. Use your meter to test the continuity between the connectors. If you find a reading other than 0 ohms, carefully remove the connector and inspect it for loose wires, broken wires, and broken or dirty contacts. Resolder or replace the connector if it is damaged. Use a recommended cleaner to clean contact points.

9.2.5 If the problem still persists, the next logical step is to examine the wires and components on the main PCB. Are there any obviously broken wires? Test with a meter to be sure. Look closely at the capacitors and resistors mounted on the board. Occasionally, you can spot a burned out component by looking for black charring on and around it. Generally, you cannot spot a blown transistor or integrated circuit in this manner because the damage does not usually extend to the exterior of the device.

9.3. If you find that the disc loading door or drawer will not open or close, under no circumstances should you try to force the drawer or door manually. Doing so may seriously damage the loading mechanism or seriously bend a catch or latch.

9.3.1 An object of some type, including a warped disc, could be obstructing the free path of the loading drawer/door. Remove the top cover of the player and examine the loading mechanism. If a disc is on the spindle, remove it by gently lifting the flapper (clamping lever) and easing out the disc. Examine the disc for warpage. Turn the machine on and try opening the drawer/door again.

If the drawer/door still won't operate, inspect

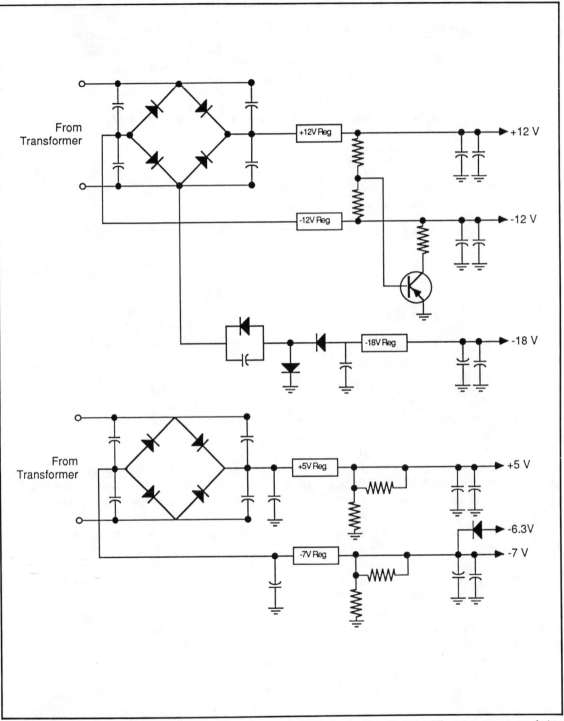

Fig. 9-2. Schematic of the power supply circuit used in a typical CD player. Note that six different voltages are fed to different points on the player's PCB.

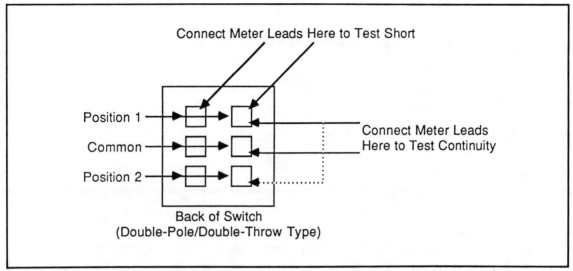

Fig. 9-3. Connect the probes of the meter as shown to test for continuity or shorts in a double-pole/double-throw switch.

the path of the mechanism, including all gears, cams, slideways, and other parts in and around the loader. Carefully remove any objects that may have lodged in place.

9.3.2 When you push the Open/Close button, does the loading motor operate? If it does, but nothing happens, suspect the belt that connects the motor to the loading mechanism. Belts can break or slip off the metal or plastic pulleys. Look at the belt as you depress the Open/Close switch. If the motor shaft turns, but the belt doesn't budge, the belt may be too loose or may be slippery from oil or grease build-up. Inspect the belt and clean it if necessary.

A number of machines use plastic gears to drive the loading mechanism from the motor. A gear is mounted on the motor shaft, and meshes with a straight toothed rail. When the motor shaft turns, the gear inches the loading mechanism along the rail, thus opening the drawer or door (Fig. 9-5). Inspect the gear and rail to be sure that none of the teeth are broken and that the gear teeth are meshing properly.

9.3.3 Even if the loading mechanism looks fine, the gears and rails may still bind against one another. Would oiling or greasing help? Apply a small dab of grease on the gear surfaces or oil to shafts and levers.

9.3.4 If the motor does not turn when you depress the Open/Close button, it may not be getting the command to do so. Check the Open/Close switch first, to make sure that it hasn't gotten dirty, broken, or corroded. To test the switch, connect the test leads of the ohm-meter to either side of the switch terminals. The meter should alternate between 0 and infinite ohms when the switch is pushed.

Keep an eye out for cracked or pinched wires leading to the switch, as well as poor solder joints. Test the joints and wires using the meter, as usual. Opens and shorts are indications that the wiring is bad and must be repaired.

9.3.5 The wires from the Open/Close switch routes back to the main PCB, and eventually is connected to the system microprocessor. You can test the wiring leading from the microprocessor and back out to the disc loading motor. Inspect these wires carefully and look for obvious damage. Use the volt-ohm meter to test continuity. You should get a reading of 0 ohms when the test leads are connected to either end of the wires. Broken or cold solder joints on the motor terminals should be resoldered.

To ensure that the proper drive signals are being applied to the motor when the Open/Close switch is depressed, connect the volt-ohm meter to

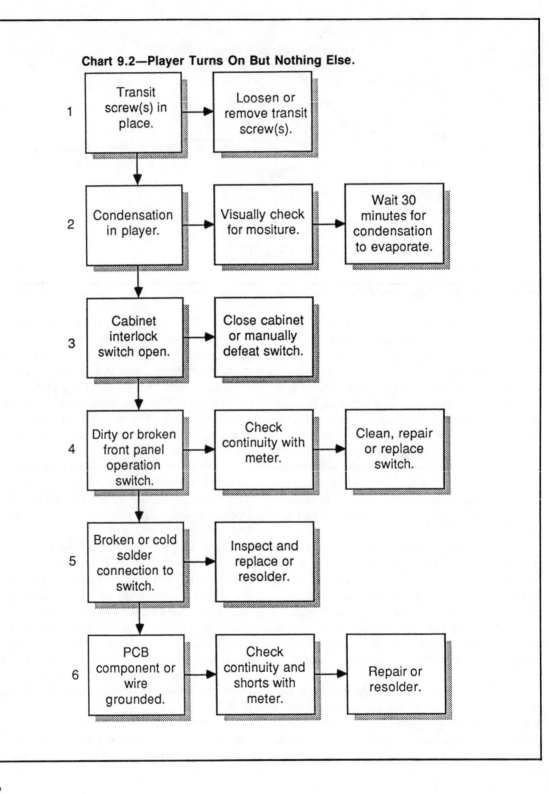

Chart 9.2—Player Turns On But Nothing Else.

1. Transit screw(s) in place. → Loosen or remove transit screw(s).

2. Condensation in player. → Visually check for mositure. → Wait 30 minutes for condensation to evaporate.

3. Cabinet interlock switch open. → Close cabinet or manually defeat switch.

4. Dirty or broken front panel operation switch. → Check continuity with meter. → Clean, repair or replace switch.

5. Broken or cold solder connection to switch. → Inspect and replace or resolder.

6. PCB component or wire grounded. → Check continuity and shorts with meter. → Repair or resolder.

Fig. 9-4. In most players, the front panel controls and indicators are mounted on a separate PCB. The front panel and main PCBs are electrically connected using wires or flexible printed wire boards (PWBs).

both motor terminals (Fig. 9-6). Select the dc volts function on the meter, with a range of no less than 12 volts. With the player plugged in and turned on, depress the Open/Close switch once. With most machines, your meter should read a voltage (it may be as small as 3 volts but as high as 12 volts).

9.3.6 If no other defects can be found up to this point, the problem may lie in the loading motor itself. You can test the motor by connecting a "C" or "D" size battery to the motor terminals, as illustrated in Fig. 9-7. The polarity of the battery determines which direction the motor turns, so if the motor seems to labor when power is applied in one polarity, reverse the connection to the terminals and try again.

9.4. It's aggravating when the CD plays a disc for only a few seconds or minutes, then either turns off mysteriously, or comes to a grinding halt. Fortunately, the problem is almost always mechanical in nature and is often easily corrected.

9.4.1 A disc that's been scratched may play for a while then abruptly stop. This can happen especially if the scratch is a deep one, and throws the pickup seriously out of tracking or focus. With a number of players, a complete and irrecoverable loss of tracking and focus will cease playback.

Likewise, a warped disc may play for a while. Then, as the amount of warpage increases as the pickup moves to the outer edge of the disc, the pickup can no longer keep the disc in track or focus. If a disc won't play, inspect it, and if possible clean or repair it. A seriously warped or scratched disc is not repairable and must be discarded.

9.4.2 A dirty objective lens can prevent the laser from tracking or focusing the disc. If the tracking or focus error spans many thousands of bits, the system microprocessor in the player may stop playback. If the problem persists with many discs, a dirty lens may be the cause. Inspect and clean the objective lens.

9.4.3 An open or defective interlock switch may prevent the CD from playing more than just a few seconds of the beginning of the disc. The system microprocessor senses that the interlock switch is open, and stops playback. Interlock switches are typically located in the disc loading drawer/door mechanism, and sometimes in the cabinet.

Be sure that all interlock switches are properly closed. If you are testing the player with the top cover off, look for a safety interlock switch and close or defeat it (you can defeat it by attaching a jumper between its terminals, as shown in Fig. 9-8).

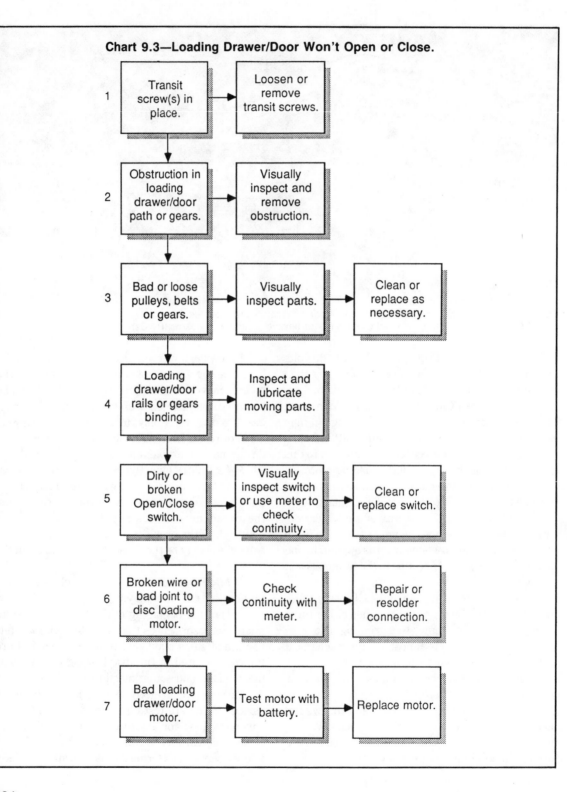

Chart 9.3—Loading Drawer/Door Won't Open or Close.

1. Transit screw(s) in place. → Loosen or remove transit screws.

2. Obstruction in loading drawer/door path or gears. → Visually inspect and remove obstruction.

3. Bad or loose pulleys, belts or gears. → Visually inspect parts. → Clean or replace as necessary.

4. Loading drawer/door rails or gears binding. → Inspect and lubricate moving parts.

5. Dirty or broken Open/Close switch. → Visually inspect switch or use meter to check continuity. → Clean or replace switch.

6. Broken wire or bad joint to disc loading motor. → Check continuity with meter. → Repair or resolder connection.

7. Bad loading drawer/door motor. → Test motor with battery. → Replace motor.

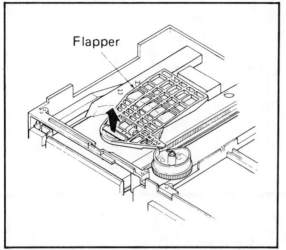

Fig. 9-5. The location of the flapper in a drawer-type disc loading mechanism.

Interlock switches in the disc loading mechanism should be closed if a disc is properly inserted.

Test the interlock switches to make sure that they work properly. Connect the test leads of the ohm-meter to either side of the switch terminals. The meter should read 0 ohms when the switch is in the on position, and infinite ohms when the switch is in the off position. For testing purposes, you can override a broken switch by connecting a jumper between its terminals (see the figure above). For normal operation, a dirty or broken switch should be cleaned or replaced.

9.4.4. Insert a disc and press play. Listen for the sound of the pickup motor turning. If motor turns but the pickup does not move, check pulleys, belts, rollers, or gears for signs of wear and/or excessive slippage. Also check for obstructions or foreign matter that may prevent the pickup from moving freely.

9.4.5 The speed of the disc during playback is carefully monitored by the system microprocessor, and any fluctuations are adjusted during playback to provide highly accurate disc rotation speed. In most players, the disc spindle motor attaches to the disc spindle by a pulley or belt. If the pulley or belt is worn, cracked, broken, loose, or oily, the spindle may move in a herky-jerky fashion, and the system microprocessor may not be able to correct for the fluctuations. When the playback speed exceeds certain upper and lower limits, the microprocessor will cease playback.

With the cover of the player off, and a disc

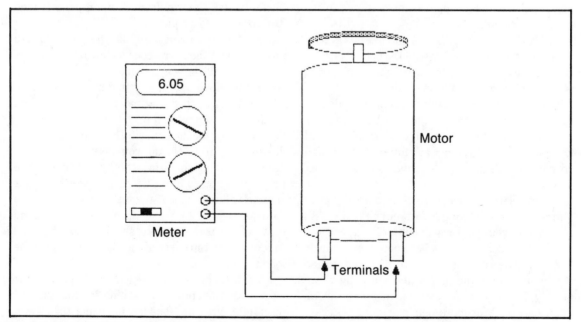

Fig. 9-6. How to test the voltage level reaching the disc loading motor.

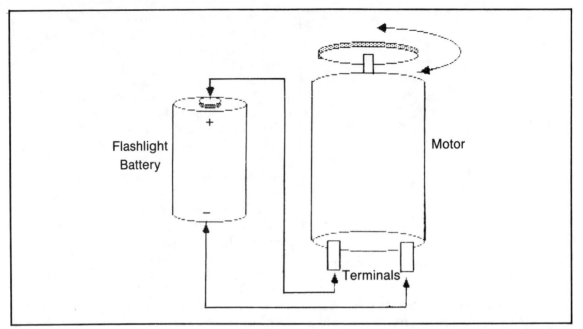

Fig. 9-7. Testing the disc loading motor with a flashlight battery. The polarity of the wires determines the direction of motor rotation.

loaded, press play and watch the drive motor, pulley, belt, and spindle. You should be able to see any mechanical defects. If the belt seems like it's slipping, apply some non-slip cleaner to it, or replace it with a new one.

9.4.6 The compact disc system depends greatly on the light output of the laser in the optical pickup. If the light output gets too high or low, playback is impaired and the data from the disc may not properly reach the player electronics. A laser diode that gets too hot acts erratically, and its light output is not steady. In these cases, the preamplifier and EFM demodulator cannot accurately process and decode the disc data, and the player is forced to shut down.

Many players, particularly the models designed for the car, have a laser overheat circuit that ceases playback. If your player has such a circuit, and you suspect the laser diode may have gotten excessively hot, turn the player off for 30 to 60 minutes, and try again. Should the player get unusually warm quickly, it may be suffering from another problem. See Chart 9.17 for more details.

9.5. Diagnosing a disc spindle that doesn't turn

when you push the Play button is a rather straightforward procedure. Compared to many CD player problems, however, there are a number of possible faults—all the way from an improperly loaded disc to a bad laser pickup.

9.5A.1 First make sure that the disc is loaded properly (with the mirrored side down) and that the door closes all the way. While the disc is out, inspect it for obvious warpage and heavy scratches.

9.5A.2 A warped disc may prevent the loading mechanism from retracting all the way. A malfunction in the mechanism itself also keeps the drawer/door from closing completely. Unless the drawer/door mechanism is fully retracted, the player will not go into Play mode, and the motor spindle will not spin. If the disc shows no sign of damage, check to make sure that the loading drawer/door is closing as it should. You may need to remove the top cover of the player to inspect the loading mechanism.

9.5A.3 A dirty objective lens might prevent the laser diode from properly tracking and focusing the disc. If the disc spins for a few moments, then stops, even after pushing the Play button, it's a good in-

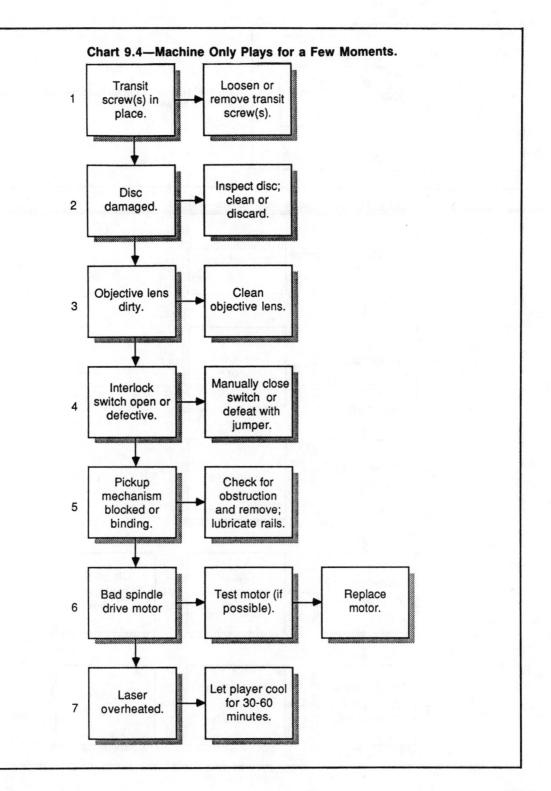

Chart 9.4—Machine Only Plays for a Few Moments.

1. Transit screw(s) in place. → Loosen or remove transit screw(s).

2. Disc damaged. → Inspect disc; clean or discard.

3. Objective lens dirty. → Clean objective lens.

4. Interlock switch open or defective. → Manually close switch or defeat with jumper.

5. Pickup mechanism blocked or binding. → Check for obstruction and remove; lubricate rails.

6. Bad spindle drive motor → Test motor (if possible). → Replace motor.

7. Laser overheated. → Let player cool for 30-60 minutes.

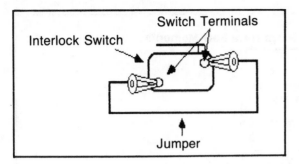

Fig. 9-8. How to defeat an interlock switch by connecting a jumper between its terminals.

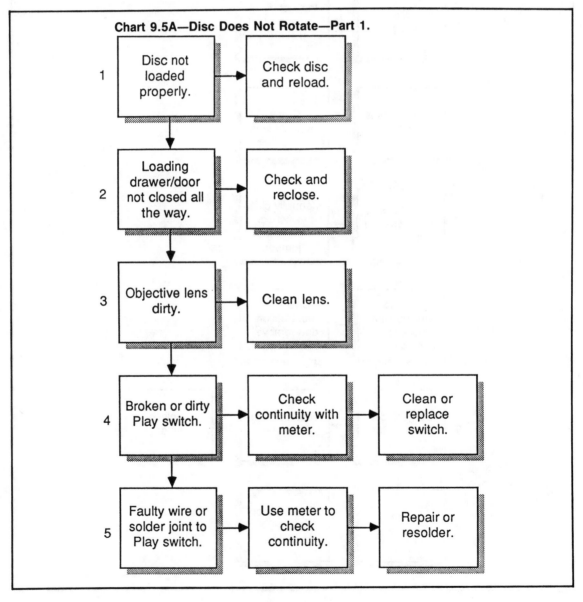

Chart 9.5A—Disc Does Not Rotate—Part 1.

1. Disc not loaded properly. → Check disc and reload.

2. Loading drawer/door not closed all the way. → Check and reclose.

3. Objective lens dirty. → Clean lens.

4. Broken or dirty Play switch. → Check continuity with meter. → Clean or replace switch.

5. Faulty wire or solder joint to Play switch. → Use meter to check continuity. → Repair or resolder.

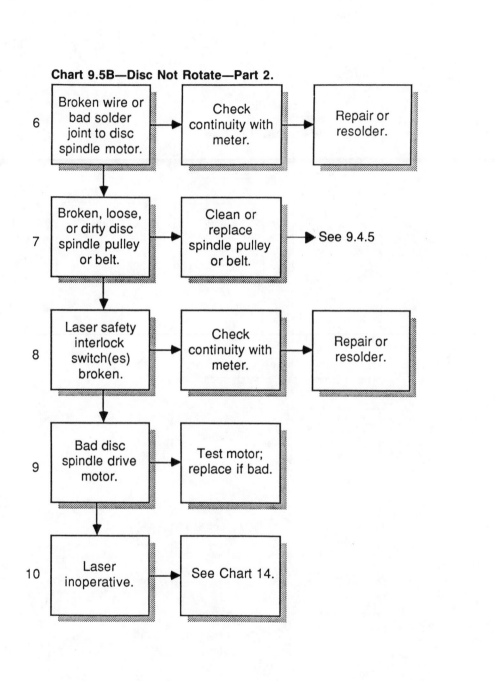

Chart 9.5B—Disc Not Rotate—Part 2.

6 — Broken wire or bad solder joint to disc spindle motor. → Check continuity with meter. → Repair or resolder.

7 — Broken, loose, or dirty disc spindle pulley or belt. → Clean or replace spindle pulley or belt. → See 9.4.5

8 — Laser safety interlock switch(es) broken. → Check continuity with meter. → Repair or resolder.

9 — Bad disc spindle drive motor. → Test motor; replace if bad.

10 — Laser inoperative. → See Chart 14.

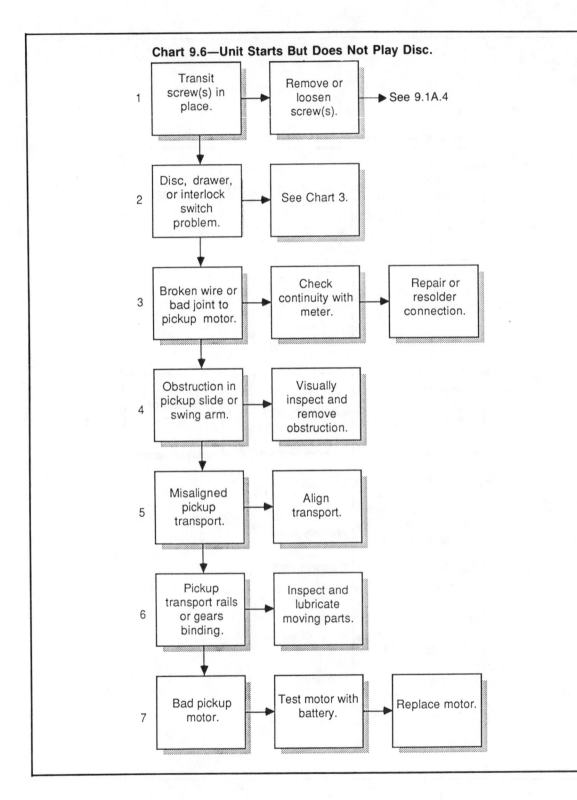

Chart 9.6—Unit Starts But Does Not Play Disc.

1. Transit screw(s) in place. → Remove or loosen screw(s). → See 9.1A.4

2. Disc, drawer, or interlock switch problem. → See Chart 3.

3. Broken wire or bad joint to pickup motor. → Check continuity with meter. → Repair or resolder connection.

4. Obstruction in pickup slide or swing arm. → Visually inspect and remove obstruction.

5. Misaligned pickup transport. → Align transport.

6. Pickup transport rails or gears binding. → Inspect and lubricate moving parts.

7. Bad pickup motor. → Test motor with battery. → Replace motor.

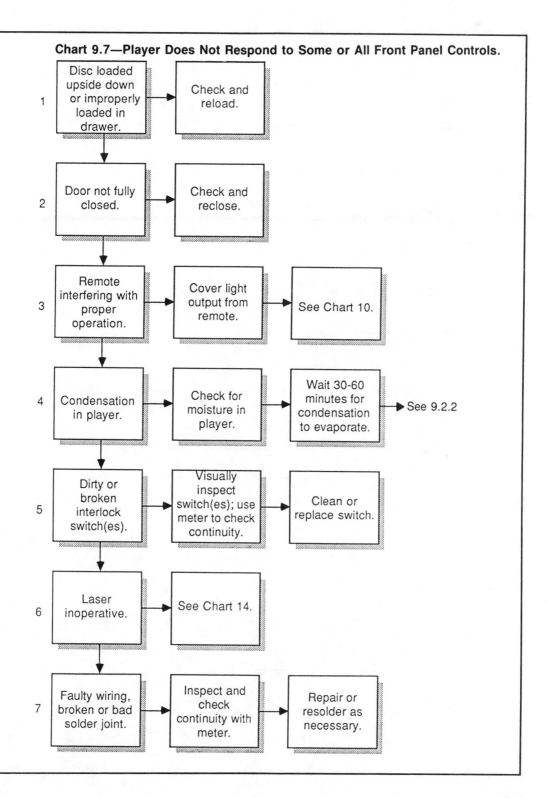

Chart 9.7—Player Does Not Respond to Some or All Front Panel Controls.

1. Disc loaded upside down or improperly loaded in drawer. → Check and reload.

2. Door not fully closed. → Check and reclose.

3. Remote interfering with proper operation. → Cover light output from remote. → See Chart 10.

4. Condensation in player. → Check for moisture in player. → Wait 30-60 minutes for condensation to evaporate. → See 9.2.2

5. Dirty or broken interlock switch(es). → Visually inspect switch(es); use meter to check continuity. → Clean or replace switch.

6. Laser inoperative. → See Chart 14.

7. Faulty wiring, broken or bad solder joint. → Inspect and check continuity with meter. → Repair or resolder as necessary.

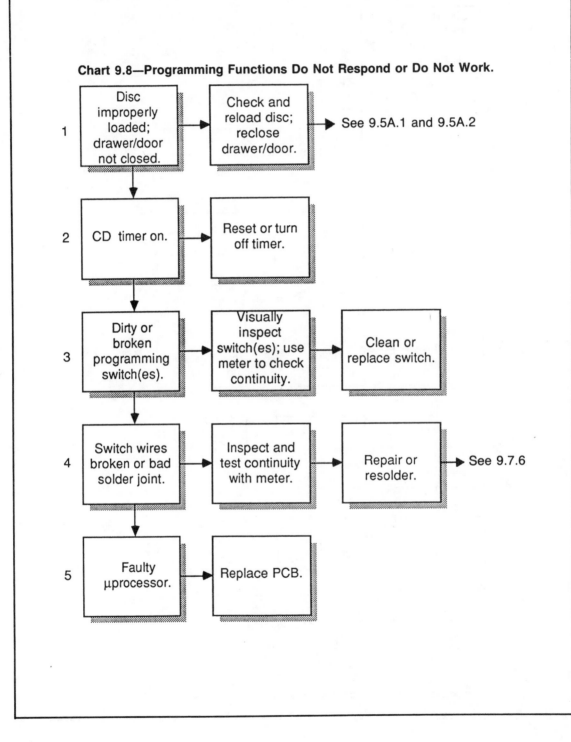

Chart 9.8—Programming Functions Do Not Respond or Do Not Work.

1. Disc improperly loaded; drawer/door not closed. → Check and reload disc; reclose drawer/door. → See 9.5A.1 and 9.5A.2

2. CD timer on. → Reset or turn off timer.

3. Dirty or broken programming switch(es). → Visually inspect switch(es); use meter to check continuity. → Clean or replace switch.

4. Switch wires broken or bad solder joint. → Inspect and test continuity with meter. → Repair or resolder. → See 9.7.6

5. Faulty µprocessor. → Replace PCB.

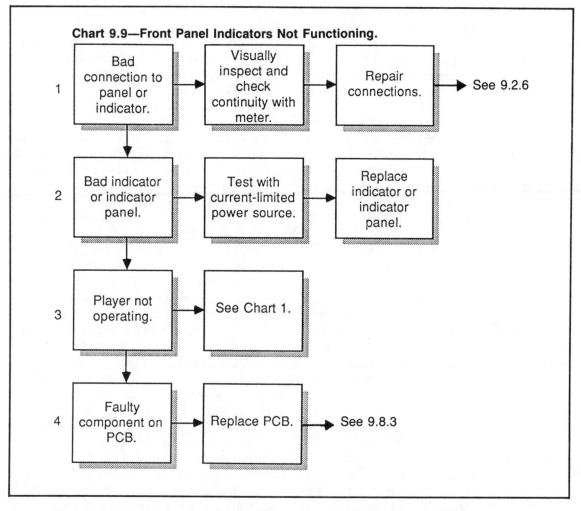

Chart 9.9—Front Panel Indicators Not Functioning.

1. Bad connection to panel or indicator. → Visually inspect and check continuity with meter. → Repair connections. → See 9.2.6

2. Bad indicator or indicator panel. → Test with current-limited power source. → Replace indicator or indicator panel.

3. Player not operating. → See Chart 1.

4. Faulty component on PCB. → Replace PCB. → See 9.8.3

dication that the problem lies within the optical pickup mechanism. Later steps in this flowchart deal with faults in the optical pickup, but the first course of action is to clean the lens.

9.5A.4 Switches can get broken, dirty, or corroded. Test the Play switch to make sure that it works properly. Connect the test leads of the ohmmeter to either side of the switch terminals. The meter should read 0 and infinite ohms when the Play switch is depressed. If pushing the Play switch doesn't yield these results, it may be dirty or the contacts inside broken.

If the contacts are not sealed, spray a bit of electrical contact cleaner inside the switch. You can be fairly certain that the problem is limited to just the Play switch (and/or its wiring) if the other front panel controls operate properly.

9.5A.5 While at the Play switch, look for broken wires and faulty solder joints. Check the connections at the switch (usually direct-soldered to the front panel PCB) and the wires that lead to the main PCB. Check the wires themselves for open circuits using the volt-ohm meter. With the test leads connected to either end of the wires, the meter should read 0 ohms. If it does not, it is an indication that the wire is broken inside its insulation. Replace it with a new wire.

The wiring harness connecting the front panel PCB and the main PCB may be the flexible membrane type (called a printed wire board, or PWB).

The connecting wires are actually copper bands, or traces, glued onto a flexible mylar base. These flexible ribbon connectors can be easily damaged if abused, and are extremely difficult to repair. If you suspect a broken trace on the ribbon, double check the continuity using a volt-ohm meter. A faulty ribbon must be replaced.

9.5B.1 If the disc spindle does not move when the Play button is depressed, the spindle motor or the wires leading to it may be defective. For now, concentrate on bad wiring to the disc spindle motor. Locate the motor and find the wires leading from it to the main PCB. Visually examine the wires and motor terminals and look for obvious breaks or bad solder joints.

Use your volt-ohm meter to test that the wires leading from the motor to the main PCB are good and that nothing is shorted. With the test leads connected to either end of each motor wire, the reading should be 0 ohms. If you get a reading of infinite ohms, it is an indication that there is an internal break in the wiring or cold soldering joints. Replace the wire or resolder the joint as necessary.

Now connect the test leads across the motor terminals (many motors will have only two terminals, but if the motor in your player has more, refer to a schematic; the other leads are for the motor's built-in tachometer). You should get a low reading, but it should not be 0. If the reading is 0 or over 1,000 ohms, it is an indication that either the motor is burned out, or that there is a short in the wiring on the main PCB. You can usually isolate problems in the motor by disconnecting it from the main PCB. Most players use snap-on connectors that can be easily removed and replaced.

9.5B.2 Many players are built with interlock switches that prevent the laser from turning on and subsequent playback if a disc is not loaded into the tray or if the top cover has been removed. If the cover is open, depress the switch to close the interlock loop.

If the cover is on, and a disc is properly loaded in the tray, the fault may lie in a broken interlock switch. To test a switch, make sure the player is off and unplugged. Use the volt-ohm meter to test the continuity of the switch. With the leads of the

meter connected to both terminals of the switch, the reading should be 0 ohms when the switch is closed, and infinite ohms when the switch is open. The interlock switches for the disc loading mechanism are usually located along the length and back of the sliding mechanism.

9.5B.3 Check for excessive play in the motor shaft. Grasp the shaft and rock it back and forth. Any noticeable amount of movement is a good indication that the bearings in the motor are worn out. If this is the case, the motor must be replaced.

Even if the motor shaft checks out, the motor itself may be bad. You can test the motor with your ohm-meter. Follow the procedure given in Step 6 of this flowchart.

9.5B.4 If the laser is inoperative, for just about any reason, the disc spindle may not rotate, or only for a few seconds, see Chart 9.14 for details.

9.6. If disc spindle turns but the machine refuses to play the disc, there is likely a problem in the optical pickup or pickup mechanism. Note that this symptom is not the same as when the unit plays a disc but no sound comes out. You can easily distinguish between the two if the player has an elapsed time indicator. If the indicator advances each second as it should, but no sound comes out, refer to Chart 9.11. If the indicator stays on 0:00, or stops at some point even though you have not pressed the Pause button.

9.6.1 A damaged disc, or a disc inserted upside down, will also prevent playback. Similarly, playback will not begin if there is a problem with the drawer/door loading mechanism or interlock switch. Refer to Chart 9.3 for troubleshooting details.

9.6.2 The optical pickup is operated by a motor (and in some cases a coil), which passes the assembly across the disc. A broken wire or a bad solder joint to this motor or coil will prevent proper operation of the pickup. Visually inspect the wiring at the motor/coil, and note any cold soldering joints.

Use your volt-ohm meter to test that the wires leading from the motor/coil to the main PCB are good and that nothing is shorted out. With the test leads connected to either end of each wire, the reading should be 0 ohms. If you get a reading of infinite ohms, it is an indication that there is an internal break in the wiring or of cold joints on the solder terminals. Replace the wire or resolder the joint as necessary.

Connect the test leads across the motor/coil terminals (most motors and coils will have only two terminals). You should get a low reading, but it should not be 0. If the reading is 0 or over 1,000 ohms, it is an indication that either the motor is burned out, or that there is a short in the wiring or on the main PCB.

9.6.3 An object that blocks the free movement of the pickup assembly will prevent it from scanning the disc. Visually inspect the pickup transport mechanism and look for foreign objects, loose components, and other obstructions.

9.6.4 Slide (or sled) pickups are mounted on a pair of rails, and travel back and forth along the rails while the player reads the disc. If these rails have become misaligned, the pickup may jam and fail to move. If the rails look bent, or the rails are no longer parallel, the player must be serviced. The alignment of the rails is critical, and almost always involves using a special alignment tool, available only from the manufacturer.

9.6.5 The slide pickup may be frozen along the track because the transport gears are binding. Visually inspect for loose parts and tighten them (doing so may require realignment). Lubricate the gears if necessary.

9.6.6 A pickup that never budges may be caused by a faulty pickup motor or coil. If the pickup is operated by a motor, check for excessive play in the motor shaft. Grasp the shaft and rock it back and forth. Any noticeable amount of movement is a good indication that the bearings in the motor are worn out. If this is the case, the motor will need to be replaced.

Even if the motor shaft checks out, the motor itself may be bad. You can test the motor with your meter, using the procedure given in Step 3 of this flowchart.

9.7. Failure to respond to some or all of the front panel controls is often a mechanical fault, but it can also be caused by the electronics on the main PCB. If only some of the switches are affected, the problem might lie in the switches themselves, or the functions associated with the switch (optical pickup with the Play button is depressed, for example). If all of the switches do not respond, refer to charts 9.1 through 9.6.

9.7.1 If the disc is loaded upside down, or is off-center on the disc spindle, the front panel controls may not appear to work properly. Remove the disc and reinsert it. A damaged or warped disc may also cause the controls to behave erratically.

9.7.2 The disc loading drawer/door must be completely closed or the front panel controls will not function. Many players incorporate internal safety interlock switches that close only when the loading mechanism is completely closed. The switches may also be dirty or broken. See Step 5 in this troubleshooting chart.

9.7.3 If your compact disc player has a remote control, it may be overriding the front switches. To rule out the possibility of a faulty remote control, remove its batteries, take it to another room, or—if the control is the wireless infrared type—cover up the end to block the light. If the control is the wired type, disconnect it from the player. Refer to Chart 9.10 if disabling the remote frees the operation of the front panel controls on the player (it is an indication that the remote is faulty).

9.7.4 Given the right set of circumstances, switches can get broken, dirty, and corroded. Test the switch to make sure that it works properly. Connect the test leads of the ohm-meter to either side of the switch terminals. As you depress the switch, the meter should read either 0 ohms or infinite ohms. If not, it is an indication that the switch is faulty.

Unsealed switches can be cleaned using an electrical contact spray cleaner. Liberally squirt the cleaner inside the switch. Broken switches must be replaced.

9.7.5 The system microprocessor in the CD player might ignore the commands from the front panel switches if the laser diode is not working properly. If you suspect that this may be the case, refer to Chart 9.14. In this instance, all of the front panel controls are generally inoperative.

9.7.6 If the switches themselves check out, the problem may be caused by faulty wiring. Carefully inspect the wiring leading to and from the front panel control switches. Look for obvious breaks, kinks, and cold solder joints. Use a meter to test the continuity of all affected switches.

The wiring harness connecting the front panel PCB and the main PCB might be the flexible membrane type. The connecting wires are copper bands that are glued onto a flexible mylar base. These flexible ribbon connectors can be easily damaged if abused, and are extremely difficult to repair. If you suspect a broken trace on the ribbon, double check the continuity using a volt-ohm meter. A faulty ribbon must be replaced.

9.8. Most mid to high-end CD players incorporate a programming function, where you can select specific tracks for playback. With most players, you can program the tracks to play in a certain sequence. The programming feature is controlled either by the system microprocessor or a special sub-processor. In most cases, programming problems are caused by mechanical defects, and can be readily repaired.

9.8.1 Compact disc players with built-in timers may ignore the programming sequence you enter if the timer is on. Turn the timer off then try the programming buttons.

9.8.2 The switch(es) that control the programming functions may be broken, dirty, and corroded. Test all the switches to make sure they work properly. Connect the test leads of the ohm-meter to either side of the switch terminals. When the switch is depressed, the meter should alternate between 0 and infinite ohms. If it does not, there is a good chance that the switch under test is defective. If the switch is unsealed, you can clean its contacts with an electronic contact cleaning spray.

9.8.3 If the switches and wiring check out, it's safe to assume the problem lies further on in the main PCB, possibly the system or programming microprocessors. If this is the case, the main PCB must be replaced.

9.9. You put in a disc, press Play, and everything works. That is, everything but the front panel indicators.

9.9.1 The indicators used in most compact disc players are the LED, LCD, or fluorescent type. These have exceptionally long lives, so it is unlikely that they have simply "burned out" like a lightbulb. The most probable cause is a bad wire or connection leading to the front panel or indicator.

9.9.2 Rarely will all the LEDs and number segments go out all at once. The more common occurrence is that only one indicator lamp or one segment in one numeral will fail. Check first to make sure that the wiring is not at fault. Use the volt-ohm meter as before. You can also test LED and LCD indicators and segments using the current-limited power source illustrated in Fig. 9-9. Don't forget the resistor; connecting the battery directly to the connections on the panel will burn out the segments.

If one or more indicators or segments are indeed bad, the entire module must be replaced. You cannot repair or replace individual indicators or segments within the module.

9.9.3 A blank indicator panel might also be due to a fault on the player. Be sure that the player responds properly to all the front panel controls. If it does not, refer to Charts 9.1 through 9.6 for more information.

9.10. Problems with the remote control functions can be due either to a faulty remote transmitter, or bad receiver circuits in the player. Fortunately, problems with the remote control are almost always caused by the transmitter, which is not only easier to repair, but cheaper to replace should it be seriously defective.

If the remote control transmitter is the infrared type, you can test for proper operation by using the light sensor described in Chapter 5.

9.10.1 If the remote control is not working properly, first make sure that you are operating the transmitter within the prescribed limits. Most transmitters don't work when operated at distances beyond 20 feet from the player, or at angles greater than 30 degrees off to either side of the receiving sensor. If you must place the player off angle to the direct beam of the transmitter, you can try "bouncing" the infrared light off a card. The card is placed near the front of the player, as shown in Fig. 9-10.

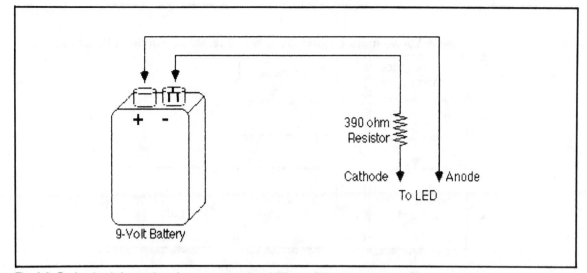

Fig. 9-9. Basic circuit for testing the segments of an LED or LCD indicator panel. Use a schematic for the location of the test points, and be sure to include the current-limiting resistor.

9.10.2 Batteries that are low or dead will obviously cause the controller to fail. Even batteries that have some kick left may cause some trouble, so even after testing them with a meter, try a fresh set.

9.10.3 While the batteries are out of the transmitter, inspect the battery contacts. They should be bright and shiny. If not, there may be insufficient current getting to the transmitter circuits. Clean the contacts and reinsert the batteries.

9.10.4 Most remote controllers for CD players work by emitting short pulses of infrared light. Sunlight striking against the player may overload the receiving sensor, so the commands from the transmitter are not adequately received. Always shade the sensor from direct sunlight. If the player is subjected to sunlight, the remote control function might not operate properly even after the light has been blocked. Wait five to 10 minutes for the sensor and surrounding components in the player to cool down.

9.10.5 Dirty switch contacts in the remote control might cause all or some of the functions to fail. Open the remote and liberally spray the switches with an electrical contact cleaner. Inspect the wiring and solder joints and make repairs as necessary.

9.10.6 Broken wires and bad solder joints between the receiver sensor and the main PCB may also cause problems. Open the player only until af-

ter you are certain that the transmitter is operating properly (use the light sensor described in Chapter 5 to be absolutely sure). Inspect the wires and solder joints; test the continuity with a volt-ohm meter. With the test probes connected to either end of each wire, the reading should be 0 ohms. A reading of infinite ohms is an indication of an open circuit.

9.11. The player does everything it should, with one important exception; it's quiet as a mouse. With CD players at least, this is an undesirable circumstance. Unlike most other audio components, if you are plagued with no sound, the fault is almost always external to the compact disc player. Remembering how a CD player works, the great majority of its internal electronics and mechanisms must function properly to even make the disc spin.

9.11.1 The disc is upside down in the player. Although this usually causes the player to stop, an upside down disc can also prevent audio playback, and the player might function properly otherwise. To the player, the label writing seems like a giant scratch. So much of the disc is affected, that even though tracking and focus can be minimally retained, the high number of errors trigger the muting circuits, and you don't hear anything. End of lecture; reinsert the disc the right way.

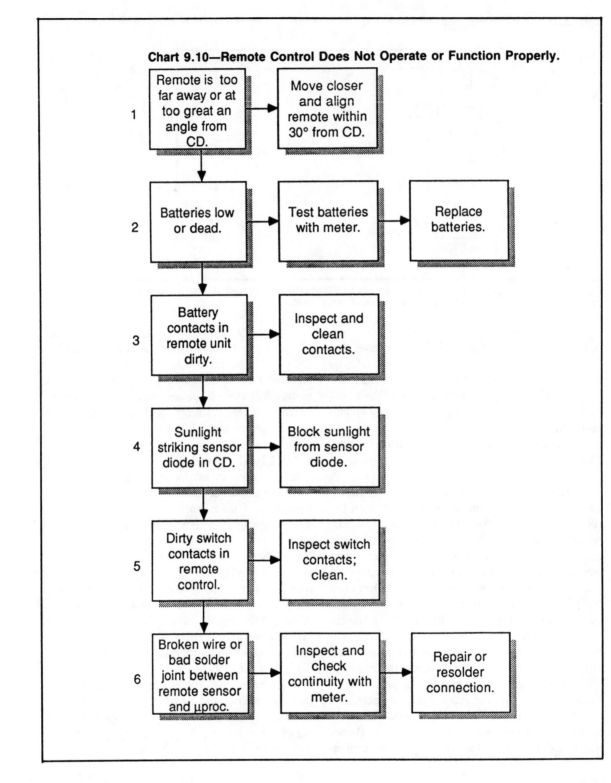

Chart 9.10—Remote Control Does Not Operate or Function Properly.

1. Remote is too far away or at too great an angle from CD. → Move closer and align remote within 30° from CD.

2. Batteries low or dead. → Test batteries with meter. → Replace batteries.

3. Battery contacts in remote unit dirty. → Inspect and clean contacts.

4. Sunlight striking sensor diode in CD. → Block sunlight from sensor diode.

5. Dirty switch contacts in remote control. → Inspect switch contacts; clean.

6. Broken wire or bad solder joint between remote sensor and µproc. → Inspect and check continuity with meter. → Repair or resolder connection.

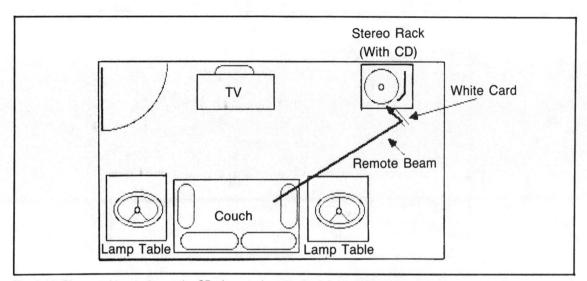

Fig. 9-10. Place a white card near the CD player to bounce the infrared light from the remote control into the sensor.

9.11.2 Loose audio cables between the CD and the amplifier is a common cause of no sound. Visually inspect the cables and test them using a meter. Replace or repair bad cables. If your CD has a headphone jack, connect a pair of headphones to it. You'll hear sound if the CD is operating properly.

9.11.3 Be sure the function switches on the amplifier are set correctly. Specifically, be sure that you've selected the CD player (push CD, AUX, TAPE, or other button as required) and that the mute switch is out.

9.11.4 Many amplifiers have two speaker switches—one for speaker pair "A" and another for speaker pair "B." Make sure the "A" switch is down to route the sound to speaker pair "A." If there are no speakers connected to the "B" speaker terminals in the rear of the amp, and the "B" switch is pushed in, the protection circuits in the amplifier may cut off the sound. This prevents a circuit overload.

If you still can't hear anything, inspect the speaker wires and make sure they are not broken. If your amplifier has a headphone jack, connect a pair of phones to it. If you hear sound, you know that the audio from the CD is at least getting to the amplifier.

9.11.5 A number of compact disc players have a sound level adjustment. This control alters the

level of audio signal to the amplifier. If the control is set too low, the player might not provide the amplifier with a strong enough signal. Turn the control up and see if it has any effect. With some players, the headphone level knob also controls the output level to the amplifier.

9.11.6 The audio output wires in the player might be shorted out. This will not only prevent sound from reaching the amplifier, but you might also hear a low humming sound through the speakers. Immediately turn the player off and unplug it. Remove the cover and visually inspect in and around the audio output jacks for shorted wires or foreign metallic objects.

Use a meter to test the resistance of the jacks. With the test leads connected to the inner and outer connectors of one jack, the resistance should measure between 10,000 and 50,000 ohms. Test the other output jack as well. A very low or zero reading is an indication that the output is shorted. If the cause cannot be found, the audio output circuit must be serviced. With some players, the circuit is on its own printed circuit board; in others, the audio output circuitry is contained on the main PCB.

9.12. The audio from a CD player is not supposed to be distorted in the least, but several factors can contribute to bad sound. If there are repeated unconcealed errors in the audio output,

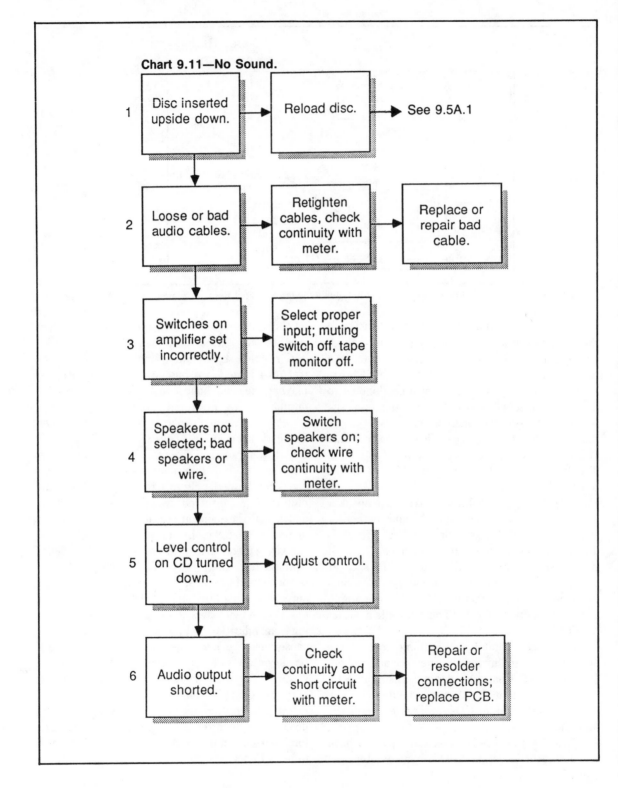

Chart 9.11—No Sound.

1	Disc inserted upside down.	Reload disc.	See 9.5A.1
2	Loose or bad audio cables.	Retighten cables, check continuity with meter.	Replace or repair bad cable.
3	Switches on amplifier set incorrectly.	Select proper input; muting switch off, tape monitor off.	
4	Speakers not selected; bad speakers or wire.	Switch speakers on; check wire continuity with meter.	
5	Level control on CD turned down.	Adjust control.	
6	Audio output shorted.	Check continuity and short circuit with meter.	Repair or resolder connections; replace PCB.

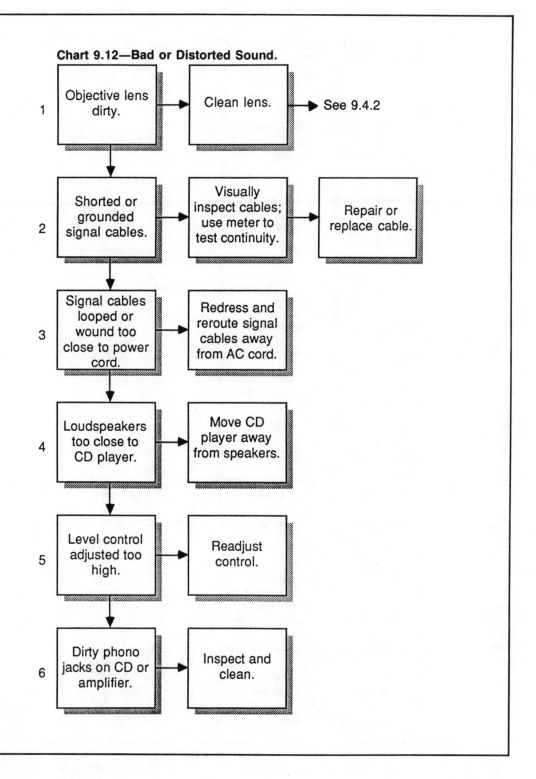

Chart 9.12—Bad or Distorted Sound.

1. Objective lens dirty. → Clean lens. → See 9.4.2

2. Shorted or grounded signal cables. → Visually inspect cables; use meter to test continuity. → Repair or replace cable.

3. Signal cables looped or wound too close to power cord. → Redress and reroute signal cables away from AC cord.

4. Loudspeakers too close to CD player. → Move CD player away from speakers.

5. Level control adjusted too high. → Readjust control.

6. Dirty phono jacks on CD or amplifier. → Inspect and clean.

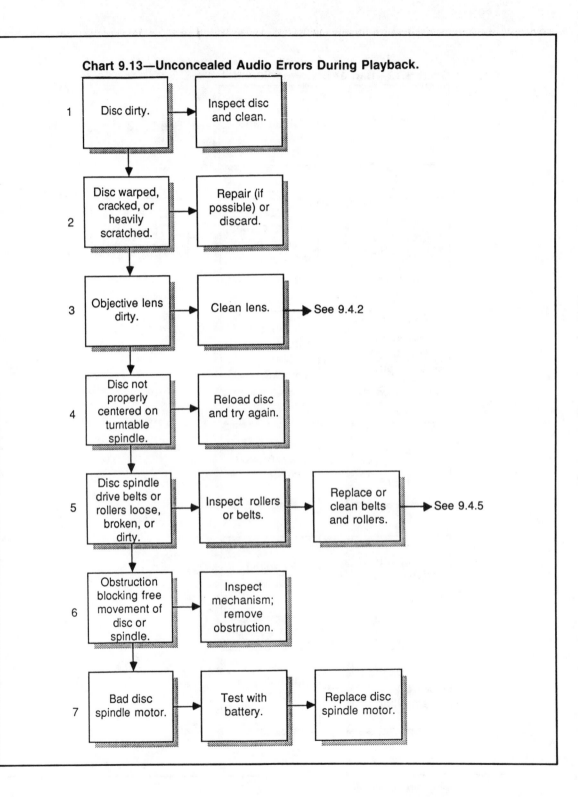

Chart 9.13—Unconcealed Audio Errors During Playback.

1. Disc dirty. → Inspect disc and clean.

2. Disc warped, cracked, or heavily scratched. → Repair (if possible) or discard.

3. Objective lens dirty. → Clean lens. → See 9.4.2

4. Disc not properly centered on turntable spindle. → Reload disc and try again.

5. Disc spindle drive belts or rollers loose, broken, or dirty. → Inspect rollers or belts. → Replace or clean belts and rollers. → See 9.4.5

6. Obstruction blocking free movement of disc or spindle. → Inspect mechanism; remove obstruction.

7. Bad disc spindle motor. → Test with battery. → Replace disc spindle motor.

refer to Chart 9.13. The troubleshooting chart you are now reading assumes that the disc is free of defects and that it has been loaded properly.

9.12.1 Loose, shorted, or grounded audio cables between the CD and the amplifier is a common cause of hum and distortion. Visually inspect the cables and test them using a meter. Replace or repair bad cables. If your CD has a headphone jack, connect a pair of headphones to it. The sound should be clear and undistorted.

9.12.2 Excessive hum can also be caused by poorly shielded signal cables, or cables routed closely to ac power cords. The hum is caused by the close proximity of the alternating current field. If hum is a problem, examine the quality of the cables. The better the cable, the better the shielding, and the greater the rejection of ac-induced hum. Route the cables as far from ac cords as possible, and keep the cable lengths as short as possible.

9.12.3 Components inside the CD player may be adversely affected if they are subjected to sonic vibrations from the loudspeaker. If your speakers are too close to the player, the vibrations may distort the digital and analog signals, and cause data errors and high frequency ringing. The best remedy is to move the CD or speakers so that there is at least six to eight feet of distance between them. Separate them even further if you like to listen to your music at high volume.

9.12.4 A number of compact disc players have a sound level adjustment. This control alters the level of audio signal to the amplifier. If the control is set too high, the player may overload the input circuits of the amplifier. Distorted sound is the likely result. Turn the control down and see if it has any effect. With some players, the headphone level knob also controls the output level to the amplifier.

9.12.5 Dirty phono jacks on the CD player or amplifier may impede the signal and cause noticeable audio distortion. Clean the jacks with an electronic contact cleaner. Inspect the cable connectors; clean them too if they look dirty.

9.13. Unconcealed audio errors are clicks and pops that you hear when listening to a disc. Skips and long periods of silence—where there should be none—are other forms of unconcealed errors. None should be present in a CD player that's working properly and playing an undamaged disc.

9.13.1 About 98 percent of all the skips, clicks, and pops you'll hear are caused by a dirty disc. Before every use, wipe your discs with a soft cloth. If a disc gets dirty, clean it with a recommended CD cleaner.

9.13.2 A disc that is warped, cracked, or heavily scratched might also exhibit extensive unconcealed audio errors—if the disc plays at all. Inspect the disc for damage. You can sometimes salvage a scratched or warped disc. See Chapter 5 for details. Manufacturing defects can also cause heavy popping, clicking, and skipping. About the only serious manufacturing defects you can see are air bubbles in the protective plastic and an off-centered stamping.

9.13.3 With some drawer loading players, the clamping flapper may not engage the disc against the drive spindle properly, and the disc may spin off center in the tray. A certain amount of eccentricity can be compensated for by the pickup and tracking circuits, but a large amount of wobble ends up as unconcealed audio errors. Remove the disc and reinsert it.

If the problem persists, carefully inspect the disc. Look closely at the stamping encased inside the protective plastic. It should be exactly centered. Sometimes, the stamping is centered in the plastic, but the hub is not in the exact center of the disc. You can check for this by putting the disc in the machine and playing it. Look closely at the edge of the disc as it spins in the player, as depicted in Fig. 9-11. Direct a flashlight into the tray if necessary. Some slight wobble is normal, but an excessive amount is a good indication that the disc was improperly stamped.

9.13.4 Something may be blocking the free movement of the disc or spindle. You can usually hear the motor or disc scrape against the obstruction.

9.13.5 A bad spindle motor may spin, but not at the correct speed. Worn bearings may cause the motor shaft to wobble, again causing speed imperfections. You can isolate the problem to the spin-

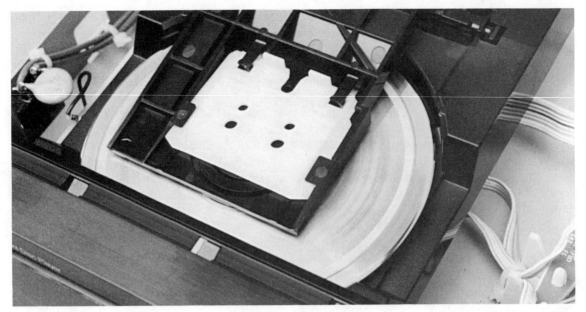

Fig. 9-11. Carefully watch the disc as it spins for signs of faulty manufacturing. Don't touch the disc while it is in motion.

dle motor by disconnecting the drive and press the Play button. Check for any movement in the shaft that could indicate worn bearings. If the motor makes excessive noises while spinning, its a good indication that it is bad.

The motor will spin only for a few seconds, until the system microprocessor discovers something is amiss. The system processor won't activate the motor unless the interlock switches are closed. If you don't have a disc inserted in the tray, manually defeat the switches by attaching a jumper between the switch terminals.

9.14. Some problems can be narrowed down to the laser diode—it doesn't emit light when it should. Since laser diodes have an average design life of over 5,000 hours, it's unlikely that the laser will burn out in the average use of the player— although it is a distinct possibility with a player that's five or six years old.

There are many reasons why the laser diode may not emit light, and only a few of them have to do with the laser itself or the pickup mechanism. You can test for laser light output by using the infrared light sensor described in Chapter 5.

9.14.1 Inspect the wires leading to the pickup mechanism. If any look broken, loose, or crimped,

the laser diode may not be getting the proper signals, or may not be receiving power. Test the continuity of the wires with a volt-ohm meter. With the test probes connected to either end of each wire, the reading should be 0 ohms. A reading of infinite ohms means that there is probably a break somewhere in the wire, or that the solder joints are cold. Replace the wires or resolder the connects as necessary.

9.14.2 The laser diode as well as the components on the PCB may be faulty. The laser may not be getting the signals from the system microprocessor to turn on, or the laser diode itself may be burned out. A failure in the laser diode means that the optical pickup must be replaced. This can be expensive and requires specialized tools. A faulty component on the main PCB generally involves replacing the entire board.

9.15. Mechanical noises are those terrible grinding, crunching, rattling, and squeaking noises that can emanate from the player. A well designed player is nearly silent in operation, and any noticeable noise is indicative of a malfunction inside the unit.

9.15.1 A disc that's off-centered on the spindle may wobble during playback. The sound you

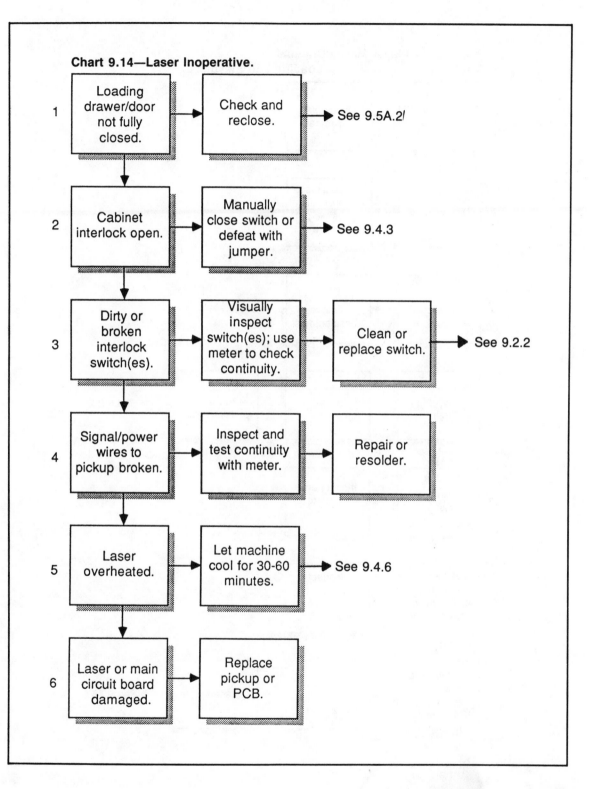

Chart 9.14—Laser Inoperative.

1. Loading drawer/door not fully closed. → Check and reclose. → See 9.5A.2/

2. Cabinet interlock open. → Manually close switch or defeat with jumper. → See 9.4.3

3. Dirty or broken interlock switch(es). → Visually inspect switch(es); use meter to check continuity. → Clean or replace switch. → See 9.2.2

4. Signal/power wires to pickup broken. → Inspect and test continuity with meter. → Repair or resolder.

5. Laser overheated. → Let machine cool for 30-60 minutes. → See 9.4.6

6. Laser or main circuit board damaged. → Replace pickup or PCB.

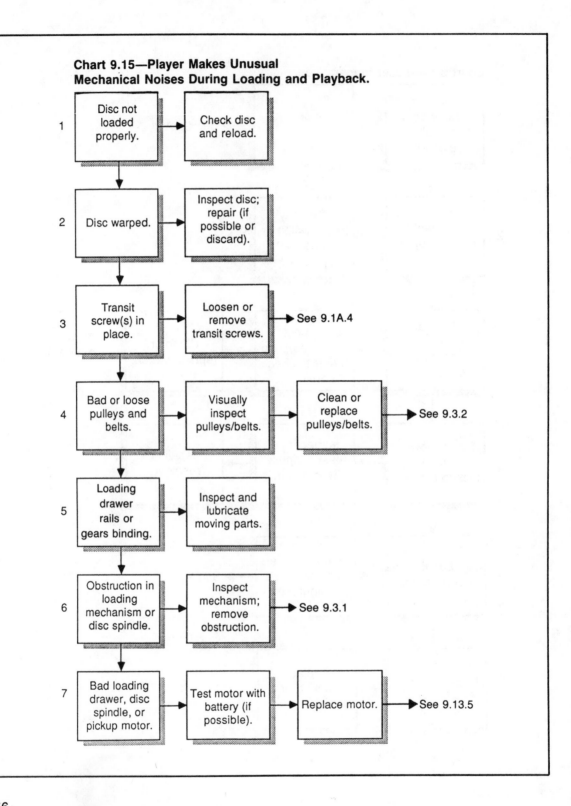

Chart 9.15—Player Makes Unusual Mechanical Noises During Loading and Playback.

1. Disc not loaded properly. → Check disc and reload.

2. Disc warped. → Inspect disc; repair (if possible or discard).

3. Transit screw(s) in place. → Loosen or remove transit screws. → See 9.1A.4

4. Bad or loose pulleys and belts. → Visually inspect pulleys/belts. → Clean or replace pulleys/belts. → See 9.3.2

5. Loading drawer rails or gears binding. → Inspect and lubricate moving parts.

6. Obstruction in loading mechanism or disc spindle. → Inspect mechanism; remove obstruction. → See 9.3.1

7. Bad loading drawer, disc spindle, or pickup motor. → Test motor with battery (if possible). → Replace motor. → See 9.13.5

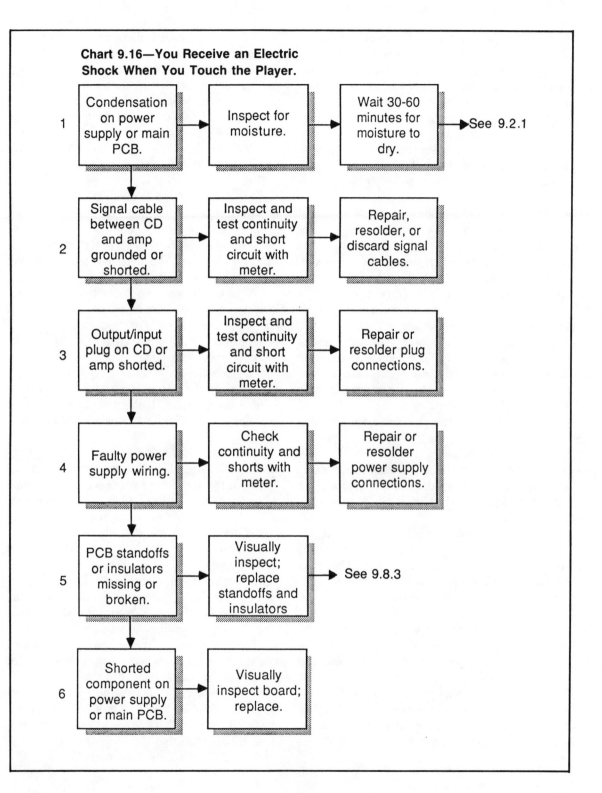

Chart 9.16—You Receive an Electric Shock When You Touch the Player.

1. Condensation on power supply or main PCB. → Inspect for moisture. → Wait 30-60 minutes for moisture to dry. → See 9.2.1

2. Signal cable between CD and amp grounded or shorted. → Inspect and test continuity and short circuit with meter. → Repair, resolder, or discard signal cables.

3. Output/input plug on CD or amp shorted. → Inspect and test continuity and short circuit with meter. → Repair or resolder plug connections.

4. Faulty power supply wiring. → Check continuity and shorts with meter. → Repair or resolder power supply connections.

5. PCB standoffs or insulators missing or broken. → Visually inspect; replace standoffs and insulators → See 9.8.3

6. Shorted component on power supply or main PCB. → Visually inspect board; replace.

hear may be the bearings in the spindle groaning under the increased stress. Reinsert the disc and the problem should go away. If it does not, the disc clamping mechanism may need adjustment. Open the player and locate the flapper. This spring loaded mechanism clamps the disc in place after loading and during play. Look for loose or broken parts. Unlike the loading mechanism and optical pickup assemblies, the adjustment and repair of the flapper are non-critical, and does not generally require special tools.

9.15.2 Like an off-centered disc, a warped disc can cause the bearings in the spindle to groan. Remove the disc and inspect the disc for warpage. Slight warpage can sometimes be cured by applying pressure to the disc (as described in Chapter 6). An unrepairable disc should be discarded.

9.15.3 A number of machines use plastic gears to drive the loading mechanism from the motor. A gear is mounted on the motor shaft, and meshes with a straight toothed rail. When the motor shaft turns, the gear inches the loading mechanism along the rail, thus opening the drawer or door. Inspect the gear and rail to be sure that none of the teeth are broken and that the gear teeth are meshing properly.

Even if the loading mechanism looks fine, the gears and rails may still bind against one another, and cause grinding sounds. If necessary, apply a small dab of grease on the gear surfaces or oil to shafts and levers.

9.16. The words "thrilling" and "breathtaking" are often used to describe the experience of listening to music on a compact disc. The word "shocking" should not be in the CD users vocabulary, unless there is something wrong with the player.

A CD that gives you a shock—even a mild one—should not be used. Some or all of the ac power has been shorted to the metal cabinet, so when you touch the player, you get a shock (and if the jolt is big enough, you get to do the "killowatt dance," which looks a little like the jitterbug but can *really* put you in the hospital). Before playing another disc, unplug the machine, isolate the cause, and fix it.

You can test for ac leakage current with the following procedures.

The ac leakage current test determines if any part of the ac line has come in contact with the metal cabinet or base. It is a safety check to prevent a potential shock hazard. It requires the use of a volt-ohm meter.

With the CD player unplugged, short the two flat prongs on the end of the ac cord, as illustrated in Fig. 9-12. On the meter, select the kOhms function and a range of no less than 1,000 kOhms. Connect one test lead from the meter to the jumper on the ac cord. Connect the other test lead to any and all bare (not painted) metal parts of the player. For a typical CD player, the meter will read about 500 to 1,000 kOhms—if you get any reading at all.

A reading substantially lower than this is a good indication that the power supply has come into contact with the metal parts of the player. If this happens, inspect the power cord as it leads into the player, as well as the Power switch, the transformer (usually bolted onto the back of the machine), and the wires leading from the transformer to the printed circuit board. If the wires are broken, or are shorted to the cabinet, repair the fault before using the player.

Not all exposed metal parts of the CD will return a high value. Touching the center conductor of one of the audio output connectors could yield a low resistance, of 40 or 50 kOhms. This is considered normal with some machines.

Water is a poor conductor of electricity, but it's good enough to short the ac power cord or the power supply terminals against the player cabinet. Condensation can also form a light film of moisture that can conduct some current, and although the shock may be slight to the human body, it could damage the player electronics.

9.16.1 The signal cable between the CD player and amplifier may be shorted. Inspect the cable for obvious damage and test it with a volt-ohm meter. Connect the test leads across the center and middle conductor of each cable. You should get a reading of infinite ohms. If you get any other reading, it is an indication that the cable is shorted.

9.16.2 Determining if the output of the CD is

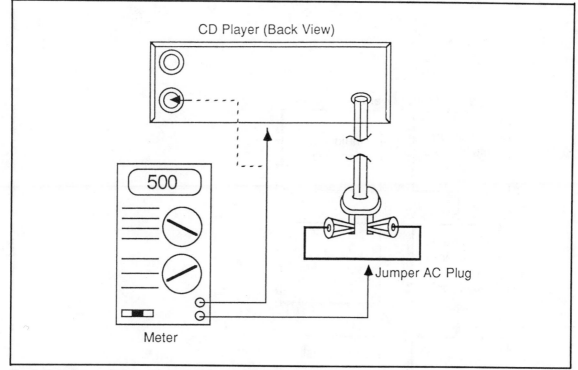

Fig. 9-12. Using a volt-ohm meter to test for possible leakage current.

shorted is a little tougher. The resistance values can vary, but they should be within 10,000 to 50,000 ohms when the test leads are attached across the center and outer connectors of each output. A substantially lower reading, or a reading of 0 ohms, indicates a short.

9.16.3 The wiring leading to and from the power supply may be faulty. Inspect the ac cord leading to the power transformer and power switch. Use your meter to check for short circuits. Examine the power transformer for obvious damage. Check the solder terminals to make sure that none are touching the cabinet. Look closely because even one small strand of wire in the ac cord can cause at least a partial short circuit.

Examine the wiring from the transformer to the power supply circuitry. This is sometimes located on its own PCB, other times on the main PCB. Use your meter to check for obvious short circuits. At least one of the wires from the power transformer will act as the circuit ground for the player. You should receive a low reading when checking this wire. The other wires should yield reasonably high resistances.

9.16.4 The power supply and main PCBs are generally insulated from the cabinet and base using plastic standoffs. When secured with metal hardware, the boards are electrically isolated from the cabinet with plastic or rubber insulators. Inspect the mounting hardware to see if any part of the boards are touching the base or cabinet. Inspect the insulators and look for breaks and cracks. Replace any broken standoffs or insulators.

9.17. A player that gets abnormally hot is not only a potential fire hazard, but will exhibit erratic behavior. You can easily tell if the player is getting warmer than normal by touching its cabinet. It should not be noticeably hot to the touch. If it is, you should investigate the problem before playing any more discs. Continued use of the player might damage it beyond repair.

9.17.1 CD players don't consume much power,

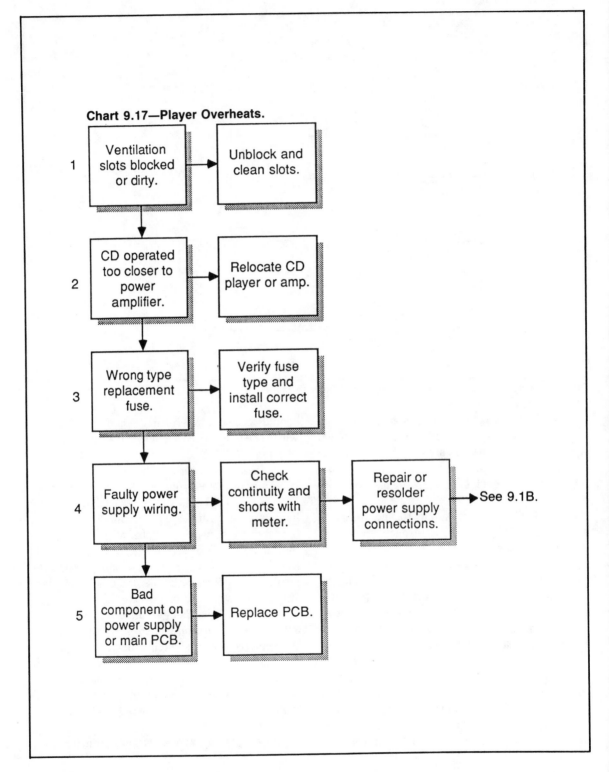

Chart 9.17—Player Overheats.

1. Ventilation slots blocked or dirty. → Unblock and clean slots.

2. CD operated too closer to power amplifier. → Relocate CD player or amp.

3. Wrong type replacement fuse. → Verify fuse type and install correct fuse.

4. Faulty power supply wiring. → Check continuity and shorts with meter. → Repair or resolder power supply connections. → See 9.1B.

5. Bad component on power supply or main PCB. → Replace PCB.

so cooling is not as critical as it is with, say, a 100 watt power amplifier. Most players rely on ventilation slots for proper operation. It is important that these slots not be blocked, either by some outside object or by dust and dirt. If the slots become blocked with dust, use a brush or vacuum to clean them.

9.17.2 A CD operated too close to a large power amplifier might get overly warm because of the heat put out by the high power circuits in the amp. For proper operation of your CD player, as well as the other components in your stereo system, you should keep your amplifier separate as much as possible.

9.17.3 Many CD players use external or internal fuses. If a fuse blows, it is important to replace it with the same value of fuse as the original. This is particularly true if the fuse is the current-limiting type.

9.17.4 Faulty components on the power supply board or main PCB may cause excessive overheating. You can often identify the responsible component by carefully touching each one. To test, power the player for a while until the heat rises, then turn it off. Unplug it from the wall socket. Lightly touch each component. Except for the voltage regulators none should be hot to the touch (some ICs may be quite warm, but they should not burn your fingers). The voltage regulators, usually mounted on the power supply board, can get hot but are usually kept within a safe operating temperature by the use of aluminum heat sinks.

Chapter 10

CD Player Reference Guide

This chapter contains information on several popular home, portable, and automotive CD players. Included are basic features, operating controls, specifications and, where appropriate, data on the location and removal of transit screws and disassembly instructions. The specifications listed are from the manufacturer; tests by independent labs and reviewers may produce different results.

JVC XLV-400

Features:

Filtering: Digital
Sampling Rate: 2X oversample—88.2 kHz
Number of D/A Converters: N/A
Beams: 3
Operating Controls: Power; open/close; stop; pause; skip down; play; skip up; search up; search down; display; repeat; index; programming—resume, cancel, call; headphone level control
Indicator: Track number; index number; elapsed time
Remote: Yes
Headphone jack: Yes

Specifications:

Loading Type: Front; drawer-type
Dynamic Range: 95 dB
Frequency Response: 5 Hz to 20 kHz
Signal to Noise Ratio: 95 dB
Channel Separation: 90 dB
Output Level: 2 V fixed
Dimensions: 17.2 × 2.35 × 11.5 inches
Weight: 8.9 pounds
Transit Screw: Loosen transit screw 1/2 turn.
Disassembly Instructions: Remove two screws on each side and two screws on back near top. Slide cover off towards the rear of the player.

JVC XLV-500

Features:

Filtering: Digital
Sampling Rate: 2X oversample—88.2 kHz
Number of D/A Converters: 1
Beams: 3
Operating Controls: Power; open/close; stop; pause; skip down; play; skip up; search up; search down; fast search up; fast search down; display; introscan; repeat; index; programming—resume, cancel, call, 10 key programming pad; headphone volume (slide); play mode
Indicator: Track number; index number; elapsed time
Remote: Yes
Headphone jack: Yes

Specifications:

Loading Type: Front; drawer-type
Dynamic Range: 95 dB
Frequency Response: 5 Hz to 20 kHz
Signal to Noise Ratio: 96 dB
Channel Separation: 90 dB
Output Level: 2 V fixed
Dimensions: 16.3 × 3.5 × 11.7
Weight: 13 pounds
Transit Screw: Loosen transit screw 1/2 turn.
Disassembly Instructions: Remove two screws on each side and two screws on back near top. Slide cover off towards the rear of the player.

Kenwood DP-1000

Features:

Filtering: Analog
Sampling Rate: 44.1 kHz
Number of D/A Converters: 1
Beams: 3
Operating Controls: Power; open/close; pause; play; time; A/B; space; repeat; reserve; stop; search up; search down; headphone output level (knob)
Indicator: Track number; index number; time; space; repeat, manual play
Remote: Yes (10 key pad)
Headphone jack: Yes

Specifications:

Loading Type: Front; drawer-type
Dynamic Range: 95 dB
Frequency Response: 4 Hz to 20 kHz; +/− 0.5 dB
Signal to Noise Ratio: N/A
Channel Separation: 95 dB at 1 kHz
Output Level: 2 V fixed
Dimensions: 17.3 × 3.5 × 12.3 inches
Weight: 13.2 pounds

Magnavox CDB650

Features:

Filtering: Digital
Sampling Rate: N/A
Number of D/A Converters: 2
Beams: 1
Operating Controls: Power; open/close; stop; pause; play/replay; index down; index up; track down; track up; 112 key programming pad; headphone level adjust
Indicator: Track number; index number; time
Remote: Yes
Headphone jack: Yes

Specifications:

Loading Type: Front; drawer-type
Dynamic Range: Greater than 100 dB
Frequency Response: 2 Hz to 20 kHz; +/– 0.3 dB
Signal to Noise Ratio: Greater than 100 dB
Channel Separation: 94 dB at 1 kHz
Output Level: 2 V fixed
Dimensions: 16.5 × 3.5 × 11.75 inches
Weight: 9 pounds

Panasonic CQ-E800 (Car Player)

Features:

Filtering: Analog
Sampling Rate: 44.1 kHz
Number of D/A Converters: 1
Beams: 1
Operating Controls: Volume; fader; balance; treble;
    bass; pause; repeat, memo; recall; scan; tune;
    seek; skip/search; eject
Indicator: Track number; FM freq.
Remote: None
Headphone jack: None

Specifications:

Loading Type: Front
Dynamic Range: 90 dB
Frequency Response: 5 Hz to 20 kHz
Signal to Noise Ratio: 90 dB A-weighted
Channel Separation: 75 dB
Output Level: 2 V
Dimensions: 1.0 × 7.0 × 5.12 inches
Weight: N/A

Pioneer PD-M6 (6-disc multiplay)

Features:

Filtering: Analog
Sampling Rate: 44.1 kHz
Number of D/A Converters: 1
Beams: 3
Operating Controls: Power; eject; repeat; program memory; track down; track up; manual search down; manual search up; stop; display; programming—check, clear; random play; play; pause; disc selector (6); track number selector (10-key); headphone level adjust
Indicator: Disc play; track number; index number; time
Remote: Yes
Headphone jack: Yes

Specifications:

Loading Type: Front; cartridge-type (holds 6 discs)
Dynamic Range: Greater than 94 dB
Frequency Response: 4 Hz to 20 kHz
Signal to Noise Ratio: Greater than 98 dB at 1 kHz
Channel Separation: Greater than 92 dB at 1 kHz
Output Level: 2 V fixed
Dimensions: 16.5 × 3.8 × 12.7
Weight: 17.6 pounds

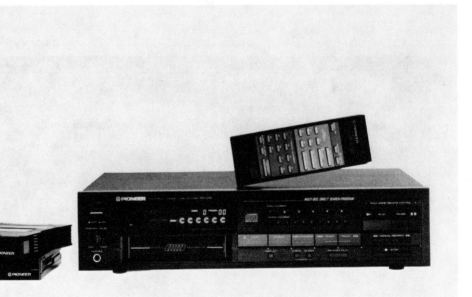

Pioneer PD-C7 (Portable)

Features:

Filtering: Analog
Sampling Rate: 44.1 kHz
Number of D/A Converters: 1
Beams: 3
Operating Controls: Stop; play; track up; track down; mode; display; on/off; open; volume
Indicator: Track; time; time remaining; mode
Remote: None
Headphone jack: Yes

Specifications:

Loading Type: Top
Dynamic Range: Greater than 90 dB
Frequency Response: 20 Hz to 20 kHz; +1 dB, −3 dB
Signal to Noise Ratio: 85 dB
Channel Separation: Greater than 85 dB
Output Level: 2 V (line)
Dimensions: 5.0 × 1.5 × 5.25 inches
Weight: 1.4 pounds

Pioneer CD-X1 (Car Player)

Features:

Filtering: Analog
Sampling Rate: 44.1 kHz
Number of D/A Converters: 1
Beams: 3
Operating Controls: Scan; pause; eject; track up/down; search up/down; display
Indicator: Track number; time
Remote: None
Headphone jack: None

Specifications:

Loading Type: Front
Dynamic Range: 90 dB
Frequency Response: 10 Hz to 20 kHz; +/− 2 dB
Signal to Noise Ratio: 90 dB
Channel Separation: 90 dB
Output Level: N/A
Dimensions: 7.1 × 2.0 × 6.5 inches
Weight: 4.6 pounds

Philips CD-10 (Car Player)

Features:

Filtering: Analog
Sampling Rate: 44.1 kHz
Number of D/A Converters: 1
Beams: 1
Operating Controls: Volume; balance; bass; treble; skip forward; skip back; track up; track down; pause; repeat; eject
Indicator: Track number, time
Remote: None
Headphone jack: None

Specifications:

Loading Type: Top
Dynamic Range: 90 dB
Frequency Response: 20 Hz to 20 kHz; +/– 0.5 dB
Signal to Noise Ratio: Greater than 90 dB A-weighted
Channel Separation: Greater than 90 dB
Output Level: 1.6 V fixed
Dimensions: 5.0 × 1.6 × 7.5 inches
Weight: 1.6 pounds

Philips DCO-85 (Car Player)

Features:

Filtering: Analog
Sampling Rate: 44.1 kHz
Number of D/A Converters: 1
Beams: 1
Operating Controls: Volume; balance; bass; treble;
    skip forward; skip back; track up; track down;
    pause; repeat; eject; compress
Indicator: Track number; elapsed time
Remote: None
Headphone jack: None

Specifications:

Loading Type: Front
Dynamic Range: N/A
Frequency Response: 20 Hz to 20 kHz; +/− 0.5 dB
Signal to Noise Ratio: Greater than 90 dB A-
    weighted
Channel Separation: 90 dB
Output Level: N/A
Dimensions: N/A
Weight: N/A

Sansui CDV550R

Features:

Filtering: Analog
Sampling Rate: 44.1 kHz
Number of D/A Converters: N/A
Beams: 3
Operating Controls: Power; open/close; display; auto spacing; play; pause/stop; index down; index up; track down; track up; repeat; memory; headphone level adjust
Indicator: Track number; index number; time
Remote: Yes
Headphone jack: Yes

Specifications:

Loading Type: Front; drawer type
Dynamic Range: 96 dB
Frequency Response: 5 Hz to 20 kHz; +/– 0.5 dB
Signal to Noise Ratio: 100 dB
Channel Separation: 90 dB
Output Level: 2 V fixed
Dimensions: 16.9 × 3.2 × 12.2 inches
Weight: 8.8 inches
Disassembly Instructions: Remove four screws on bottom and one screw on top. Slide off top cover towards the rear.

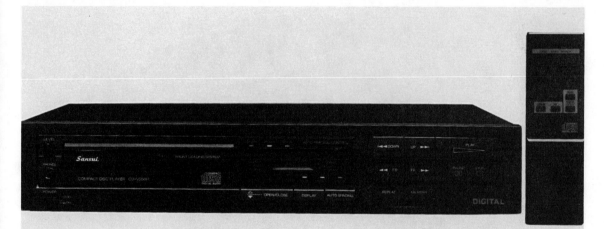

Sanyo CP10 (Portable)

Features:

Filtering: Analog
Sampling Rate: 44.1 kHz
Number of D/A Converters: 1
Beams: 3
Operating Controls: Open; top; play; skip up; skip
    down; mode; repeat; remain; volume
Indicator: Track number; time
Remote: None
Headphone jack: Yes

Specifications:

Loading Type: Top
Dynamic Range: 90 dB
Frequency Response: 20 Hz to 20 kHz
Signal to Noise Ratio: 88 dB
Channel Separation: 80 dB
Output Level: 1.6 V (line out)
Dimensions: 7.25 × 1.5 × 5.0
Weight: 2 pounds

Sanyo MCD-40 (Portable)

Features:

Filtering: Analog
Sampling Rate: 44.1 kHz
Number of D/A Converters: 1
Beams: 3
Operating Controls: (For CD) Stop; open; play/pause; skip/search up/down; repeat; mode; remain
Indicator: Track number; time
Remote: None
Headphone jack: Yes

Specifications:

Loading Type: Front; door type
Dynamic Range: 90 dB
Frequency Response: 20 Hz to 20 kHz
Signal to Noise Ratio: 88 dB
Channel Separation: 78 dB
Output Level: 1 V
Dimensions: N/A
Weight: 9.1 pounds

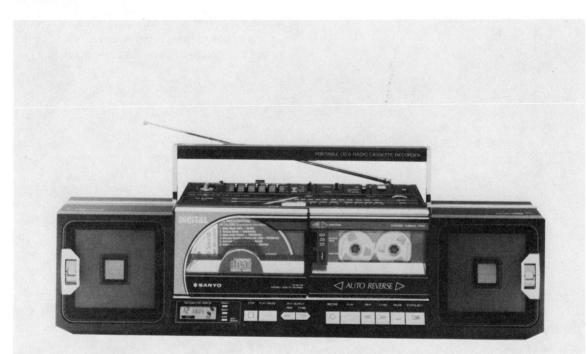

Sharp DX-620

Features:

Filtering: Analog
Sampling Rate: 44.1 kHz
Number of D/A Converters: 1
Beams: 1
Operating Controls: Power; open/close; memory; clear; play; repeat; call; track up; track down
Indicator: Track number; time; repeat
Remote: Yes
Headphone jack: Yes

Specifications:

Loading Type: Front; drawer-type
Dynamic Range: 96 dB
Frequency Response: 5 Hz to 20 kHz
Signal to Noise Ratio: 97 dB
Channel Separation: 90 dB at 1 kHz
Output Level: 2 V fixed
Dimensions: 17.0 × 3.1 × 11.75 inches
Weight: 9.3 pounds
Transit Screws: One screw on bottom under drawer; turn 3/4 revolution in direction of arrow.
Disassembly Instructions: Remove two screws on each side of case; remove one screw in center of back edge of case. Lift cover off.

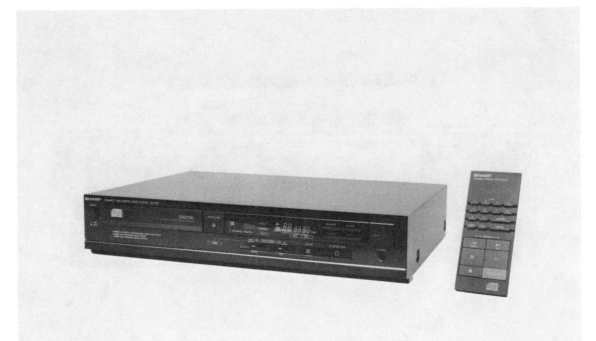

Sony CDP55

Features:

Filtering: Digital

Sampling Rate: 2X oversample—88.2 kHz

Number of D/A Converters: 1

Beams: 3

Operating Controls: Power; open/close; play; pause; music search up; music search down; index up; index down; fast scan up; fast scan down; stop; repeat; programming—program, check, clear; shuffle (random); time; auto space; headphone level adjust

Indicator: Track number; program selection number; index number; time

Remote: Yes

Headphone jack: Yes

Specifications:

Loading Type: Front; drawer-type

Dynamic Range: Greater than 96 dB

Frequency Response: 2 Hz to 20 kHz; +/− 0.3 dB

Signal to Noise Ratio: Greater than 96 dB

Channel Separation: Greater than 93 dB

Output Level: 2 V fixed

Dimensions: 17.0 × 3.25 × 11.25 inches

Weight: 11 pounds

Transit Screw: Loosen red screw; slide bar to the right; retighten screw.

Disassembly Instructions: Remove two screws on each side and slide off top.

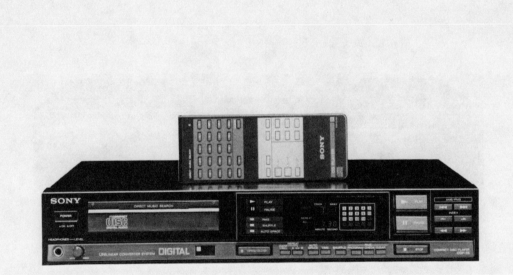

Features:

Filtering: Digital
Sampling Rate: 2X oversample—88.2 kHz
Number of D/A Converters: 1
Beams: 3
Operating Controls: Power; open/close; play; pause; stop; track up; track down; index up; index down; programming—set, clear, start; headphone level adjust
Indicator: Track number; index number; time
Remote: Yes
Headphone jack: Yes

Specifications:

Loading Type: Front; drawer-type
Dynamic Range: 96 dB
Frequency Response: 2 Hz to 20 kHz
Signal to Noise Ratio: 96 dB
Channel Separation: 95 dB
Output Level: 2 V fixed
Dimensions: 17.0 × 3.2 × 13.25 inches
Weight: 15 pounds
Transit Screws: Loosen screw in slot on bottom of drawer. Loosen and slide in direction of arrow; retighten.
Disassembly Instructions: Remove two screws on each side of cover, then remove three screws on top back edge. Lift top off.

Sony D5

Features:

Filtering: Analog
Sampling Rate: 44.1 kHz
Number of D/A Converters: 1
Beams: 3
Operating Controls: Stop; play; track up; track down; mode; display; on/off
Indicator: Track; time; time remaining; mode
Remote: None
Headphone jack: Yes

Specifications:

Loading Type: Top
Dynamic Range: Greater than 90 dB
Frequency Response: 20 Hz to 20 kHz; +1 dB, -3 dB
Signal to Noise Ratio: 85 dB
Channel Separation: Greater than 85 dB
Output Level: 2 V (line)
Dimensions: 5.0 × 1.5 × 5.25 inches
Weight: 1.4 pounds

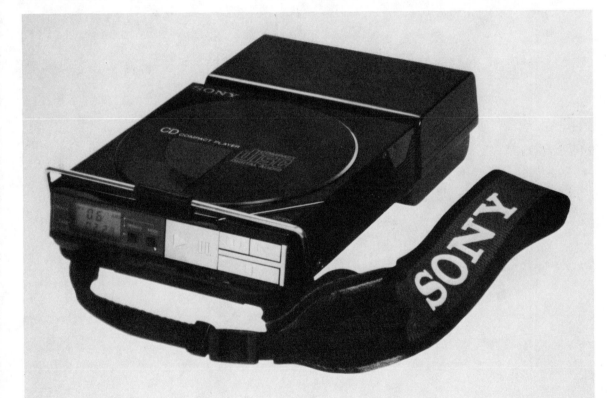

Sony D7

Features:

Filtering: Analog
Sampling Rate: 44.1 kHz
Number of D/A Converters: 1
Beams: 3
Operating Controls: Stop; play; track up; track down; mode; display; on/off
Indicator: Track; time; time remaining; mode
Remote: None
Headphone jack: Yes

Specifications:

Loading Type: Top
Dynamic Range: Greater than 90 dB
Frequency Response: 20 Hz to 20 kHz; +1 dB, −3 dB
Signal to Noise Ratio: 85 dB
Channel Separation: Greater than 85 dB
Output Level: 2 V (line)
Dimensions: 5.0 × 1.3 × 5.0 inches
Weight: 1.5 pounds

Sony D77 (with AM/FM)

Features:

Filtering: Analog
Sampling Rate: 44.1 kHz
Number of D/A Converters: 1
Beams: 3
Operating Controls: Stop; play; track up; track down; mode; display; on/off
Indicator: Track; time; time remaining; mode
Remote: None
Headphone jack: Yes

Specifications:

Loading Type: Top
Dynamic Range: Greater than 90 dB
Frequency Response: 20 Hz to 20 kHz; +1 dB, −3 dB
Signal to Noise Ratio: 85 dB
Channel Separation: Greater than 85 dB
Output Level: 2 V (line)
Dimensions: 5.0 × 1.3 × 5.0 inches
Weight: 1.5 pounds

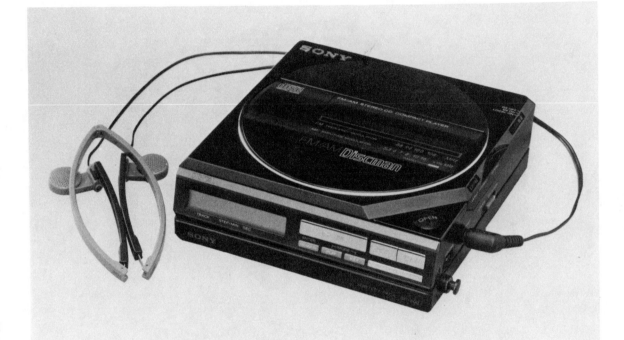

Sony D170

Features:

Filtering: Analog
Sampling Rate: 44.1 kHz
Number of D/A Converters: 1
Beams: 3
Operating Controls: Stop; play; track up; track down; mode; display; on/off
Indicator: Track; time; time remaining; mode
Remote: None
Headphone jack: Yes

Specifications:

Loading Type: Top
Dynamic Range: Greater than 90 dB
Frequency Response: 20 Hz to 20 kHz; +1 dB, −3 dB
Signal to Noise Ratio: 85 dB
Channel Separation: Greater than 85 dB
Output Level: 2 V (line)
Dimensions: 7.5 × 2.25 × 9.0 inches
Weight: 10 pounds

Sony CDX-A10 (10 disc changer)

Features:

Filtering: Analog
Sampling Rate: 44.1 kHz
Number of D/A Converters: 1
Beams: 3
Operating Controls: On remote—Disc select; search up/down; index up/down; memory; disc/track/tuner preset keys; select
Indicator: Mode; FM freq; track; time
Remote: Yes
Headphone jack: No

Specifications:

Loading Type: Front; cartridge-type (10 disc capacity)
Dynamic Range: Greater than 85 dB
Frequency Response: 5 Hz to 20 kHz
Signal to Noise Ratio: Greater than 90 dB
Channel Separation: Greater than 78 dB
Output Level: 1.2 V
Dimensions: Play unit—12.7 × 5.25 × 8.75 inches
Weight: Play unit—12.5 pounds

Technics SL-P500

Features:

Filtering: Digital
Sampling Rate: 2X oversample—88.2 kHz
Number of D/A Converters: 1
Beams: 1
Operating Controls: Power; open/close; stop; pause; play; A-B repeat; time mode; repeat; auto cue; music scan; auto space; index up/down; skip up/down; track up/down; programming—clear, recall, memory, index; 10-key programming pad; headphone level adjust
Indicator: Track number; programmed tracks; cue; space; time
Remote: Yes
Headphone jack: Yes

Specifications:

Loading Type: Front; drawer-type
Dynamic Range: 96 dB
Frequency Response: 4 Hz to 20 kHz; +/− 0.5 dB
Signal to Noise Ratio: 102 dB
Channel Separation: 110 dB
Output Level: 2 V fixed
Dimensions: 16.9 × 3.5 × 11
Weight: 10.1 pounds
Transit Screws: Push button on underside of player once to unlock transport; again to lock transport.
Disassembly Instructions: Remove two screws on each side of player. Lift top cover from the back and slide off toward the rear.

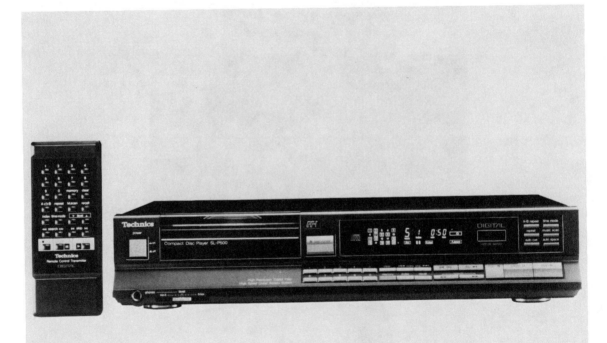

Technics SL-P16 (50 disc changer)

Features:

Filtering: Digital
Sampling Rate: N/A
Number of D/A Converters: N/A
Beams: 3
Operating Controls: Power; open/close; play; pause; stop; track up; track down; index up; index down; recall; program; track and index keypads; headphone level adjust; pitch; play mode
Indicator: Disc in play; track number; index number; time
Remote: Yes
Headphone jack: Yes

Specifications:

Loading Type: Front; cartridge-type (50 disc capacity)
Dynamic Range: 96 dB
Frequency Response: 4 Hz to 20 kHz
Signal to Noise Ratio: 96 dB
Channel Separation: 90 dB
Output Level: 2 V fixed
Dimensions: N/A
Weight: 49 pounds

Technics SL-P300

Features:

Filtering: Digital
Sampling Rate: 2X oversampling—88.4 kHz
Number of D/A Converters: N/A
Beams: 1
Operating Controls: Power; open/close; play; pause; stop; skip up; skip down; search up; search down; A-B repeat; repeat; auto space; programming—memory, index; time mode
Indicator: Track number; index number; time; programmed tracks
Remote: Yes (with direct access keypad)
Headphone jack: Yes

Specifications:

Loading Type: Drawer; drawer-type
Dynamic Range: 96 dB
Frequency Response: 4 Hz to 20 kHz
Signal to Noise Ratio: 100 dB
Channel Separation: 100 dB
Output Level: 2 V
Dimensions: 16.9 × 3.0 × 10.4
Weight: 9.3 pounds
Transit Screws: Push button on underside of player once to unlock transport; again to lock transport.
Disassembly Instructions: Remove two screws on each side of player. Lift top cover from the back and slide off toward the rear.

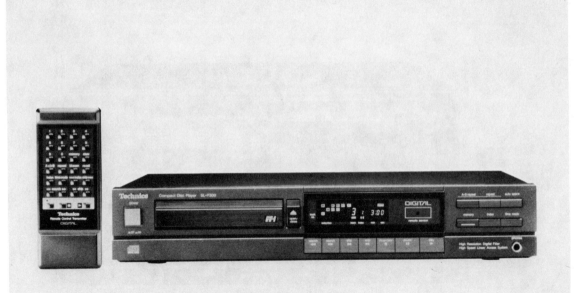

Technics SL-PJ11

Features:

Filtering: Digital
Sampling Rate: 2X oversample—88.2 kHz
Number of D/A Converters: 1
Beams: 1
Operating Controls: Power; open/close; play; pause; stop/clear; skip down; skip up; search up; search down; memory; index; repeat; remaining time
Indicator: Track number; index number; time; programmed tracks
Remote: No
Headphone jack: No

Specifications:

Loading Type: Front; drawer-type
Dynamic Range: 96 dB
Frequency Response: 4 Hz to 20 kHz; +/− 0.5 dB
Signal to Noise Ratio: 96 dB
Channel Separation: 100 dB
Output Level: 2 V fixed
Dimensions: 12.4 × 2.0 × 10.5 inches
Weight: 7.9 pounds
Transit Screws: Push button on underside of player once to unlock transport; again to lock transport.
Disassembly Instructions: Remove two screws on each side of player. Lift top cover from the back and slide off toward the rear.

Technics SL-XP8 (Portable)

Features:

Filtering: Digital
Sampling Rate: 2X oversample—88.2 kHz
Number of D/A Converters: 1
Beams: 1
Operating Controls: Stop/clear; skip/search up; skip/search down; play/pause; open; memory/recall; remain time; repeat; volume; high filter; track selectors
Indicator: Track number; AM/FM; programmed track; time
Remote: None
Headphone jack: Yes

Specifications:

Loading Type: Top
Dynamic Range: 90 dB
Frequency Response: 4 Hz to 20 kHz; +0.5 dB, −1.0 dB
Signal to Noise Ratio: 90 dB
Channel Separation: 90 dB
Output Level: 1.8 V
Dimensions: 4.9 × 1.1 × 4.9 inches
Weight: N/A

Technics CQ-DP5 (Car Player)

Features:

Filtering: Analog
Sampling Rate: 44.1 kHz
Number of D/A Converters: 1
Beams: 1
Operating Controls: Volume; fader; balance; treble;
    bass; pause; repeat, memo; recall; scan; tune;
    seek; skip/search; eject
Indicator: Track number; FM freq.
Remote: None
Headphone jack: None

Specifications:

Loading Type: Front
Dynamic Range: 90 db
Frequency Response: 5 Hz to 20 kHz
Signal to Noise Ratio: 90 dB A-weighted
Channel Separation: 75 dB
Output Level: 2 V
Dimensions: 1.0 × 7.0 × 5.12 inches
Weight: N/A

Yamaha CD-300

Features:

Filtering: Digital

Sampling Rate: 2X oversample—88.2 kHz

Number of D/A Converters: 1

Beams: 3

Operating Controls: Power; open/close; play; pause/stop; search up; search down; track up; track down; display, repeat, program

Indicator: Track number; elapsed time; total time, repeat play; index search

Remote: No

Headphone jack: Yes

Specifications:

Loading Type: Front; drawer-type

Dynamic Range: Greater than 95 dB

Frequency Response: 5 Hz to 20 kHz; +0.5 dB −1.0 dB

Signal to Noise Ratio: 98 dB; 100 dB A-weighted

Channel Separation: 90 dB at 1 kHz

Output Level: 2 V fixed

Dimensions: 13.3 × 3.6 × 11.25 inches

Weight: 7.7 pounds

Disassembly Instructions: Remove three screws on back. Slide off top toward rear of player.

Yamaha CD-400

Features:

Filtering: Digital
Sampling Rate: 2X oversample—88.2 kHz
Number of D/A Converters: 1
Beams: 3
Operating Controls: Power; open/close; play; pause; stop; search up; search down; track up; track down; index up/down; display; repeat
Indicator: Track number; elapsed time; total time; repeat play; index search
Remote: No
Headphone jack: Yes

Specifications:

Loading Type: Front; drawer-type
Dynamic Range: Greater than 95 dB
Frequency Response: 5 Hz to 20 kHz; +0.5 dB, −1.0 dB
Signal to Noise Ratio: Greater than 98 dB; 100 dB A-weighted
Channel Separation: 90 dB at 1 kHz
Output Level: 2 V fixed
Dimensions: 17.1 × 3.75 × 11.25
Weight: 9.25 pounds
Disassembly Instructions: Remove three screws on back. Slide off top toward rear of player.

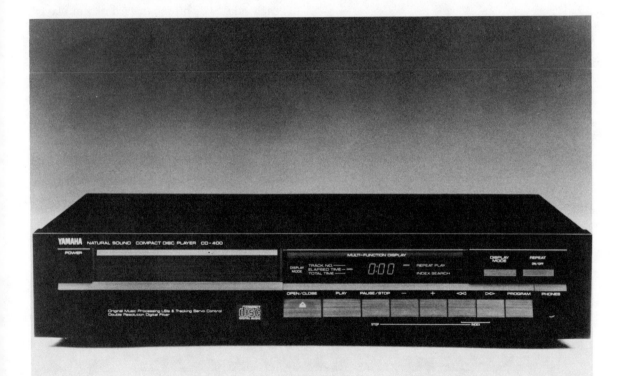

Yamaha CD-500

Features:

Filtering: Digital
Sampling Rate: 2X oversample—88.2 kHz
Number of D/A Converters: 1
Beams: 3
Operating Controls: Power; open/close; play; pause/stop; index up; index down; repeat; A-B repeat; programming—set, clear, 10 key keypad; headphone level adjust
Indicator: Track number; elapsed time; total time; repeat play; index search
Remote: Yes
Headphone jack: Yes

Specifications:

Loading Type: Front; drawer-type
Dynamic Range: Greater than 96 dB
Frequency Response: 5 Hz to 20 kHz; +0.5 dB, −1.0 dB
Signal to Noise Ratio: Greater than 100 dB; 102 dB A-weighted
Channel Separation: 92 dB at 1 kHz
Output Level: 2 V fixed
Dimensions: 17.1 × 3.7 × 11.25 inches
Weight: 10.5 pounds

Disassembly Instructions: Remove one screw on back cover near top; remove two screws on each side. Slide off top toward rear of player.

Yamaha CD-700

Features:

Filtering: Digital

Sampling Rate: 2X oversample—88.2 kHz

Number of D/A Converters: 1

Beams: 3

Operating Controls: Power; open/close; play; pause/stop; index up; index down; track up/down; repeat; A-B repeat; programming—set, clear; headphone level adjust

Indicator: Track number; time; remaining time; repeat

Remote: Optional

Headphone jack: Yes

Specifications:

Loading Type: Front; drawer-type

Dynamic Range: Greater than 96 dB

Frequency Response: 4 Hz to 20 kHz; +0.5 dB, −1.0 dB

Signal to Noise Ratio: Greater than 100 dB; Greater than 103 dB A-weighted

Channel Separation: 92 dB at 1 kHz

Output Level: 2 V fixed

Dimensions: 17.1 × 3.7 × 11.4

Weight: 10.5 pounds

Transit Screws: Remove one transit screw located on bottom plate under drawer.

Disassembly Instructions: Remove four screws on bottom near outside edges. Slide off top toward rear of player.

Yamaha YCD-1000

Features:

Filtering: Digital
Sampling Rate: 2X oversample—88.2 kHz
Number of D/A Converters: 1
Beams: 3
Operating Controls: Volume; bass; treble; skip forward; skip back; track up; track down; pause; repeat; stop; open; repeat
Indicator: N/A
Remote: None
Headphone jack: None

Specifications:

Loading Type: Front; cartridge-type
Dynamic Range: Greater than 92 dB
Frequency Response: 20 Hz to 20 kHz; -3.0 dB
Signal to Noise Ratio: Greater than 92 dB
Channel Separation: 75 dB at 1 kHz
Output Level: 2 V
Dimensions: 7.1 × 2.0 × 7.2
Weight: 3.4 pounds

Yamaha CD-2000

Features:

Filtering: Digital
Sampling Rate: 2X oversample—88.2 kHz
Number of D/A Converters: 2
Beams: 3
Operating Controls: Power; open/close; play; pause/stop; index up/down; track up/down; search up/down; A-B repeat; programming—set, clear; output level up/down; space insert
Indicator: Track number; time; remaining time; repeat; output level; remote control
Remote: Yes
Headphone jack: Yes

Specifications:

Loading Type: Front; drawer-type
Dynamic Range: Greater than 97 dB
Frequency Response: 2 Hz to 20 kHz; +/− 0.3 dB
Signal to Noise Ratio: Greater than 102 dB; 105 dB A-weighted
Channel Separation: 95 dB at 1 kHz
Output Level: 2 V fixed; 0-5 V variable
Dimensions: 17.1 × 4.0 × 11.5 inches
Weight: 11.4 pounds

Sanyo CP700

Features:

Filtering: Analog
Sampling Rate: 44.1 kHz
Number of D/A Converters: 2
Beams: 1
Operating Controls: Power; open/close; skip up; skip down; track up; track down; stop; play; memory; repeat
Indicator: track number; index number
Remote: No
Headphone jack: No

Specifications:

Loading Type: Front; drawer-type
Dynamic Range: 95 dB
Frequency Response: 5 Hz to 20 kHz
Signal to Noise Ratio: 96 dB
Channel Separation: 92 dB
Output Level: 2 V fixed
Dimensions: 16.8 × 3.0 × 10.8 inches
Weight: 7.2 pounds
Transit screws: Remove the two transit screws and place them into the receptacles.
Disassembly Instructions: Remove two screws on either side of the player. Slide the top cover off towards the rear.

Sanyo CP710

Features:

Filtering: Analog
Sampling Rate: 44.1 kHz
Number of D/A Converters: 2
Beams: 1
Operating Controls: Power; open/close; play/pause; stop; skip up; skip down; memory; repeat
Indicator: Track number; index number; time
Remote: Yes
Headphone jack: No

Specifications:

Loading Type: Front; drawer type
Dynamic Range: 95 dB
Frequency Response: 5 Hz to 20 kHz
Signal to Noise Ratio: 95 dB
Channel Separation: 92 dB
Output Level: 2 V fixed
Dimensions: 16.8 × 3.0 × 10.8 inches
Weight: 7.2 pounds
Transit screws: Remove the two transit screws and place them into the receptacles.
Disassembly Instructions: Remove two screws on either side of the player. Slide the top cover off towards the rear.

Sanyo CD-P1

Features:

Filtering: Analog
Sampling Rate: 44.1 kHz
Number of D/A Converters: 1
Beams: 3
Operating Controls: (For CD) Stop; open;
    play/pause; skip/search up/down; repeat; mode;
    remain; programming—memory, call, clear,
    repeat
Indicator: Track number; time
Remote: None
Headphone jack: Yes

Specifications:

Loading Type: Top
Dynamic Range: 90 dB
Frequency Response: 20 Hz to 20 kHz
Signal to Noise Ratio: 88 dB
Channel Separation: 78 dB
Output Level: 1 V
Dimensions: N/A
Weight: N/A

Sanyo FTEC-1 (Car Player)

Features:

Filtering: Analog
Sampling Rate: 44.1 kHz
Number of D/A Converters: 1
Beams: 3
Operating Controls: N/A
Indicator: N/A
Remote: None
Headphone jack: None

Specifications:

Loading Type: Front
Dynamic Range: 90 dB
Frequency Response: 5 Hz to 20 kHz; +/- 1 dB
Signal to Noise Ratio: 90 dB
Channel Separation: 80 dB
Output Level: 5-15 V variable
Dimensions: 6.75 × 2.0 × 5.2 inches
Weight: N/A

Sharp DX-110

Features:

Filtering: Digital
Sampling Rate: 44.1 kHz
Number of D/A Converters: 1
Beams: 1
Operating Controls: Power; open/close; pause; play;
    index down; index up; track down; track up
Indicator: Track number; index number
Remote: No
Headphone jack: Yes

Specifications:

Loading Type: Front; drawer-type
Dynamic Range: 96 dB
Frequency Response: 5 Hz to 20 kHz
Signal to Noise Ratio: 97 dB
Channel Separation: 90 dB at 1 kHz
Output Level: 2 V fixed
Dimensions: 13.0 × 3.1 × 11.75 inches
Weight: 10.4 pounds
Transit Screws: One screw on bottom under
    drawer; turn 3/4 revolution in direction of
    arrow.
Disassembly Instructions: Remove two screws on
    each side of case; remove one screw in center
    of back edge of case. Lift cover off.

Sony CDP-25

Features:

Filtering: Analog
Sampling Rate: 44.1 kHz
Number of D/A Converters: 1
Beams: 3
Operating Controls: Power; on/off; play; pause;
    stop; track up; track down; index up; index
    down; memory; clear; timer; repeat
Indicator: Track number; index number; time
Remote: No
Headphone jack: No

Specifications:

Loading Type: Front; drawer type
Dynamic Range: Greater than 93 dB
Frequency Response: 2 Hz to 20 kHz; +/− 0.5 dB
Signal to Noise Ratio: Greater than 93 dB
Channel Separation: Greater than 90 dB
Output Level: 2 V fixed
Dimensions: 17.0 × 2.8 × 11.2 inches
Weight: 8.8 pounds
Disassembly Instructions: Remove two screws on
    each side and slide off top.

Sony CDP-520ESII

Features:

Filtering: Digital
Sampling Rate: 2X oversample—88.2 kHz
Number of D/A Converters: 1
Beams: 3
Operating Controls: N/A
Indicator: N/A
Remote: Yes
Headphone jack: N/A

Specifications:

Loading Type: Front; drawer-type
Dynamic Range: Greater than 96 dB
Frequency Response: 2 Hz to 20 kHz; +/− 0.3 dB
Signal to Noise Ratio: 96 dB
Channel Separation: Greater than 95 dB
Output Level: 2 V fixed
Dimensions: 17.0 × 3.25 × 13.25 inches
Weight: 15 pounds

Teac PD500

Features:

Filtering: Digital
Sampling Rate: 2X oversample—88.2 kHz
Number of D/A Converters: N/A
Beams: N/A
Operating Controls: N/A
Indicator: N/A
Remote: Yes
Headphone jack: N/A

Specifications:

Loading Type: Front; drawer-type
Dynamic Range: 96 dB
Frequency Response: 3 Hz to 20 kHz
Signal to Noise Ratio: 96 dB
Channel Separation: 95 dB
Output Level: 2 V fixed
Dimensions: 17.2 × 3.5 × 11.3 inches
Weight: 10.6 pounds

Toshiba XR-P9 (Portable)

Features:

Filtering: Analog
Sampling Rate: 44.1 kHz
Number of D/A Converters: 1
Beams: 3
Operating Controls: N/A
Indicator: N/A
Remote: None
Headphone jack: Yes

Specifications:

Loading Type: Top
Dynamic Range: Greater than 84 dB
Frequency Response: 5 Hz to 20 kHz; +0 .5 dB,
  −1.5 dB
Signal to Noise Ratio: N/A
Channel Separation: Greater than 75 dB at 1 kHz
Output Level: 1 V
Dimensions: 4.9 × 1.5 × 7.1 inches
Weight: 1.1 pounds

Toshiba XR-V22

Features:

Filtering: Analog
Sampling Rate: 44.1 kHz
Number of D/A Converters: 1
Beams: 3
Operating Controls: Power; open/close; play; pause;
  stop; track up/down; index up/down; display;
  memory; repeat; headphone level
Indicator: Track number; index number; time
Remote: No
Headphone jack: No

Specifications:

Loading Type: Front; drawer-type (two drawer)
Dynamic Range: Greater than 96 dB
Frequency Response: 20 Hz to 20 kHz; +/− 1.0 dB
Signal to Noise Ratio: 95 dB
Channel Separation: Greater than 90 dB
Output Level: 2 V fixed
Dimensions: 13.2 × 4.4 × 14.1 inches
Weight: 13.4 inches
Transit Screws: Turn screw counterclockwise to
  loosen; clockwise to tighten.
Disassembly Instructions: Remove one screw on
  each side and four screws along back edge of
  cover; slide cover off towards the rear.

ADC CD-100X

Features:

Filtering: Analog
Sampling Rate: 44.1 kHz
Number of D/A Converters: 1
Beams: 3
Operating Controls: N/A
Indicator: N/A
Remote: None
Headphone jack: None

Specifications:

Loading Type: Front
Dynamic Range: 96 dB
Frequency Response: 10 Hz to 20 kHz; +/− 0.8 dB
Signal to Noise Ratio: 95 dB A-weighted
Channel Separation: 85 dB at 1 kHz
Output Level: 2V
Dimensions: 13.4 × 3.2 by 11.5 inches
Weight: 8 pounds
Transit screws: Remove three screws on underside of player. Disassembly Instructions: Remove two screws on each side of the case and lift.

---

dbx DX 3

Features:

Filtering: Digital
Sampling Rate: 2X oversample—88.2 kHz
Number of D/A Converters: 1
Beams: 3
Operating Controls: Power; open/close; play; pause/stop; repeat; program display mode; skip up; skip down; track up; track down; dynamics control; ambience control
Indicator: Track number; index number; time
Remote: No
Headphone jack: Yes

Specifications:

Loading Type: Front; drawer type
Dynamic Range: 96 dB
Frequency Response: 10 Hz to 20 kHz
Signal to Noise Ratio: N/A
Channel Separation: 90 dB
Output Level: 2 V fixed
Dimensions: 17.2 × 3.75 × 11.5 inches
Weight: 10 pounds
Transit Screws: One screw on bottom panel, under drawer
Disassembly Instructions: Remove four screws on the bottom in the corners; slide case back to remove

Denon DCD-1000

Features:

Filtering: Analog
Sampling Rate: 44.1 kHz
Number of D/A Converters: 1
Beams: 1
Operating Controls: Power; open/close; stop; pause;
    play; track up; track down; skip up; skip down;
    programming—memory, repeat, call, display
Indicator: Track number; index number
Remote: Optional
Headphone jack: Yes

Specifications:

Loading Type: Front; drawer type
Dynamic Range: 95 dB
Frequency Response: 5 Hz to 20 kHz
Signal to Noise Ratio: 95 dB
Channel Separation: 90 dB
Output Level: 2 V fixed
Dimensions: 13.5 × 12.0 × 3.5 inches
Weight: N/A
Transit Screws: Remove red screw on bottom under drawer.
Disassembly Instructions: Remove two screws on
    back corners of top. Swing back of cover up
    slightly and slide cover off.

Denon DCD-1500

Features:

Filtering: Digital
Sampling Rate: 2X oversample—88.2 kHz
Number of D/A Converters: 2
Beams: 3
Operating Controls: Power; open/close; play/pause;
    track up/down; index up/down; 10-key pro-
    gramming keypad; A-B repeat; headphone vol-
    ume level
Indicator: Track number; index number; time
Remote: Yes
Headphone jack: Yes

Specifications:

Loading Type: Front; drawer type
Dynamic Range: 96 dB
Frequency Response: 5 Hz to 20 kHz; +/− 0.3 dB
Signal to Noise Ratio: 96 dB
Channel Separation: 95 dB
Output Level: 2 V fixed; 0-2 V variable
Dimensions: 17.4 × 3.5 × 14.0 inches
Weight: 13.2 pounds
Transit Screws: Remove red screw on bottom under drawer.
Disassembly Instructions: Remove four screws on
    the top; lift cover off.

Denon DCD-1100

Features:

Filtering: Analog
Sampling Rate: 44.1 kHz
Number of D/A Converters: 1
Beams: N/A
Operating Controls: Power; open/close; play/pause; index up/down; track up/down; program; memory; repeat; timer; timer mode; headphone control
Indicator: N/A
Remote: Yes
Headphone jack: Yes

Specifications:

Loading Type: Front; drawer type
Dynamic Range: 95 dB
Frequency Response: 5 Hz to 20 kHz
Signal to Noise Ratio: 95 dB
Channel Separation: 90 dB
Output Level: 2 V fixed
Dimensions: 17.5 × 14.0 × 3.5
Weight: N/A
Transit Screws: Remove red screw on bottom under drawer.
Disassembly Instructions: Remove four screws on the top and lift off cover.

Denon DCD-1800

Features:

Filtering: Digital
Sampling Rate: 2X oversample—88.2 kHz
Number of D/A Converters: 2
Beams: 3
Operating Controls: Power; open/close; play/pause; track up/down; index up/down; 10-key programming keypad; headphone volume level; A-B repeat; repeat; intro
Indicator: Track number; index number; time
Remote: Optional
Headphone jack: Yes

Specifications:

Loading Type: Front; drawer type
Dynamic Range: 96 dB
Frequency Response: 5 Hz to 20 kHz
Signal to Noise Ratio: 96 dB
Channel Separation: 94 dB
Output Level: 2 V fixed
Dimensions: 19.0 × 15.0 × 14.5 inches
Weight: N/A
Transit Screws: Remove red screw on bottom under drawer next to red screw mounted in slot. Loosen screw and slide in direction of arrow, tighten.
Disassembly Instructions: Remove two screws on either side of cover; lift off cover.

Fisher AD815

Features:

Filtering: Analog
Sampling Rate: 44.1 kHz
Number of D/A Converters: 1
Beams: 1
Operating Controls: Power; open/close; pause; play;
    track up; track down; search up; search down;
    repeat; timer; memory
Indicator: Track number; index numnber; display;
    time; repeat
Remote: Yes
Headphone jack: Yes

Specifications:

Loading Type: Front; drawer type
Dynamic Range: N/A
Frequency Response: N/A
Signal to Noise Ratio: Greater than 90 dB
Channel Separation: Greater than 80 dB
Output Level: 2 V fixed
Dimensions: 17.3 × 3.4 × 11.3 inches
Weight: 9 pounds
Transit Screws: Remove three screws located un-
    der drawer. Turn white lock fully counter-
    clockwise.
Disassembly Instructions: Remove two screws on
    each side. Remove one screw from back edge.
    Slide the top cover off toward the back.

Hitachi DA-501

Features:

Filtering: Analog
Sampling Rate: 44.1 kHz
Number of D/A Converters: 1
Beams: 3
Operating Controls: Power; open/close; play/pause;
    stop; index up/down; track up/down; 10 key
    programming pad; program; repeat, headphone
    control
Indicator: N/A
Remote: Yes
Headphone jack: Yes

Specifications:

Loading Type: Front; drawer-type
Dynamic Range: 95 dB
Frequency Response: 5 Hz to 20 kHz
Signal to Noise Ratio: 95 dB
Channel Separation: 92 dB
Output Level: 2.5 V fixed
Dimensions: 17.1 × 3.25 × 10.3 inches
Weight: 10 pounds
Disassembly Instructions: Remove two screws on
    each side of case; slide case back and off.

Toshiba XR-30

Features:

Filtering: Analog
Sampling Rate: 44.1 kHz
Number of D/A Converters: 1
Beams: 3
Operating Controls: Power; open/close; play; pause; stop; track up/down; index up/down; display; memory; repeat; headphone level
Indicator: Track number; index number; time
Remote: No
Headphone jack: Yes

Specifications:

Loading Type: Top
Dynamic Range: Greater than 84 dB
Frequency Response: 5 Hz to 20 kHz; +0.5 dB, −1.5 dB
Signal to Noise Ratio: Greater than 84 dB
Channel Separation: Greater than 75 dB at 1 kHz
Output Level: 2 V fixed
Dimensions: $9.8 \times 1.8 \times 5.1$ inches
Weight: 2.9 pounds
Transit Screws: Turn screw counterclockwise to loosen; clockwise to tighten.
Disassembly Instructions: Remove one screw on each side and four screws along back edge of cover; slide cover off toward the rear.

Toshiba XR-35

Features:

Filtering: Analog
Sampling Rate: 44.1 kHz
Number of D/A Converters: 1
Beams: 3
Operating Controls: Power; open/close; play; pause/stop; track up; track down; index up; index down; display; memory; repeat; headphone level adjust
Indicator: Track number; index number; time
Remote: No
Headphone jack: No

Specifications:

Loading Type: Front; drawer-type
Dynamic Range: Greater than 96 dB
Frequency Response: 20 Hz to 20 kHz; +/− 0.5 dB
Signal to Noise Ratio: Greater than 96 dB
Channel Separation: Greater than 90 dB
Output Level: 2 V fixed
Dimensions: $16.5 \times 3.2 \times 12.1$ inches
Weight: 9 pounds
Transit Screws: Turn screw counterclockwise to loosen; clockwise to tighten.
Disassembly Instructions: Remove one screw on each side and four screws along back edge of cover; slide cover off towards the rear.

Appendix A

Sources

Accuphase/Madrigal Ltd.
PO Box 781
Middletown, CT 04657

ADC Product Division
71 Chapel St. Box 100C
Newton, MA 02195

ADS/Analog & Digital Systems, Inc.
One Progress Way
Wilmington, MA 01887

Aiwa America Ltd.
35 Oxford Dr.
Moonachie, NJ 07074

Akai America Ltd.
800 W. Artesia Blvd.
Compton, CA 90220

Alpine Electronics of America
19145 Gramercy Place
Torrance, CA 90501

Audio-Technica US Inc.
1221 Commerce Dr.
Stowe, OH 44224

Bang & Olufsen of America
1150 Feehanville Dr.
Mt. Prospect, IL 60056

Blaupunkt
PO Box 4601
North Suburban, IL 60198

California Audio Lab
21962 Annette Ave.
El Toro, CA 92630

Cambridge Audio
c/o Michael Basikin Co.
4650 Arrow Highway #F4
Monclair, CA 91765

Carver Corp.
19210 33 Avenue West
PO Box 1237
Lynwood, WA 98036

Citizen Consumer Products
CBM America Corp.
2999 Overland Ave.
Los Angeles, CA 90064

dbx Inc.
PO Box 100C
Newton, MA 02195

Denon America Inc.
27 Law Dr.
Fairfield, NJ 07006

Discrete Technologies
2911 Oceanside Rd.
Oceanside, NY 11571

DUAL Electronics
Ortophon Corp.
122 Dupont St.
Plainview, NY 11803

Emerson Radio Corp.
One Emerson Lane
Secaucus, NJ 07094

Fisher Corp.
21214 Lassen St.
Chatsworth, CA 91311

General Electric
One Wellner Dr.
Portsmouth, VA 23705

Goldstar Electronics Inc.
c/o Richard Weiner, Inc.
888 7th Ave.
New York, NY 10106

Harmon/Kardon Inc.
240 Crossway Park West
Woodbury, NY 11797

Hitachi Sales of America
401 W. Artesia Blvd.
Compton, CA 90220

JVC Company of America
41 Slater Dr.
Elmwood Park, NJ 07407

Kenwood Electronics
1315 Watsoncenter Rd.
Carson, CA 90745

Kinergetics
6029 Reseda Blvd.
Tarzana, CA 91356

Kyocera International Inc.
100 Randolph Rd., CN 6700
Somerset, NJ 08873-1284

Luxman/Alpine
19145 Gramercy Pl.
Torrance, CA 90504

Madrigal Ltd.
P.O. Box 781
Middletown, CT 06457

NAP Consumer Electronics (Magnavox)
Interstate 40 & Straw Plains Pike
PO Box 6950
Knoxville, TN 37914

Marantz Inc.
20525 Nordoff St.
Chatsworth, CA 91311

McIntosh Laboratory Inc.
2 Chambers St.
Binghampton, NY 13903

Mission Electronics Corp. of America
5985 Atlantic Drive, Unit 6
Mississauga, Ontario, Canada L4W 1S4

Mitsubishi Electric Sales of America
3030 E. Victoria St.
Rancho Dominquez, CA 90221

NAD, USA
675 Canton St.
Norwood, MA 02062

Nakamichi USA Corp.
19701 South Vermont Ave.
Torrance, CA 90502

NEC Home Electronics USA
1401 Estes Ave.
Elk Grove Village, IL 60007

Nikko Audio
5830 So. Triangle Drive
Commerce, CA 90040

Onkyo Corp.
200 Williams Dr.
Ramsey, NJ 07446

Panasonic
One Panasonic Way
Secaucus, NJ 07094

Parasound Products
945 Front Street
San Francisco, CA 94111

Pioneer Electronics USA
PO Box 1720
Long Beach, CA 90801

Pioneer Video, Inc.
200 West Grand Ave.
Montvale, NJ 07645

Proton Corp.
737 W. Artesia Blvd.
Compton, CA 90220

Quasar Company
9401 West Grand Ave.
Franklin Park, IL 60131

RCA
600 North Sherman Dr.
Indianapolis, IN 46201

Radio Shack/Realistic
1800 One Tandy Center
Fort Worth, TX 76102

Revox/Studer Revox America
1425 Elm Hill Pike
Nashville, TN 37210

Rotel of America
Mosobanke International Inc.
PO Box 653
New York, NY 14240

Sampo Corp of America
5550 Peachtree
Norcross, GA 30071

Sansui Electronics Corp.
1250 Valley Brook Ave.
Lyndhurst, NJ 07071

Sanyo Electric Inc.
1200 W. Artesia Blvd.
PO Box 5177
Compton, CA 90220

H.H. Scott
20 Commerce Way
Woburn, MA 01888

Sears, Roebuck & Co.
Sears Tower
Chicago, IL 60684

Sharp Electronics Corp.
10 Sharp Plaza
PO Box 588
Paramus, NJ 07652

Sherwood
13845 Artesia Blvd.
Cerritos, CA 90701

Shure Brothers Inc.
222 Hartley Ave.
Evanston, IL 60202-3696

Sonograph
Conrad-Johnson Design, Inc.
1474 Pathfinder Lane
McLean, VA 22101

Sony Corp. of America
Sony Drive
Park Ridge, NJ 07656

Sylvania Electronic Components
Philips ECG, Inc.
1025 Westminister Drive
PO Box 3277
Williamsport, PA 17701

Symphonic Electronic
1825 So. Acacia Ave.
Compton, CA 90220

Teac Corp. of America
7733 Telegraph Rd.
Montebello, CA 90640

Technics/Panasonic
One Panasonic Way
Secaucus, NJ 07094

Toshiba America Inc.
82 Towtowa Rd.
Wayne, NJ 07470

Vector Research
20600 Nordoff St.
Chatsworth, CA 91311

ULTRX
1200 West Artesia Blvd.
Compton, CA 90220

Yamaha Electronics Corp.
6660 Orangethorpe Ave.
Buena Park, CA 90620

Appendix B

Further Reading

Interested in learning more about compact discs? Sure you are. Here is a selected list of magazines and books that can enrich your understanding and enjoyment of CD.

MAGAZINES

Audio
PO Box 5316
Boulder, CO 80302

Monthly magazine (plus special issues) on all audio interests. Regular reviews of CD hardware and software, but not enough. Machine reviews by Len Feldman and Ivan Berger usually on the mark; Feldman tends to be "easier" on mediocre CD players than some other cut-throat reviewers in other publications. Ken Pohlmann's columns are must-reading, though usually on the technical or esoteric side.

Audio/Video Buyer's Guide
Harris Publications
1115 Broadway
New York, NY 10010

Seasonal buyer's guide issues on home and car audio, available at newstands. Light reading and somewhat out of date when you get it. No subjective reviews of CD hardware or software.

Digital Audio & Compact Disc Review
Wayne Green Enterprises
PO Box 976
Farmingdale, NY 11737-0976

Monthly magazine with reviews and features articles on compact disc players and software. Very good regular columns by Ken Pohlmann and others. Publisher Green (known for his ham radio and computer publications) always has something to say about something, and his mark (whether you like it or not) is felt throughout the pages of Digital Audio. Recommended reading in any case.

High Fidelity
825 Seventh Ave., 8th Floor
New York, NY 10019

A general interest home audio magazine geared to serious hobbyists and audiophiles. Regular reviews of CD hardware and software. Machine reviews are technically sound.

Modern Electronics
76 North Broadway
Hicksville, NY 11801
Monthly magazine for electronics hobbyists. Occasional technical article on compact disc.

Radio-Electronics
500 Bi-County Blvd.
Farmingdale, NY 11735
Monthly magazine for electronics hobbyists. Occasional technical article on compact disc.

BOOKS

Basic Electronic Test Procedures—2nd Ed. by Irving M. Gottlieb, TAB book No. 1927, 368 pgs./234 illus.
How to take in- and out-of-circuit electronic measurements using volt-ohm meters, oscilloscopes, and other common test gear.

Beginners Guide to Reading Schematics by Robert J. Traister, TAB book No. 1536, 140 pgs./123 illus.
How to read and interpret schematic diagrams.

Digital Audio Technology by H. Nakajima, T. Doi, J. Fukuda, A Iga, TAB book No. 1451, 320 pgs./210 illus. (Also issued as The Sony Book of Digital Audio Technology, TAB book No. 1451B.)

Explains the technology behind digital audio and compact discs. Written by Sony engineers.

Digital Electronics Troubleshooting by Joseph J. Carr, TAB book No. 1250, 250 pgs./331 illus.
Theory and practice of troubleshooting digital circuits.

Handbook of Electronic Safety Procedures by Edward A. Lacy, TAB books No. 1420, 288 pgs./170 illus.
Covers safety precautions and procedures when troubleshooting and repairing electric and electronic devices.

How to Troubleshoot & Repair Electronic Circuits by Robert L. Goodman, TAB book No. 1218, 378 pgs./250 illus.
General troubleshooters guide; both analog and digital.

Principles and Practice of Electrical and Electronics Troubleshooting, by D. Tomal and D. Gedeon, TAB books No. 1842, 256 pgs./275 illus.
General tips on taking electronic measurement and troubleshooting procedures.

Understanding Digital Electronics, by R.H. Warring, TAB book No. 1593, 154 pgs./140 illus.
Introduction to the principles of digital theory.

Appendix C

Maintenance Log

Use the maintenance log on the following pages to keep track of the routine upkeep and servicing you do on your compact disc player. Feel free to make photocopies of these pages and keep the copies with your player's instruction manual. Maintenance logs are of little use unless you stick to them religiously, so make sure you write down anything and everything you do to your player.

Maintenance Log

Compact Disc Player Maintenance and Repair Log

Player Vital Statistics

Brand_____

Model_____

Date Purchased_____Serial Number_____

Where Purchased_____

Sales Person_____Warranty Period_____

New_____Used_____ If Used, How Old When Purchased?_____

Type: AC Operated Home_____Portable_____Auto_____

Player Design

Type of Pickup: 1-Beam_____ 3-Beam_____ Other_____

Type of Filtering: Analog_____2X Oversample_____ 4X Oversample____

D/A Converter: Single___Dual___ Single-Chip____Double-Chip____

Audio Output Level (Volts)_____Variable?_____ Headphones?_____

PM Schedule Supplies (Type or Brand and Source)

Household Spray Cleaner_____

Non Petroleum-Based Solvent Cleaner_____

Optical Lens Cleaner_____

Oil Lubricant_____

Grease Lubricant_____

Electrical Contact Cleaner_____

Compressed Air_____

Non-Slip Cleaner (Rubber)_____

Other:_____

_____

_____

_____

_____

_____

_____

_____

Tools (List)

_____

_____

_____

General Maintenance

Date				
Clean PCB				
Clean Pickup Transport				
Clean Lens				
Check/Clean Rollers				
Check/Clean Belts				
Inspect Wiring				

Lubrication

Date				
Slide Ass'y				
Loading Ass'y				
Clamping Ass'y				
Other_____				

Contact Cleaning

Date				
PowerSwitch				
Front Panel Switches				
Interlock Switches				
Remote Switches				
Connectors				
Pickup Ass'y				
Remote Battery Terminals				

Compact Disc Player Maintenance and Repair Log

Page 3

Repair/Replacement

Date				
Loading Drawer Belt				
Loading Drawer Roller				
Disc Spindle Belt				
Switches________				
Main PCB				
Pickup				
Other__________				
Other__________				
Other__________				

Problem Occurance

Date____________
Description of Problem____
____
____
Action Taken____
____
____
Meter Readings, Measurements, Etc.____________________________
____

Date____________
Description of Problem____
____
____
Action Taken____
____
____
Meter Readings, Measurements, Etc.____________________________
____

Problem Occurance (Continued)

Date_____
Description of Problem_____ .
_____
_____
Action Taken_____
_____
_____
Meter Readings, Measurements, Etc._____
_____

Date_____
Description of Problem_____ .
_____
_____
Action Taken_____
_____
_____
Meter Readings, Measurements, Etc._____
_____

Date_____
Description of Problem_____ .
_____
_____
Action Taken_____
_____
_____
Meter Readings, Measurements, Etc._____
_____

Special Notes

_____
_____
_____
_____
_____

Appendix D

Soldering Tips and Techniques

Successful repair of your compact disc player depends largely on how well you can solder two wires together. Soldering sounds and looks simple enough, but there really is a science about it. If you are unfamiliar with soldering, or want a quick refresher course, read this short soldering primer.

TOOLS AND EQUIPMENT

Good soldering requires the proper tools. If you don't have them already, they can be purchased at Radio Shack and most any electronics store.

Soldering Iron

You'll need a soldering iron, of course, but not just any old soldering iron. Get a soldering "pencil" with a low-wattage heating element. For electronics work, the heating element should not be higher than about 30 watts. Most soldering pencils are designed so that you can change heating elements as easy as changing a lightbulb.

DO NOT use the instant-on type soldering guns, favored in the old tube days. They create far too much unregulated heat, and they are too large to effectively solder most joints on a PCB.

If your soldering iron has a temperate control and readout, dial it to between 665 and 680 degrees. This provides maximum heat with the minimum danger of damage to the electronic components. When you are not using your soldering iron, keep it in an insulated stand. Don't rest the iron in an ashtray or precariously on the carpet. You or some precious belonging is sure to be burned.

Soldering Tip

The choice of soldering tip is important. For best results, use a fine tip designed specifically for printed circuit board use. Tips are made to fit certain types and brands of heating elements, so make sure you get the kind for your iron. If the tip doesn't come pre-tinned, tin it by attaching the tip to the iron and heating it up. After the iron is hot, apply a thin coat of solder to the entire tip.

Sponge

Keep a damp sponge by the soldering station

and use it to wipe off extra solder. You'll have to re-wet the sponge now and then if you are doing lots of soldering.

Solder

You should use only rosin core solder. It comes in different thicknesses; for best results, use the thin type (0.050″) for PCB work. NEVER use acid core or silver solder on electronic equipment.

Soldering Tools

Basic soldering tools include a good pair of small needle-nose pliers, tweezers, wire strippers and wire cutters (sometimes called side or diagonal cutters). The stripper should have a dial that lets you select the gauge of wire you are using. A pair of "nippy" cutters, which cut wire leads flush to the surface of the board, are handy but not absolutely essential.

Cleaning Supplies

After soldering, and when the components and board are cool, you should spray or brush on some flux remover. Isopropyl alcohol can also be used for cleaning.

Solder Vacuum

A solder vacuum is a suction device that is used to pick up excess solder. It is often used when desoldering—removing a wire or component on the board. Solder can also be removed using a length of copper braid. Most electronics stores sell a spool of it specifically for solder removal.

BASIC SOLDERING

The basis of successful soldering is that the soldering iron is used to heat up the work, whether it be a component lead, a wire, or whatever. You then apply the solder to the work. DO NOT apply solder directly to the soldering iron. If you take the shortcut by melting the solder on the iron, you might end up with a "cold" solder joint. A cold joint doesn't adhere well to the metal surfaces of the part or board, so electrical connection is impaired.

Once the solder flows around the joint (and some will flow to the tip), remove the iron and let the joint cool. Avoid disturbing the solder as it cools; a cold joint might result. Do not apply heat any longer than necessary. Prolonged heat can permanently ruin electronic components. A good rule of thumb is that if the iron is on any one spot for more than five seconds, it's too long.

If at all possible, you should keep the iron at a 30 to 40 degree angle to work, as shown in Fig. D-1. Most tips have a beveled tip for this purpose.

Apply only as much solder to the joint as is required to coat the lead and circuit board pad. A heavy-handed soldering job may lead to soldering bridges, which is when one joint melds with joints around it. At best, solder bridges cause the circuit to not work; at worse, they cause short circuits that can burn out the entire board.

REPLACING COMPONENTS

Replacing a soldered component first requires that you remove all the solder holding it in place. Use the soldering iron to melt the joint, and as the solder flows, suck it up with a solder vacuum or wick it up with a copper mesh. Remove enough solder so that the component lead is free. If you can't get all the solder up the first time, let the joint cool and try again.

Clean the old joint and the leads of the replacement component in alcohol. This removes any oil that might impair the grip of the joint after soldering.

Insert the new component gently. Don't pull on the lead or you may damage the component. Once the part is seated on the board, bend the leads slightly to keep it in place. Solder as usual. If you are resoldering a wire onto a terminal, wrap the stripped end of the wire around the eyelet of the terminal prior to soldering.

A GOOD SOLDER JOINT

A good solder joint should be bright and shiny. A joint that looks dull is probably cold and should be remade. The joint should not have any sharp

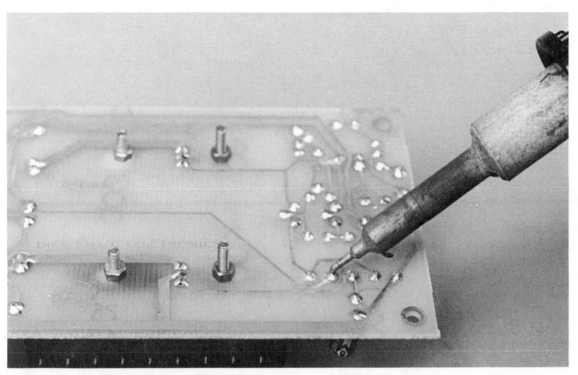

Fig. D-1. Hold the soldering angle at a 30 to 40 degree angle to the PCB.

"peaks." If so, the solder didn't flow well enough to make a good connection. Remake the joint, being sure to apply the iron to the work and not to the iron. Excess solder that forms on the tip (another cause for the "peaks") should be removed using the damp sponge.

ELECTROSTATIC DISCHARGE

Electrostatic discharge—better known as a "carpet shock"—can ruin electronic components. You should remove the excess static buildup from your body by touching some grounded metal object prior to soldering, or before handling electronic parts and boards. If you are soldering transistors and integrated circuits, you should use a grounded soldering iron, as well as an anti-static wrist band and table mat.

TIP MAINTENANCE AND CLEANUP

After soldering, let the iron cool. Loosen the tip from the heating element and store it for next use. After several soldering sessions, the tip should be cleaned using a soft brush. Don't file it or sand it down with emery paper.

Invariably, little nuggets of solder will be left around after a repair job. Make sure that these balls of once-molten solder balls are not left on the PCB or in the CD player cabinet. The solder may bridge wires or board traces together, and cause a serious short circuit. Inspect your work carefully and use a soft brush to wisk away stray bits of solder.

Appendix E

Charts

MAKE	MODEL	DISC LOADING	FREQUENCY RESPONSE	dB	DYNAMIC RANGE	S/N RATIO	SAMPLING RATE	OUTPUT FILTER	# DA CONV	CHANNEL SEP.	OUTPUT LEVEL
Accuphase	DP80/DC81	Front	4 Hz - 20 kHz	±0.3 dB	106 dB	106 dB	88.2	D	2	100 dB	2.5 V
Acoustic Res.	CD-04	Front	20 Hz - 20 kHz	±0.15 dB	105 dB	96 dB	176.4	D	2	94 dB	2 V
ADC	CD-100X	Front	10 Hz - 20 kHz	±0.8 dB	96 dB	95 dB(A)	44.1	A	1	85 dB	2 V
ADC	CD-16/1,16/2R	Front	20 Hz - 20 kHz	+0.5,-1 dB	96 dB	95 dB	44.1	A	1	85 dB	2 V
ADCOM	GCD-200	Front	5 Hz - 20 kHz	0.5 dB	96 dB	98 dB	N/A	D	N/A	90 dB	2.5 V
ADCOM	GCD-300	Front	5 Hz - 20 kHz	0.5 dB	96 dB	98 dB	N/A	A	N/A	90 dB	2.5 V
ADS	Atelier CD3/CD4	Front	20 Hz - 20 kHz	±0.25 dB	96 dB	>102 dB	88.2	D	2	>86 dB	0-3 V
Aiwa	DX-1200	Front	2 Hz - 20 kHz	N/A	N/A	96 dB	N/A	N/A	N/A	90 dB	var
Akai	CD-A30	Front	5 Hz - 20 kHz	±0.5 dB	90 dB	90 dB	44.1	A	1	86 dB	2 V
Akai	CD-A3X	Front	5 Hz - 20 kHz	±0.5 dB	90 dB	90 dB	44.1	A	1	86 dB	2 V
Akai	CD-A70	Front	5 Hz - 20 kHz	±0.5 dB	95 dB	95 dB	88.2	D	1	90 dB	2 V
Akai	CD-A7T	Front	5 Hz - 20 kHz	0.5 dB	90 dB	90 dB	44.1	A	N/A	85 dB	0-2 V
Akai	CD-M515	Front	5 Hz - 20 kHz	±0.5 dB	90 dB	90 dB	44.1	A	1	86 dB	2 V
Akai	CD-M88T	Front	5 Hz - 20 kHz	0.5 dB	90 dB	90 dB	44.1	A	N/A	85 dB	0-2 V
Alpine	5900	Front	5 Hz - 20 kHz	±1 dB	90 dB	90 dB	44.1	A	1	85 dB	5 V
Alpine	7900	Front	5 Hz - 20 kHz	±1 dB	90 dB	90 dB	44.1	A	1	85 dB	5 V
Audio Technica	AT-CD10	Front	5 Hz - 20 kHz	+0.5,-1dB	95 dB	100 dB	N/A	D	N/A	90 dB	2 V
Audio Technica	AT-CD20	Front	4 Hz - 20 kHz	+0.5,-1 dB	>96 dB	100 dB	88.2	D	1	>92 dB	2 V
AVA	Transcendence	Front	2 Hz - 20 kHz	±0.1 dB	100 dB	100 dB	N/A	D	N/A	100 dB	2 V
Bang & Olufsen	Beogram CDX	Top	3 Hz - 20 kHz	±0.3 dB	>96 dB	>96 dB	176.4	D	2	>94 dB	2 V
Bang & Olufsen	CD 50	Front	4 Hz - 20 kHz	±0.3 dB	>96 dB	>95 dB	88.2	D	1	>94 dB	2V
Blaupunkt	CDP 05	Front	20 Hz - 20 kHz	-0.3 dB	92 dB	>89 dB(A)	44.1	N/A	1	70 dB	2 V
Calif Audio Lab	Tempest	Front	5 Hz - 20 kHz	-0.5 dB	105 dB	100 dB(A)	176.4	A	2	96 dB	2 V
Cambridge Aud.	CD 1	Front	10 Hz - 20 kHz	0.5 V	110 dB	110 dB	176.4	D	6	105 dB	0.1-12 V
Carver	CD	Front	50 Hz - 20 kHz	0.5 dB	96 dB	96 dB	N/A	N/A	1	86 dB	1.9 V
Carver	DTL-100	Front	5 Hz - 20 kHz	±0.3 dB	96 dB	96 dB	88.2	D	1	86 dB	1.9 V
Carver	DTL-200	Front	5 Hz - 20 kHz	±0.1 dB	100 dB	100 dB	88.2	D	1	90 dB	2 V
Carver	DTL-50	Front	5 Hz - 20 kHz	±0.5 dB	94 dB	95 dB	88.2	D	1	84 dB	2 V
Citizen	CDP-120	Top	20 Hz - 20 kHz	N/A	90 dB	N/A	44.1	N/A	1	80 dB	1.6 V
Curtis Mathis	AP500	Front	4 Hz - 20 kHz	±0.3 dB	96 dB	100 dB	N/A	A	N/A	100 dB	2 V
dbx	DX3	Front	10 Hz - 20 kHz	+0.5,-1 dB	96 dB	96 dB	88.2	D	1	90 dB	2 V
dbx	DX30	Front	20 Hz - 20 kHz	+0.5,-1 dB	96 dB	100 dB	88.2	D	1	90 dB	2 V
Denon	DCD-1000	Front	5 Hz - 20 kHz	1 dB	95 dB	95 dB	44.1	A	N/A	90 dB	2 V
Denon	DCD-1100	Front	5 Hz - 20 kHz	1 dB	95 dB	95 dB	44.1	A	N/A	90 dB	2 V
Denon	DCD-1300	Front	5 Hz - 20kHz	±0.3 dB	95 dB	96 dB	88.2	D	1	90 dB	2 V
Denon	DCD-1500	Front	5 Hz - 20 kHz	±0.3 dB	96 dB	96 dB	88.2	D	2	95 dB	0-2 V
Denon	DCD-1800R	Front	5 Hz - 20 kHz	0.3 dB	96 dB	96 dB	N/A	D	N/A	94 dB	2 V
Denon	DCD-500	Front	5 Hz - 20 kHz	±0.5 dB	95 dB	95 dB	44.1	A	1	90 dB	2 V
Denon	DCD-700	Front	5 Hz - 20 kHz	±0.5 dB	95 dB	95 dB	44.1	A	1	90 dB	2 V
Discrete Tech	LS 1	Front	2 Hz - 20 kHz	0.3 dB	96 dB	96 dB	N/A	D	N/A	>98 dB	0-2 V
Distech	LS-1 Mark 2	Front	20 Hz - 20 kHz	±0.3 dB	110 dB	103 dB	176.4	D	2	103 dB	2 V
Dual	CD-130	Front	5 Hz - 20 kHz	N/A	N/A	95 dB	N/A	N/A	N/A	94 dB	2 V
Emerson	CD160	Front	5 Hz - 20 kHz	+0.5,-1 dB	95 dB	95 dB	44.1	N/A	2	92 dB	2 V
Emerson	CD170	Front	5 Hz - 20 kHz	+0.5,-1 dB	95 dB	95 dB	44.1	N/A	2	92 dB	2 V
Fisher	AD-815B	Front	N/A	N/A	N/A	>90 dB	44.1	N/A	N/A	>80 dB	N/A
Fisher	AD-823B	Front	20 Hz - 20 kHz	N/A	90 dB	90 dB	N/A	N/A	N/A	90 dB	N/A
General Electric	3-7050	Vertical	N/A	N/A	N/A	N/A	N/A	N/A	N/A	N/A	N/A
General Electric	4800/4911	Front	5 Hz - 20 kHz	±0.5	93 dB	93 dB	N/A	A	N/A	90 dB	1.8 V
Goldstar	GCD-616	Front	5 Hz - 20 kHz	±1.5 dB	>90 dB	>85 dB	N/A	D	1	85 dB	2 V
Goldstar	PCD-N1	Vertical	N/A	N/A	N/A	N/A	44.1	N/A	1	N/A	N/A
H.H. Scott	949D/A	Front	5 Hz - 20 kHz	±0.5 dB	N/A	95 dB	N/A	D	N/A	N/A	N/A
H.H. Scott	950 D/A	Front	5 Hz - 20 kHz	±0.5 dB	95 dB	95 dB	44.1	A	1	92 dB	2.5 V
H.H. Scott	959D/A	Front	3 Hz - 20 kHz	+0.5,-1 dB	N/A	98 dB	N/A	D	N/A	90 dB	2 V
H.H. Scott	960 D/A	Front	5 Hz - 20 kHz	±0.5 dB	95 dB	95dB	N/A	A	1	92 dB	2.5 V
H.H. Scott	PCD 88 Port	Top	5 Hz - 20 kHz	N/A	95 dB	95 dB	44.1	A	1	92 dB	N/A
Harman/Kardon	HD300	Front	4 Hz - 20 kHz	±0.5 dB	94 dB	100 dB	88.2	D	1	83 dB	2.4 V
Hitachi	CDD-4	Front	5 Hz - 20 kHz	N/A	94 dB	98 dB	44.1	A	1	92 dB	N/A
Hitachi	D/A 007	Front	5 Hz - 20 kHz	±0.5 dB	95 dB	95 dB	N/A	D	N/A	92 dB	2.5 V
Hitachi	D/A 400/401	Front	5 Hz - 20 kHz	+0.5, -1 dB	95 dB	95 dB	N/A	A	N/A	92 dB	2.5 V
Hitachi	D/A-005	Front	5 Hz - 20 kHz	±0.1,-0.3dB	96 dB	97dB	88.2	D	1	95 dB	2.5 V
Hitachi	D/A-405	Front	5 Hz - 20 kHz	N/A	95 dB	95 dB	44.1	A	1	92 dB	2.5 V
Hitachi	D/A-500/501	Front	5 Hz - 20 kHz	N/A	95 dB	95 dB	44.1	A	1	92 dB	2.5 V
Hitachi	D/A-5000	Front	5 Hz - 20 kHz	N/A	95 dB	95 dB	44.1	A	N/A	92 dB	2.5 V
Hitachi	D/A-6000/6001	Front	5 Hz - 20 kHz	N/A	95 dB	95 dB	44.1	A	1	90 dB	2.5 V
Hitachi	D/A-800	Front	5 Hz - 20 kHz	N/A	N/A	95 dB	N/A	N/A	N/A	92 dB	2 V
Hitachi	D/A-P100	Top	5 Hz - 20 kHz	N/A	90 dB	N/A	44.1	A	1	85 dB	2 V
JVC	V38	Front	5 Hz - 20 kHz	+0.5,-1 dB	95 dB	96 dB	N/A	D	1	90 dB	2 V
JVC	XL-200	Front	5 Hz - 20 kHz	N/A	N/A	96 dB	N/A	N/A	N/A	90 dB	2 V
JVC	XL-400B	Front	5 Hz - 20 kHz	N/A	95 dB	96 dB	88.2	D	N/A	90 dB	2 V
JVC	XL-M700BK	Cart	5 Hz - 20 Hz	N/A	95 dB	93 dB	N/A	D	N/A	90 dB	2 V
JVC	XL-V1100	Front	2 Hz - 20 kHz	N/A	96 dB	96 dB	176.4	D	N/A	95 dB	N/A
JVC	XL-V20	Front	5 Hz - 20 kHz	N/A	N/A	96 dB	N/A	N/A	N/A	90 dB	2 V
JVC	XL-V200B	Front	5 Hz - 20 kHz	+.5,-1 dB	95 dB	93 dB	88.2	D	N/A	90 dB	2 V
JVC	XL-V400B	Front	5 Hz - 20 kHz	+.5,-1 dB	95 dB	95 dB	88.2	D	N/A	90 dB	2V
JVC	XL-V500	Front	5 Hz - 20 kHz	+0.5,-1 dB	95 dB	96 dB	N/A	D	N/A	90 dB	2 V
Kenwood	DP-1000	Front	4 Hz - 20 kHz	±0.5 dB	95 dB	N/A	44.1	A	1	95 dB	2 V

# BEAMS	# PROGRAM. SELECTIONS	AUD. FAST SEARCH	INDEXING	REMOTE CONTROL	HEADPH. JACK	DIMENSIONS	WEIGHT	COMMENTS
1	99	No	Yes	Yes	No	19x5.4x14.9	67 lbs.	Two units; combined weight
N/A	99	Yes	Yes	Yes	Yes	N/A	N/A	
3	16	No	No	No	No	13.4x3.2x11.5	8 lbs.	
3	16	No	Yes	16/2R	No	17x3.3x12	8.5 lbs.	
N/A	99	Yes	Yes	Yes	N/A	17x10.5x3.25	12 lbs.	
N/A	99	Yes	N/A	Yes	N/A	17x10.5x3.25	12 lbs.	
3	30, 16(CD4)	Yes	Yes	Optional	Yes, var	17.5x2.75x14.8	20 lbs.	
N/A	N/A	N/A	N/A	No	Yes	13x2.8x11.7	13.5 lbs	
3	36	Yes	Yes	No	No	17.3x3.1x10.2	7.7 lbs.	
3	36	Yes	Yes	No	Yes	17.3x3.1x10.2	7.7 lbs.	
3	>99	Yes	Yes	Yes	Yes	17.3x3.1x10.2	8.6 lbs.	
N/A	16	No	Yes	Yes	Yes, var	17.3x3x10	12.8 lbs.	
3	36	Yes	Yes	No	No	13.7x3.3x10.2	7 lbs.	
N/A	16	No	Yes	Yes	Yes, var	13.8x2.8x10	14.3 lbs.	
3	None	Yes	No	No	No	7x2x5.5	4 lbs.	Car Player
3	None	Yes	No	No	No	7x2x5.75 (dash)	4.5 lbs.	Car Player; AM/FM tuner 7x1x5.25, 1.5 lbs.
N/A	9	Yes	Yes	N/A	Yes, var	13.3x3.7x11.5	8 lbs.	
3	9	Yes	Yes	Yes	Yes,var	17.1x3.7x11.4	9.9 lbs.	
N/A	20	Yes	Yes	No	N/A	16.5x11.9x3.75	11 lbs.	
1	40	Yes	Yes	No	No	16.5x3x12.25	13.4 lbs.	
3	99	Yes	Yes	Optional	No	16.5x3x12.75	17.8 lbs.	
3	None	Yes	No	No	No	7.2x2.1x6.4	N/A	Car Player
1	20	Yes	Yes	Optional	No	19x5.5x12	17.6 lbs.	
3	99	No	Yes	No	No	16x11x5	20 lbs.	
N/A	9	Yes	Yes	Yes	N/A	19x3.5x11.25	13 lbs.	
3	9	Yes	Yes	No	No	19x3.5x11.25	13 lbs.	
3	29	Yes	Yes	Yes	Yes	19x13.5x14.25	13 lbs.	
3	29	Yes	Yes	Yes	Yes	17x3x11.25	10 lbs.	
3	16	No	No	No	Yes, 2	5x1.2x7.3	1.9 lbs.	Portable
N/A	20	Yes	Yes	Optional	N/A	17x10.5x3	9.3 lbs.	
3	9	Yes	Yes	No	No	17.2x3.75x11.5	10 lbs.	
3	9	Yes	Yes	No	No	17.1x3.75x11	10 lbs.	
N/A	9	Yes	Yes	Optional	Yes, var	13.5x12x3.5	N/A	
N/A	9	Yes	Yes	Yes	Yes, var	17.5x14x3.5	N/A	
3	20	Yes	Yes	Yes	Yes, var	17.4x3.5x14	11.8 lbs.	
3	20	Yes	Yes	Yes	Yes, var	17.4x3.5x14	13.2 lbs.	
N/A	15	Yes	Yes	Yes	Yes, var	19x15x4.5	N/A	
3	15	Yes	No	No	Yes	17.3x3.6x12.2	7.9 lbs.	
3	15	Yes	No	Yes	Yes, var	17.3x3.6x12.2	7.9 lbs.	
N/A	20	No	Yes	N/A	No	16.5x3.5x11.9	16.5 lbs.	
1	20	No	Yes	No	No	16.1x3.6x11.8	16.5 lbs.	
N/A	N/A	N/A	N/A	Yes	Yes	17x4.3x10.4	N/A	
3	15	Yes	Yes	No	No	17.1x2.8x10.4	7.25 lbs.	
3	15	Yes	Yes	No	No	17.1x2.8x10.4	7.25 lbs.	
1	16	No	Yes	Yes	Yes	17.3x3.4x11.3	9 lbs.	
N/A	N/A	N/A	N/A	N/A	N/A	17.3x3.4x11.3	N/A	
N/A	None	No	No	No	Yes	25.8x10x6.3	N/A	Portable, with cassette player, AM/FM
3	15	Yes	Yes	4911 only	No	17.2x2.9x10.4	9.5 lbs.	
3	9	Yes	Yes	No	No	16.9x3x12	11 lbs.	
N/A	None	No	No	No	Yes	27.8x9.4x7.9	N/A	Portable
N/A	23	No	Yes	No	No	N/A	10 lbs.	
3	15	Yes	Yes	No	No	17.2x3.7x11	10.8 lbs.	
N/A	90	Yes	Yes	Yes	Yes	N/A	10.5 lbs.	
3	15	Yes	Yes	Yes	No	17.2x3.7x11	10.8 lbs.	
1	15	Yes	Yes	No	Yes	26.2x5.5x9.2	N/A	Portable
3	15	Yes	No	Yes	No	17.3x4x14	12 lbs.	
3	32	Yes	No	Yes	Yes	17.1x3.8x12.5	17 lbs.	6 disc cartridge
N/A	15	Yes	N/A	No	N/A	14.5x3.5x6.4	10 lbs.	
N/A	15	Yes	N/A	No	N/A	17.1x2.9x10.4	10 lbs.	
3	15	Yes	Yes	Yes	Yes	17.1x3.7x10.3	11 lbs.	
3	15	Yes	Yes	Yes	Yes	17.1x2.8x10.3	10 lbs.	
3	15	Yes	Yes	501 only	501 only	17.1x3.25x10.3	10 lbs.	
N/A	15	Yes	Yes	N/A	N/A	12.5x12.2x3.25	9 lbs.	
3	15	Yes	Yes	6001 only	No	14.8x2.8x10.5	9 lbs.	
N/A	N/A	N/A	N/A	Yes	Yes	17x3.5x10.4	13.7 lbs.	
3	None	Yes	No	No	Yes	7.5x1.5x6.4	2.5 lbs.	Portable
N/A	8	Yes	No	No	N/A	13.3x3.75x11.7	9.7 lbs.	
N/A	N/A	N/A	N/A	No	Yes	17x3.6x11.7	8.9 lbs.	
3	15	No	Yes	Yes	Yes	17x3.25x11.5	8.9 lbs.	
3	32	Yes	N/A	Yes	Yes	17.25x12.1x4.3	17 lbs.	6 Disc changer, cartridge
3	15	Yes	Yes	Yes	Yes,var	17.2x3.9x14.8	17.7 lbs.	
N/A	N/A	N/A	N/A	No	Yes	13.3x3.14x11.7	7.9 lbs.	
3	15	No	Yes	No	Yes	17.2x3.25x11.5	8.4 lbs.	
3	15	No	Yes	Yes	Yes,var	17.2x3.25x11.5	8.9 lbs.	
N/A	15	Yes	Yes	Yes	Yes, var	17.25x3.7x11.75	13 lbs.	
3	16	Yes	No	Yes	Yes,var	17.3x3.5x12.3	13.2 lbs.	

230

Kenwood	DP-1100II	Front	2 Hz - 20 kHz	0.5 dB	95 dB	95 dB	N/A	D	N/A	90 dB	2 V
Kenwood	DP-750	Front	5 Hz - 20 kHz	±0.5 dB	>96 dB	N/A	44.1	A	N/A	>90 dB	N/A
Kenwood	DP-840	Front	5 Hz - 20 kHz	0.5 dB	96 dB	N/A	N/A	D	N/A	90 dB	2 V
Kenwood	DP-850	Front	5 Hz - 20 kHz	±1.0 dB	92 dB	N/A	44.1	A	N/A	90 dB	1.5 V
Kenwood	DP-900	Front	4 Hz - 20 kHz	0.5 dB	95 dB	95 dB	N/A	D	N/A	90 dB	2 V
Kinergetics	KCD-1	Front	3 Hz - 20 kHz	N/A	100 dB	100 dB	N/A	D	N/A	94 dB	0-2 V
Kinergetics	KCD-20	Front	2 Hz - 20 kHz	±0.5 dB	100 dB	100 dB	176.4	D	2	94 dB	4 V
Kyocera	DA-01	Front	20 Hz - 20 kHz	0.4 dB	90 dB	90 dB	N/A	D	N/A	90 dB	0-2 V
Kyocera	DA-610	Front	5 Hz - 20 kHz	±0.5 dB	>90 dB	>90 dB	44.1	A	2	>90 dB	2 V
Kyocera	DA-610 CX	Front	5 Hz - 20 kHz	N/A	>90 dB	>90 dB	44.1	A	2	>90 dB	2 V
Kyocera	DA-810	Front	5 Hz - 20 kHz	±0.5 dB	>90 dB	>95 dB	176.4	D	2	>90 dB	2 V var
Kyocera	DA-910	Front	5 Hz - 20 kHz	±0.5 dB	>90 dB	>95 dB	176.4	D	2	>90 dB	2 V var
Luxman	D-03	Front	5 Hz - 20 kHz	-0.5 dB	>97 dB	>97 dB	44.1	A	1	>93 dB	2 V
Luxman	D-100	Front	5 Hz - 20 kHz	±0.5 dB	>90 dB	>91 dB	44.1	A	1	>85 dB	2 V
Luxman	D-102	Front	5 Hz - 20 kHz	-0.5 dB	>91 dB	>91 dB	44.1	A	1	>88 dB	2 V
Luxman	D-109	Front	5 Hz - 20 kHz	-0.5 dB	>96 dB	>96 dB	44.1	A	1	>95 dB	2 V
Luxman	D-404	Front	5 Hz - 20 kHz	-0.5 dB	>96 dB	>96 dB	44.1	A	1	>90 dB	2 V
Luxman	D-405	Front	5 Hz - 20 kHz	0.5 dB	96 dB	96 dB	44.1	A	N/A	90 dB	2 V
Luxman	D-408	Front	5 Hz - 20 kHz	-0.5 dB	>96 dB	>96 dB	44.1	A	1	>90 dB	2 V
Magnavox	CD-9510	Top	20 Hz - 20 kHz	N/A	88 dB	N/A	N/A	N/A	1	88 dB	2 V
Magnavox	FD1010SL	Front	20 Hz - 20 kHz	±0.3 dB	90 dB	>90 dB	176.4	D	N/A	>90 dB	2 V
Magnavox	FD1040	Front	20 Hz - 20 Khz	0.15 dB	105 dB	96 dB	176.4	D	N/A	94 dB	2 V
Magnavox	FD1041BK	Front	20 Hz - 20 kHz	0.15 dB	105 dB	96 dB	176.4	D	2	94 db	2 V
Magnavox	FD1051BK	Front	20 Hz - 20 kHz	±0.3 dB	105 dB	>100 dB	176.4	D	2	>96 dB	2 V
Magnavox	FD2040SL	Front	20 Hz - 20 kHz	0.15 dB	105 dB	96 dB	N/A	D	N/A	94 dB	2 V
Magnavox	FD2041BK	Front	20 Hz - 20 kHz	±0.3 dB	105 dB	>90 dB	176.4	D	2	>90 dB	2 V
Magnavox	FD3040SL	Front	3 Hz - 20 kHz	±0.3 dB	90 dB	>90 dB	176.4	D	N/A	90 dB	2 V
Magnovox	CD9555	Vertical	40 Hz - 20 kHz	N/A	N/A	N/A	44.1	A	1	N/A	N/A
Magnovox	CDB650	Front	2 Hz - 20 kHz	±0.3 dB	>100 dB	>100 dB	176.4	D	2	>94 dB	2 V
Marantz	CD-150	Front	5 Hz - 20 kHz	N/A	96 dB	96 dB	176.4	D	2	90 dB	2 V
Marantz	CD-152	Front	5 Hz - 20 kHz	N/A	96 dB	96 dB	176.4	D	2	90 dB	2 V
Marantz	CD-30	Front	5 Hz - 20 kHz	N/A	96 dB	96 dB	88.2	D	2	90 dB	2 V
Marantz	CD-44	Front	20 Hz - 20 kHz	N/A	N/A	90 dB	N/A	N/A	N/A	90 dB	2 V
Marantz	CD-50	Front	5 Hz - 20 kHz	N/A	96 dB	96 dB	88.2	D	2	90 dB	2 V
Marantz	CD-54	Front	4 Hz - 20 kHz	N/A	N/A	90 dB	N/A	N/A	N/A	90 dB	2 V
Marantz	CD-74	Front	4 Hz - 20 kHz	±1.0 dB	>90 dB	>90 dB	176.4	D	2	>90 dB	2 V
Marantz	CD-84	Front	4 Hz - 20 kHz	N/A	N/A	90 dB	N/A	N/A	N/A	90 dB	2 V
McIntosh	MCD 7000	Front	2 Hz - 20 kHz	N/A	96 dB	96 dB	176.4	D	2	94 dB	2 V
Melos Audio	CD-1	Front	20 Hz - 20 kHz	0.3 dB	90 dB	90 dB	N/A	D	N/A	90 dB	2 V
Meridian	207 PRO	Front	20 Hz - 20 kHz	±0.3	N/A	N/A	176.4	D	2	N/A	N/A
Meridian	MCD	Top	20 Hz - 90 kHz	+0.3 dB	90 dB	90 dB	N/A	D	N/A	90 dB	2 V
Mission	DAD 7000R	Front	20 Hz - 20 kHz	±0.3 dB	>90 dB	>90 dB	176.4	D	2	>90 dB	2 V
Mission	PCM 4000	Front	20 Hz - 20 kHz	N/A	>96 dB	>96 dB	176.4	D	2	>90 dB	2 V
Mission	PCM 7000	Front	20 Hz - 20 kHz	N/A	>96 dB	>96 dB	176.4	D	2	>90 dB	2 V
Mitsubishi	DP-107	Front	5 Hz - 20 kHz	+0.5,-1 dB	>95 dB	N/A	44.1	N/A	1	>90 dB	2 V
Mitsubishi	DP-109	Front	5 Hz - 20 kHz	±0.5 dB	>95 dB	95 dB	44.1	N/A	N/A	>90 dB	N/A
Mitsubishi	DP-205	Front	5 Hz - 20 kHz	N/A	N/A	94 dB	N/A	N/A	N/A	90 dB	2 V
Mitsubishi	DP-209R	Front	5 Hz - 20 kHz	±5 dB	95 dB	95 dB	44.1	N/A	N/A	>90 dB	N/A
Mitsubishi	DP-309/DP-409R	Front	5 Hz - 20 kHz	±0.5 dB	94 dB	98 dB	44.1	N/A	N/A	>90 dB	2 V
Mitsubishi	E-CD 100	Cart	5 Hz - 20 kHz	±0.5 dB	>95 dB	98 dB	44.1	N/A	N/A	>90 dB	N/A
Mitsubishi	E-CD 50	Cart	5 Hz - 20 kHz	±0.5 dB	95 dB	98 dB	N/A	N/A	N/A	>90dB	N/A
NAD	5255	Front	20 HZ - 20 kHz	N/A	N/A	98 dB	N/A	N/A	N/A	90 dB	2 V
NAD	5330	Front	5 Hz - 20 kHz	±5 dB	98 dB	98 dB(A)	44.1	A	1	90 dB	2 V
NAD	5355	Front	5 Hz - 20 kHz	±0.5 dB	>98 dB	98 dB	88.2	A	2	90 dB	2 V
Nakamichi	OMS 3A	Front	5 Hz - 20 kHz	N/A	>92 dB	>95 dB	88.2	D	1	>90 dB	2 V
Nakamichi	OMS 4A	Front	5 Hz - 20 kHz	±0.5 dB	>94 dB	>97 dB	88.2	D	2	>93 dB	2 V
Nakamichi	OMS 5A II	Front	5 Hz - 20 kHz	±0.5 dB	>96 dB	>102 dB	176.4	D	2	>100 dB	2 V
Nakamichi	OMS 7A II	Front	5 Hz - 20 kHz	±0.5 dB	>96 dB	>102 dB	176.4	D	2	>100 dB	2 V
Nakamichi	OMS-5	Front	5 Hz - 20 kHz	0.5 dB	92 dB	92 dB	N/A	D	N/A	92 dB	2 V
Nakamichi	OMS-7	Front	5 Hz - 20 kHz	0.5 dB	92 dB	92 dB	N/A	D	N/A	92 dB	2 V
NEC	CD-500E	Front	5 Hz - 20 kHz	±0.5 dB	90 dB	96 dB	N/A	A	1	88 dB	0-2 V
NEC	CD-509E	Front	5 Hz - 20 kHz	0.5 dB	90 dB	95 dB	N/A	D	N/A	86 dB	2 V
NEC	CD-607	Front	5 Hz - 20 kHz	±0.5 dB	>90 dB	95 dB	88.2	D	1	90 dB	2.5 V
NEC	CD-650E	Front	5 Hz - 20 kHz	+0.5, -1 dB	90 dB	96 dB	88.2	D	2	88 dB	2 V
NEC	CD-705	Front	5 Hz - 20 kHz	±5 dB	>90	95 dB	88.2	D	1	90 dB	2.5 V
Nikko Audio	NCD-100	Front	5 Hz - 20 kHz	0.5 dB	96 dB	92 dB	N/A	D	N/A	90 dB	2 V
Nikko Audio	NCD-200	Front	10 hZ - 18 kHz	0.5 dB	96 dB	92 dB	N/A	D	N/A	90 dB	2 V
Nikko Audio	NCD-200R	Front	5 Hz - 20 kHz	±0.5 dB	98 dB	92 dB	N/A	D	N/A	90 dB	2 V
Nikko Audio	NCD-600	Rack	10 Hz - 20 kHz	±0.5 dB	85 dB	85 dB	N/A	D	N/A	90 dB	0-5 V
Onkyo	DX-120	Front	5 Hz - 20 kHz	N/A	96 dB	93 dB	88.2	D	1	87 dB	2 V
Onkyo	DX-150	Front	10 Hz - 20 kHz	2 dB	93 dB	93 dB	88.2	D	1	87 dB	2 V
Onkyo	DX-200	Front	2 Hz - 20 kHz	0.5 dB	96 dB	96 dB	88.2	D	1	93 dB	0-2 V
Onkyo	DX-220	Front	2 Hz - 20 kHz	N/A	96 dB	93 dB	88.2	D	1	87 dB	2 V
Onkyo	DX-320	Front	2 Hz - 20 kHz	N/A	96 dB	96 dB	88.2	D	1	83 dB	2 V
Onkyo	Integra DX-320	Front	2 Hz - 20 kHz	N/A	96 dB	96 dB	88.2	D	1	83 dB	2 V
Panasonic	CQE8000	Front	5 Hz - 20 kHz	N/A	N/A	90 dB	N/A	N/A	N/A	75 dB	N/A
Panasonic	RX-CD70	Vertical	4 Hz - 20kHz	+0.5,-1dB	>90 dB	>90 dB	44.1	A	1	>90 dB	N/A
Panasonic	SL-NP10	Top	4 Hz - 20 kHz	+0.5,-1dB	>96 dB	>96 dB	88.2	D	1	90 dB	N/A
Panasonic	SL-NP20	Front	4 Hz - 20 kHz	+0.5,-1dB	>96 dB	>96 dB	N/A	D	1	90 dB	N/A

N/A	16	Yes	Yes	Yes	Yes, var	17.3x12.25x3.5	15 lbs.	
3	16	Yes	Yes	No	Yes	16.5x3.1x12.2	2.3 lbs.	
N/A	8	No	No	No	Yes, var	16.7x12.2x3.25	10.5 lbs.	
3	16	Yes	No	No	Yes, var	16.5x2.9x12.25	9.7 lbs.	
N/A	16	Yes	Yes	No	Yes, var	17.5x12.25x3.5	13.2 lbs.	
N/A	20	Yes	No	Yes	N/A	19x3.25x15	25 lbs.	Separate power supply
1	20	Yes	Yes	Optional	No	19x3.75x15	25 lbs.	
N/A	24	No	Yes	No	No	18.25x5.25x12.7	N/A	
3	16	Yes	No	Yes	Yes, var	18.2x3.25x12.5	18 lbs.	
3	16	Yes	Yes	Yes	Yes, var	18.2x3.5x12.1	13.2 lbs.	
1	24	Yes	Yes	No	Yes	18.5x4.5x12.6	18.7 lbs.	
1	24	Yes	Yes	Yes	Yes	17x5.5x13	20.9 lbs.	
1	20	Yes	Yes	Yes	Yes, var	17.8x3.4x12.9	13.32 lbs.	
3	16	Yes	Yes	Yes	Yes, var	17.25x3.3x12.4	9.7 lbs.	
3	16	Yes	Yes	Yes	Yes	17.25x3.3x12.4	9.9 lbs.	
3	20	Yes	Yes	Yes	Yes	17.25x4x15.3	23.2 lbs.	
3	8	Yes	No	Yes*	Yes	17.7x3.4x12.3	13.2 lbs.	With R-406 amp
N/A	15	No	Yes	No	Yes	17.9x3.3x12.3	13.2	
1	1	Yes	Yes	Yes	Yes, var	16.5x6.6x17.6	34.7 lbs.	
1	10	Yes	No	No	Yes	5x1.6x7.6	1.5 lbs.	Portable
1	20	Yes	No	No	No	12.5x3x11.75	N/A	
1	20	Yes	No	No	No	12.5x11.75x3.5	20 lbs.	
3	20	Yes	Yes	No	N/A	12.5x3.5x11.75	6.6 lbs.	
3	20	Yes	Yes	Yes	No	12.5x3.5x11.75	6.6 lbs.	
N/A	20	No	No	No	Yes	16.5x11.75x3.5	25 lbs.	
3	20	Yes	Yes	No	Yes	16.5x3.5x11.75	7.6	
1	24	No	Yes	Yes	Yes	16.5x3.25x11.75	35 lbs.	
1	20	N/A	N/A	No	Yes	24.4x8.7x7.7	N/A	Portable
1	20	Yes	Yes	Yes	Yes, var	16.5x3.5x11.75	9 lbs.	
3	16	Yes	No	No	No	16.5x4x11.6	9.5 lbs.	
3	16	Yes	No	No	No	16.5x4x11.6	9.5 lbs.	
3	16	Yes	No	No	No	16.5x3.10.8	7.7 lbs.	
N/A	N/A	N/A	N/A	No	No	12.5x3.5x11.8	14 lbs.	
3	16	Yes	N/A	Yes	No	16.5x3x10.8	7.7 lbs.	
N/A	N/A	N/A	N/A	No	No	12.5x3.3x10.8	15 lbs.	
1	24	No	Yes	Optional	Yes	16.4x3.75x11.75	20.25 lbs.	
N/A	N/A	N/A	N/A	Yes	Yes	12.5x3.3x10.8	15 lbs.	
1	20	No	Yes	Yes	Yes, var	16x5.5x13	35 lbs.	
N/A	20	No	No	No	No	16.5x12x3.5	17 lbs.	
1	99	Yes	Yes	Yes	No	N/A	N/A	2 chassis, separate transport & electronics
N/A	15	No	No	No	No	12.8x3x10.7	11 lbs.	
1	20	No	No	Yes	No	12.9x3.5x12	15 lbs.	
1	20	Yes	Yes	No	Yes	17x3.4x12	12 lbs.	
1	20	Yes	Yes	Yes, var	Yes	17x3.4x12	12 lbs.	
3	9	No	Yes	No	Yes, var	16.75x3.4x11.4	9.25 lbs.	
3	16	No	Yes	No	No	16.6x2.5x11	11 lbs.	
N/A	N/A	N/A	N/A	No	Yes	16.6x3.1x11.8	12.6 lbs.	
3	9	No	Yes	Yes	Yes, var	16.6x2.5x11	11 lbs.	
3	30	No	Yes	409R only	No	16.6x4.1x13.3	16.6 lbs.	5 disc cartridge
3	N/A	N/A	N/A	N/A	N/A	11.3x16.7x13.1	N/A	System with cassette decks, AM/FM tuner
3	N/A	N/A	N/A	N/A	N/A	13.1x11.3x11.1	25 lbs.	System with cassette decks, AM/FM tuner
N/A	N/A	N/A	N/A	No	No	16.5x3.3x13	12.3 lbs.	
3	None	Yes	No	No	No	16.5x3.3x12.2	N/A	
3	8	Yes	Yes	Yes	No	16.5x3.3x12.2	10.8 lbs.	
3	15	Yes	No	Yes	Yes, var	16.9x3.9x12.6	15.6 lbs.	
3	15	Yes	No	Yes	Yes, var	16.9x3.9x12.6	15.6 lbs.	
3	None	Yes	No	No	No	17.1x3.9x12.1	15.9 lbs.	
3	24	Yes	Ys	Yes	Yes, var	17.1x3.9x12.1	15.9 lbs.	
N/A	None	Yes	No	Yes	No	17.2x3.9x12.2	16.7 lbs.	4x oversampling
N/A	24	Yes	Yes	Yes	Yes, var	17.2x3.9x12.2	16.7 lbs.	4x oversampling
3	15	N/A	No	Yes	Yes	17x3x10.6	9.6 lbs.	
N/A	15	Yes	Yes	No	Yes, var	16.9x3.5x12.7	11 lbs.	Hi-speed CMOS D/A switching
3	15	Yes	No	Yes	Yes, var	16.9x3.5x12.6	14.77 lbs.	
3	15	Yes	N/A	Yes	Yes	17x3x12.5	9.7 lbs.	
1	15	Yes	No	Yes	Yes	16.9x4.6x14.8	22.66 lbs.	
N/A	Sequential	No	Yes	No	Yes, var	17.3x3.6x12.2	12.3 lbs.	
N/A	15	No	Yes	Yes	Yes, var	17.3x3.7x11.4	10 lbs.	
s	9	No	Yes	Yes	Yes, var	17.25x3.1x11.5	13 lbs.	
3	5	No	No	No	Yes, var	18.5x14x15	56 lbs.	60 disc rack
3	16	Yes	No	No	No	17.1x3.6x13.75	10 lbs.	
3	16	No	Yes	No	No	17.2x13.75x3.7	11 lbs.	
3	16	Yes	Yes	Yes	Yes, var	17.2x13.75x4	13.2 lbs.	
3	16	Yes	No	Yes	Yes	17.1x3.6x13.75	11 lbs.	
3	16	Yes	Yes	Yes	Yes	17.1x3.6x14	13 lbs.	
3	16	Yes	Yes	Yes	Yes	17.1x3.6x14	13 lbs.	
N/A	N/A	N/A	N/A	N/A	N/A	7x1x5.12	N/A	Car Player
1	15	Yes	No	No	Yes, var	16.2x6.8x8.9	16.5 lbs.	Portable
1	15	No	Yes	No	Yes	4.96x0.87x4.96	1.5 lbs.	Portable
1	20	No	Yes	Yes	No	4.96x1.1x4.96	N/A	Portable; With AM/FM tuner

Panasonic	SL-P3610	Front	4 Hz - 20 kHz	0.5 dB	96 dB	96 dB	44.1	A	N/A	100 dB	2 V
Panasonic	SL-P3620	Front	4 Hz - 20 kHz	±0.3 dB	>96 dB	>96 dB	44.1	D	1	100 dB	2 V
Parasound	CDD 900	Front	20 hZ - 20 kHz	0.2 dB	102 dB	102 dB	44.1	A	N/A	95 dB	0-2 V
Parasound	CDD 940	Front	5 Hz - 20 kHz	±0.5 dB	100 dB	95 dB	44.1	D	1	90 dB	2 V
Philips	CD-10	Top	20 Hz - 20 kHz	N/A	N/A	90 dB	N/A	N/A	N/A	90 dB	2 V
Philips	CD-104	Front	20 Hz - 20 kHz	N/A	N/A	90 dB	N/A	N/A	N/A	90 dB	2 V
Philips	CD-204	Front	20 Hz - 20 kHz	N/A	N/A	90 dB	N/A	N/A	N/A	90 dB	2 V
Philips	CD-304	Front	20 Hz - 20 kHz	N/A	N/A	90 dB	N/A	N/A	N/A	90 dB	2 V
Philips	CD-555	Front	20 Hz - 20 kHz	N/A	N/A	90 dB	N/A	N/A	N/A	90 dB	2 V
Philips	DCO-85	Front	20 Hz - 20 kHz	N/A	N/A	90 dB	N/A	N/A	N/A	90 dB	N/A
Pioneer	CDX-1	Front	10 Hz - 20 kHz	±2 dB	90 dB	90 dB	44.1	A	1	90 dB	N/A
Pioneer	CDX-P1	Front	10 Hz - 20 kHz	N/A	N/A	90 dB	N/A	N/A	N/A	N/A	N/A
Pioneer	CLD-909	Front	4 Hz - 20 kHz	+0.5,-1 dB	>95 dB	>98 dB	N/A	A	N/A	>92 dB	.26 V
Pioneer	DEX-77	Front	5 Hz - 20 kHz	N/A	90 dB	90 dB	N/A	N/A	N/A	N/A	N/A
Pioneer	PD-5010	Front	2 Hz - 20 kHz	±0.5 dB	95 dB	96 dB	N/A	A	N/A	93 dB	2 V
Pioneer	PD-5010BK	Front	2 Hz - 20 kHz	0.5 dB	95 dB	96 dB	44.1	A	N/A	93 dB	2 V
Pioneer	PD-5030/6030	Front	4 Hz - 20 kHz	±0.5 dB	95 dB	>97 dB	44.1	A	N/A	92 dB	1.5-2.5V
Pioneer	PD-6010BK	Front	2 Hz - 20 kHz	0.5 dB	95 dB	96 dB	44.1	A	N/A	93 dB	2 V
Pioneer	PD-7010BK	Front	2 Hz - 20 kHz	0.5 dB	95 dB	96 dB	44.1	A	N/A	93 dB	2 V
Pioneer	PD-7030	Front	4 Hz - 20 kHz	N/A	95 dB	98 dB	88.2	D	N/A	94 dB	1.5-2.5 V
Pioneer	PD-9010X	Front	2 Hz - 20 kHz	N/A	96 dB	96 dB	88.2	D	1	90 dB	2 V
Pioneer	PD-9010XBK	Front	2 Hz - 20 kHz	0.3 dB	96 dB	98 dB	N/A	D	N/A	95 dB	2 V
Pioneer	PD-M6	Front	4 Hz - 20 kHz	N/A	>94 dB	>98 dB	44.1	A	1	>92 dB	2 V
Pioneer	PD-P-DX700	Front	5 Hz - 20 kHz	N/A	93 dB	95 dB	N/A	D	N/A	93 dB	2 V
Pioneer	PD-X500	Front	20 Hz - 20 kHz	N/A	95 dB	95 dB	N/A	N/A	N/A	93 dB	2 V
Pioneer	CLD-909 (CD-LV	Front	4 Hz - 20 kHz	+0.5,-1dB	95 dB	98 dB	44.1	A	N/A	92 dB	0.2 V
Proton	830R	Front	10 Hz - 20 kHz	±0.3 dB	100 dB	100 dB	176.4	A	1	90 dB	2 V
PS Audio	CD-1	Front	20 Hz - 20 kHz	±0.3 dB	90 dB	90 dB	N/A	D	N/A	90 dB	2V
Quasar	CD6975YW	Front	4 Hz - 20 kHz	0.5 dB	96 dB	96 dB	44.1	A	N/A	90 dB	2 V
Quasar	CD8936	Top	4 Hz - 20 kHz	+0.5, -1 dB	>90 dB	>90 dB	44.1	A	1	>90 dB	2 V
Quasar	CD8956	Front	4 Hz - 20 kHz	±0.3 dB	>90 dB	>100 dB	88.2	D	1	>100 dB	2 V
Quasar	CD8975YE/YW	Front	4 Hz - 20 kHz	±0.5 dB	96 dB	96 dB	44.1	A	N/A	90 dB	2 V
Realistic	CD-1200	Front	5 Hz - 20 kHz	+0.5,-1 dB	90 dB	92 dB	44.1	A	N/A	90 dB	2 V
Realistic	CD-1400	Front	5 Hz - 20 kHz	+0.5,-1 dB	92 dB	90 dB	44.1	A	N/A	90 dB	N/A
Realistic	CD-2000	Front	5 Hz - 20 kHz	+0.5,-1 dB	90 dB	88 dB	44.1	A	N/A	90 dB	1.8 V
Realistic	CD-2200	Front	5 Hz - 20 kHz	+0.5,-1 dB	92 dB	90 dB	44.1	A	N/A	90 dB	2 V
Realistic	CD-3000	Top	5 Hz - 20 kHz	+0.5,-1.5 dB	73 dB	N/A	176.4	A	N/A	93 dB	1 V
Revox	B225	Front	20 Hz - 20 kHz	-0.6 dB	96 dB	>96 dB	176.4	D	2	90 dB	0-2 V
Rotel	RCD850	Front	5 Hz - 20 kHz	+0.5,-1 dB	>95 dB	98 dB	88.2	A	2	>90 dB	2 V
SAE	D102	Front	2 Hz - 20 kHz	±0.3 dB	100 dB	100 dB	N/A	D	N/A	96 dB	2 V
Sampo	CDP-501	Front	20 Hz - 18 kHz	N/A	>96 dB	>96 dB	N/A	N/A	N/A	>86 dB	2 V
Sansui	CD-A350	Front	5 Hz - 20 kHz	±0.5 dB	96 dB	>100 dB	44.1	N/A	N/A	90 dB	2 V
Sansui	CD-E750	Front	5 Hz - 20 kHz	±0.5 dB	95 dB	100 dB	44.1	N/A	N/A	90 dB	2 V
Sansui	CD-V350	Front	5 Hz - 20 kHz	±0.5 dB	96 dB	>100 dB	44.1	D	N/A	90 dB	2 V
Sansui	CD-V550R	Front	5 Hz - 20 kHz	±0.5 dB	96 dB	100 dB	44.1	N/A	N/A	90 dB	2 V
Sansui	CDX-V500	Front	5 Hz - 20 kHz	±0.5 dB	90 dB	>90 dB	44.1	D	N/A	90 dB	0-1.5 V
Sansui	PC-V100	Front	5 Hz - 20 kHz	N/A	95 dB	N/A	N/A	D	N/A	90 dB	2 V
Sansui	PC-V750	Front	5 Hz - 20 kHz	N/A	95 dB	N/A	N/A	D	N/A	90 dB	2 V
Sansui	PCV-1000	Front	5 Hz - 20 kHz	N/A	N/A	96 dB	N/A	N/A	N/A	90 dB	2 V
Sansui	PCV-300	Front	5 Hz - 20 kHz	N/A	N/A	96 dB	N/A	N/A	N/A	90 dB	2 V
Sansui	PCV-500	Front	5 Hz - 20 kHz	N/A	N/A	96 dB	N/A	N/A	N/A	90 dB	2 V
Sanyo	CP 10	Top	20 Hz - 20 kHz	±0.5 dB	90 dB	88 dB	44.1	A	1	80 dB	1.6 V
Sanyo	CP 660	Front	5 Hz - 20 kHz	N/A	96 dB	92 dB	44.1	A	N/A	92 dB	2 V
Sanyo	CP 667	Front	5 Hz - 20 kHz	N/A	N/A	96 dB	N/A	N/A	N/A	92 dB	2 V
Sanyo	CP 700/710	Front	5 Hz - 20 kHz	N/A	96 dB	96 dB	44.1	A	2	92 dB	2 V
Sanyo	FTEC 1	Front	5 Hz - 20 kHz	±1 dB	90 dB	90 dB	88.2	A	1	80 dB	5-15 V
Sanyo	FTEC 2	Front	5 Hz - 20 kHz	±1 dB	90 dB	90 dB	44.1	A	1	90 dB	5-15 V
Sanyo	MCD 40	Front	20 Hz - 20 kHz	N/A	90 dB	88 dB	44.1	N/A	N/A	78 dB	1 V
Sears	9751	Front	20 Hz - 20 kHz	±1.0 dB	90 dB	90 dB	N/A	D	N/A	90 dB	2 V
Sears	9752	Front	20 Hz - 20 kHz	±1.0 dB	90 dB	90 dB	N/A	D	N/A	90 dB	2 V
Sharp	DX-100	Front	5 Hz - 20 kHz	±0.5 dB	96 dB	96 dB	N/A	D	N/A	90 dB	2 V
Sharp	DX-110 BK	Front	5 Hz - 20 kHz	±0.5 dB	96 dB	97 dB	44.1	D	1	90 dB	2 V
Sharp	DX-600	Front	5 Hz - 20 kHz	±0.5 dB	96 dB	96 dB	N/A	D	N/A	90 dB	2 V
Sharp	DX-610 BK	Front	5 Hz - 20 kHz	±0.5 dB	96 dB	97 dB	44.1	D	1	90 dB	2 V
Sharp	DX-620 BK	Front	5 Hz - 20 kHz	±0.5 dB	96 dB	97 dB	44.1	D	1	90 dB	2 V
Sherwood	CDP-100	Front	5 Hz - 20 kHz	N/A	N/A	96 dB	N/A	N/A	N/A	90 dB	2 V
Sherwood	CDP-200	Front	6 Hz - 20 kHz	N/A	96 dB	100 dB	N/A	D	N/A	90 dB	2 V
Sherwood	CDP-220	Front	3 Hz - 20 kHz	0.5 dB	>96 dB	98 dB	88.2	D	1	>90 dB	2 V
Sherwood	CDP-300R/310R	Front	2 Hz - 20 kHz	±0.3 dB	>96 dB	>96 dB	176.4	D	N/A	>94 dB	2 V
Shure	D5000	Front	5 Hz - 20 kHz	±0.3 dB	93 dB	10 dB(A)	88.2	D	N/A	85 dB	2 V
Shure	D6000	Front	5 Hz - 20 kHz	±0.25 dB	102 dB	102 db(A)	88.2	D	2	85 dB	2 V
Shure	SV40	Front	5 Hz - 20 kHz	±0.3 dB	98 dB	100 dB(A)	44.1	A	N/A	85 dB	2 V
Sonographe	SD 1	Front	5 Hz - 15 kHz	±0.25 dB	94 dB	>94 dB	176.4	D	2	90 Db	>2 V
Sony	CDP-102	Front	2 Hz - 20 kHz	±0.5 dB	96 dB	96 dB	N/A	D	N/A	95 dB	2 V
Sony	CDP-203	Front	2 Hz - 20 kHz	±0.3 dB	>96 dB	>96 dB	88.2	D	1	>93 dB	2 V
Sony	CDP-25	Front	2 Hz - 20 kHz	±0.5 dB	>93 dB	>93 dB	44.1	A	1	>90 dB	2 V
Sony	CDP-30	Front	2 Hz - 20 kHz	±0.5 dB	90 dB	90 dB	44.1	A	N/A	90 dB	2 V
Sony	CDP-302II	Front	2 Hz - 20 kHz	±0.4 dB	96 dB	96 dB	88.2	D	N/A	95 dB	2 V
Sony	CDP-35	Front	2 Hz - 20 kHz	±0.5 dB	>93 dB	>93 dB	44.1	A	1	>90 dB	2 V

N/A	15	Yes	Yes	No	No	16.9x3.25x12.7	11.2 lbs.	
1	20	No	Yes	Yes	No	16.8x3x10.3	9.3 lbs.	
N/A	Sequential	Yes	Yes	No	Yes	16.7x3.7x12.25	10.6 lbs.	
3	None	Yes	No	No	Yes	17.25x3.75x10	16 lbs.	Compact Disc/Cassette Deck
N/A	N/A	N/A	N/A	No	Yes	5x5.6x1.6	5 lbs.	Car Player
N/A	N/A	N/A	N/A	No	No	12.5x3.5x11.8	16.3 lbs.	
N/A	N/A	N/A	N/A	No	Yes	12.5x3.5x11.8	18 lbs.	
N/A	N/A	N/A	N/A	Yes	Yes	12.5x3.5x11.8	18.6 lbs.	
N/A	N/A	N/A	N/A	No	Yes	12.5x8.6x3.5	N/A	
N/A	N/A	N/A	N/A	N/A	N/A	7x2x5.9	N/A	Car Player with AM/FM tuner
3	None	No	No	No	No	7.1x2.6.5	4.6 lbs.	Car Player; with AM/FM tuner
N/A	N/A	N/A	N/A	N/A	N/A	7.12x2x6.5	8.4 lbs.	Car Player
3	10	Yes	Yes	Yes	Yes, var	16.5x4.7x16.1	25.3 lbs.	CD/LV Player
3	No	No	No	Yes	No	7.1x2x5.75	N/A	Car Player; with AM/FM tuner
N/A	N/A	N/A	N/A	No	Yes	16.5x3.6x12.6	11 lbs.	
N/A	27	Yes	No	No	Yes	12.7x3.9x10.25	10.2 lbs.	
3	24	Yes	No	6030 only	Yes	16.5x3.25x11.4	11.8 lbs.	
N/A	27	Yes	No	No	Yes	16.7x3.7x12.25	10.6 lbs.	
N/A	32	Yes	Yes	Yes	Yes, var	16.7x3.7x12.25	10.6 lbs.	
3	24	Yes	Yes	Yes	Yes,var	18x3.25x11.3	11.8 lbs.	
3	32	Yes	Yes	Yes	Yes, var	17.9x3.75x12.1	12.5 lbs.	
N/A	32	Yes	Yes	Yes	Yes, var	19x12x3	18 lbs.	
3	32	Yes	No	Yes	Yes, var	16.5x3.8x12.7	17.6 lbs.	6 disc cartridge
N/A	10	Yes	Yes	No	No	18x3.75x12.25	12.8 lbs.	
N/A	N/A	N/A	N/A	No	No	14.1x3.9x10.2	10.7 lbs.	
3	10	Yes	Yes	Yes	Yes	16.5x4.7x16.1	25.3 lbs.	CD/LaserVision player
1	20	Yes	No	Optional	Yes	16.5x3.3x11.1	7.9 lbs.	
N/A	20	No	No	Yes	No	19x12x3	18 lbs.	
N/A	15	Yes	Yes	No	No	4.2x18.25x12.7	17 lbs.	
1	None	No	No	No	Yes	4.9x1.25x4.9	<1 lb.	
1	20	Yes	Yes	No	No	16.9x3.1x10.5	N/A	
N/A	15	Yes	Yes	No	No	4.2x18.25x12.7	11 lbs.	
N/A	16	Yes	Yes	No	No	14x10.5x2.7	10 lbs.	
1	15	Yes	Yes	No	N/A	14.56x2.89x10.36	N/A	
N/A	15	Yes	Yes	No	No	12.7x12x3.3	7 lbs.	
1	15	Yes	Yes	No	N/A	3.3x12.6x12.2	8.6 lbs.	
1	16	Yes	No	No	Yes	4.4x2.75x4.4	1.5 lbs.	Portable
1	19	No	Yes	Yes	Yes, var	18x4.4x13.3	17.6 lbs.	
3	9	No	Yes	No	No	17.1x3.6x11.5	9.25 lbs.	
N/A	20	Yes	Yes	Yes	N/A	19x3.5x13	20 lbs.	
N/A	16	Yes	No	No	No	13.8x3.1x11.6	7.9 lbs.	
3	16	Yes	No	No	Yes	16.9x3.2x12.2	8.8 lbs.	
3	8	N/A	Yes	Optional	No	14.9x3.5x12.1	9.9 lbs.	With amp
3	16	Yes	No	No	Yes	16.9x3.2x12.2	8.8 lbs.	
3	16	Yes	No	Yes	Yes	16.9x3.2x12.2	8.8 lbs.	
3	16	No	Yes	Yes	No	7x2x6.1	3.6 lbs.	Car Player
N/A	9	Yes	Yes	No	No	13.7x3.7x11.3	7.9 lbs.	
N/A	8	Yes	Yes	No	No	17x3.2x12.2	10.7 lbs.	
N/A	N/A	N/A	N/A	Yes	Yes	17x4.4x11.7	20 lbs.	
N/A	N/A	N/A	N/A	No	No	13.6x3.7x11.3	8.9 lbs.	
N/A	N/A	N/A	N/A	No	No	17x4.4x11.7	19.5 lbs.	
3	16	Yes	No	No	Yes, 2	7.25x1.5x5	9.1 lbs.	Portable
N/A	16	Yes	Yes	No	Yes	16.5x10.7x3.2	7.3 lbs.	
N/A	N/A	N/A	N/A	No	No	16.5x3x10.8	7.7 lbs.	
1	99	Yes	Yes	710 only	No	16.8x3x10.8	7.2 lbs.	
3	None	Yes	No	No	No	6.75x2x5.2	N/A	Car Player with AM/FM tuner
3	16	Yes	No	No	No	7x2x5.1	N/A	Car Player with AM/FM tuner
3	16	Yes	No	No	Yes	N/A	2 lbs.	Portable, AM/FM radio, cassette player
N/A	15	No	No	No	Yes	16.5x10.7x2.9	11 lbs.	
N/A	15	No	Yes	No	Yes	16.5x10.7x2.9	11 lbs.	
N/A	15	Yes	No	No	Yes	13x3.2x11.75	10.4	
1	None	Yes	No	No	Yes	13x3.1x11.75	10.4 lbs.	
N/A	15	Yes	No	No	Yes	17x3.2x11.74	11.7 lbs.	
1	None	Yes	No	No	Yes	17x3.1x11.5	11.7 lbs.	
1	9	Yes	No	Yes	Yes	17x3.1x11.75	9.3 lbs.	
N/A	N/A	N/A	N/A	No	Yes	14x3.6x11.4	8.4 lbs.	
N/A	9	Yes	Yes	No	Yes	17.3x3.2x11..75	9.3 lbs.	
3	9	Yes	Yes	Yes	Yes, var	17.4x3.6x11	9.7 lbs.	
1	20	No	Yes	310R only	No	17.4x3.25x9.75	11 lbs.	
3	15	Yes	Yes	Yes	No	16.9x3.9x10	11 lbs.	
3	15	Yes	Yes	Yes	Yes	16.9x2.9x12.6	11 lbs.	
3	15	Yes	No	Yes	Yes, var	16.9x2.9x10.6	9.6 lbs.	
1	20	Yes	Yes	Optional	Yes	18x3.5x11	8.5 lbs.	
N/A	16	Yes	Yes	Yes	No	14x3.2x13.25	13 lbs.	
3	20	Yes	Yes	Yes	Yes, var	17x3.25x11.25	11 lbs.	
3	16	Yes	Yes	No	Yes	17x2.8x11.2	8.8 lbs.	
N/A	16	Yes	Yes	No	No	14x2.9x11	9 lbs.	
3	16	Yes	Yes	Yes	Yes	17x3.2x13.25	15 lbs.	
3	30	Yes	Yes	No	Yes	14x3.25x11.2	9.9 lbs.	

Sony	CDP-45	Front	2 Hz - 20 kHz	±0.5 dB	>95 dB	>95 dB	44.1	A	1	>90 dB	2 V
Sony	CDP-50	Front	2 Hz - 20 kHz	±0.5 dB	>95 dB	>95 dB	44.1	A	1	>90 dB	2 V
Sony	CDP-502	Front	2 Hz - 20 kHz	N/A	N/A	96 dB	N/A	N/A	N/A	95 dB	Var
Sony	CDP-520ES	Front	2 Hz - 20 kHz	±0.3 dB	96 dB	95 dB	88.2	D	N/A	95 dB	2 V
Sony	CDP-520ESII	Front	2 Hz - 20 kHz	±0.3 dB	>96 dB	96 dB	88.2	D	1	>95 dB	2 V
Sony	CDP-55	Front	2 Hz - 20 kHz	±0.3 dB	>96 dB	>96 dB	88.2	D	N/A	>93 dB	2 V
Sony	CDP-620ES	Front	2 Hz - 20 kHz	±0.3 dB	96 dB	96 dB	88.2	D	2	95 dB	0.5-2 V
Sony	CDP-650ESD	Front	2 Hz - 20 kHz	±0.3 dB	96 dB	96 dB	88.2	D	0	95 dB	0.5-2 V
Sony	CDP-650ESDII	Front	2 Hz - 20 kHz	±0.3 dB	>96 dB	>96 dB	88.2	D	2	>95 dB	0.5-2 V
Sony	CDP-70	Front	2 Hz - 20 kHz	±0.5 dB	90 dB	90 dB	44.1	A	N/A	90 dB	2 V
Sony	CDP-7F	Top	2 Hz - 20 kHz	±0.5 dB	>90 dB	>90 dB	44.1	A	1	>90 dB	2 V
Sony	CDP-C10 Change	10 Disc	2 Hz - 20 kHz	±0.3 dB	>96 dB	>96 dB	88.2	D	1	>95 dB	2 V
Sony	CDX-5/CDX-R7	Front	5 Hz - 20 kHz	±0.5 dB	>90 dB	>90 dB	44.1	A	1	>85 dB	>775 mV
Sony	CDX-A10	10 Disc	5 Hz - 20 kHz	N/A	>85 dB	>90 dB	44.1	A	1	>78 dB	1.2 V
Sony	CFD-5 CD Music	Top	20 Hz - 20 kHz	±1 dB	>90 dB	>85 dB	44.1	A	1	>85 dB	2 V
Sony	CFD-W888 Musi	Front	20 Hz - 20 kHz	±1 dB	>90 dB	>85 dB	44.1	A	1	>85 dB	2 V
Sony	D-5	Top	20 Hz - 20 kHz	+1,-3 dB	>90 dB	>85 dB	44.1	A	1	>85 dB	2 V
Sony	D-50	Top	20 Hz - 20 kHz	N/A	N/A	90 dB	N/A	N/A	N/A	85 dB	2 V
Sony	D-7	Top	20 Hz - 20 kHz	-1.7 dB	>90 dB	>85 dB	44.1	A	1	>85 dB	2 V
Sony	CDP-620ESII	Front	2 Hz - 20 kHz	±0.3 dB	>96 dB	>96 dB	88.2	D	2	>95 dB	0.5-2 V
Sony	CPD-30211	Front	2 Hz - 20 kHz	±0.3 dB	>96 dB	96 dB	88.2	D	1	>95 dB	2 V
Sony	D-170	Front	20 Hz - 20 kHz	+1,-3 dB	>90 dB	>85 dB	44.1	A	1	>85 dB	2 V
Sylvania	CD1150	Front	20 Hz - 20 kHz	±0.3 dB	>90 dB	>90 dB	176.4	D	1	>90 dB	N/A
Sylvania	CD1460	Front	2 Hz - 20 kHz	±0.3 dB	>100 dB	>100 dB	176.4	D	2	>96 dB	N/A
Sylvania	CD1560	Front	2 Hz - 20 khz	±0.3 dB	>100 dB	100 dB	176.4	D	2	>96 dB	N/A
Sylvania	FDD104SL	Front	20 Hz - 20 kHz	0.15 dB	105 dB	96 dB	N/A	D	N/A	94 dB	2 V
Sylvania	FDE203SL	Front	20 Hz - 20 kHz	0.15 dB	105 dB	96 dB	N/A	D	N/A	94 dB	2 V
Symphonic	CD100	Front	10 Hz - 18 kHz	N/A	90 dB	92 dB	N/A	D	N/A	86 dB	2 V
Tandberg	TCP 3015A	Front	2 Hz - 20 kHz	±0.3 dB	96 dB	100 dB	N/A	D	N/A	94 dB	2 V
TEAC	AD-7	Front	5 Hz - 20 kHz	±0.3 dB	96 dB	96 dB	44.1	D	1	>90 dB	2 V
TEAC	PD-100	Front	8 Hz - 20 kHz	N/A	>92 dB	>92 dB	88.2	D	1	>84 dB	2 V
TEAC	PD-200	Front	5 Hz - 20 kHz	±1 dB	>92 dB	>92 dB	44.1	D	1	>85 dB	2 V
TEAC	PD-22	Front	5 Hz - 20 kHz	N/A	95 dB	N/A	N/A	D	N/A	90 dB	2 V
TEAC	PD-500	Front	3 Hz - 20 kHz	N/A	96 dB	95 dB	N/A	D	N/A	95 dB	2 V
TEAC	ZD-3000	Front	5 Hz - 20 kHz	±0.3 dB	>96 dB	>96 dB	88.2	D	2	>95 dB	55mV-2V
TEAC	ZD-5000	Front	5 Hz - 20 kHz	±0.3 dB	>96 dB	>96 daB	88.2	D	2	>95 dB	55mV-2V
TEAC	CQ-700	Front	5 Hz - 20 kHz	±0.3 dB	>96 dB	>96 dB	44.1	D	1	>94 dB	2 V
Technics	CQ-DP5 Car	Front	5 Hz - 20 kHz	N/A	90 dB	90 dB	44.1	A	1	90 dB	2 V
Technics	SL-P1	Front	4 Hz - 20 kHz	±0.5 dB	96 dB	96 dB	N/A	D	N/A	100 dB	2 V
Technics	SL-P110	Front	4 Hz - 20 kHz	±0.5 dB	92 dB	96 dB	88.2	D	1	96 dB	2 V
Technics	SL-P1200	Top	4 Hz - 20 kHz	±0.2 dB	96 dB	103 dB	88.2	D	2	110 dB	2 V
Technics	SL-P2	Front	4 Hz - 20 kHz	0.5 dB	96 dB	96 dB	N/A	D	N/A	100 dB	2 V
Technics	SL-P3	Front	40 Hz - 20 kHz	±0.5 dB	96 dB	96 dB	N/A	D	N/A	100 dB	2 V
Technics	SL-P310	Front	4 Hz - 20 kHz	±0.5 dB	94 dB	96 dB	88.2	D	1	96 dB	2 V
Technics	SL-P500	Front	4 Hz - 20 kHz	±0.5 dB	94 dB	102 dB	88.2	D	1	110 dB	2 V
Technics	SL-PJ11	Front	4 Hz - 20 kHz	±0.5 dB	96 dB	96 dB	88.2	D	1	100 dB	2 V
Technics	SL-XP5	Top	4 Hz - 10kHz	+0.5,-1dB	90 dB	90 dB	88.2	D	1	90 dB	1.8 V
Technics	SL-XP8	Top	4 Hz - 20 kHz	+0.5,-1dB	90 dB	90 dB	88.2	D	1	90 dB	1.8 V
Teledyne	CD-04	Front	N/A	N/A	N/A	N/A	176.4	N/A	2	N/A	N/A
Toshiba	XR-30	Front	5 Hz - 20 kHz	±0.5 dB	>96 dB	96 dB	N/A	A	N/A	>90 dB	2 V
Toshiba	XR-35	Front	20 Hz - 20 kHz	±0.5 dB	>96 dB	>96 dB	N/A	A	N/A	>90 dB	2 V
Toshiba	XR-40	Front	5 Hz - 20 kHz	±0.5 dB	96 dB	96 dB	44.1	A	N/A	90 dB	0-2 V
Toshiba	XR-J9	Top	5 Hz - 20 kHz	+0.5,-1.5	>84 dB	>84 dB	N/A	A	N/A	>75 dB	1 V
Toshiba	XR-P9	Top	5 Hz - 20 kHz	+0.5,-1.5	>84 dB	84 d B	N/A	A	1	>75 dB	1 V
Toshiba	XR-VII	Front	5 Hz - 20 kHz	±0.5 dB	96 dB	96 dB	44.1	A	N/A	90 dB	2 V
Toshiba	XR-V22	Front	20 Hz - 20 kHz	±1.0 dB	>96 dB	96 dB	44.1	A	1	>90 dB	2 V
ULTRX	CP400	Front	5 Hz - 20 kHz	N/A	96 dB	92 dB	44.1	A	N/A	92 dB	2 V
Vector Research	VCD-800	Front	5 Hz - 20 kHz	±0.5 dB	95 dB	95 dB	N/A	D	N/A	85 dB	N/A
Yamaha	CD-1000B	Front	2 Hz - 20 kHz	±0.5 dB	>97 dB	>102 dB	88.2	D	1	95 dB	2 V
Yamaha	CD-2	Front	3 Hz - 20 kHz	+0.5,-1 dB	96 dB	102 dB	N/A	D	N/A	95 dB	2 V
Yamaha	CD-2000	Front	2 Hz - 20 kHz	±0.3 dB	>97 dB	>102 dB	88.2	D	2	96 dB	2-5 V
Yamaha	CD-2000B	Front	2 Hz - 20 kHz	±0.3 dB	>97 dB	>102 dB	88.2	D	2	95 dB	0-5 V
Yamaha	CD-3	Front	3 Hz - 20 kHz	+0.5,-1dB	96 dB	95 dB	N/A	D	N/A	90 dB	2 V
Yamaha	CD-300B	Front	5 Hz - 20 kHz	+0.5,-1.0	>95 dB	98 dB	88.2	D	1	90 dB	2 V
Yamaha	CD-37	Front	3 Hz - 20 kHz	+0.5,-1 dB	96 dB	100 dB	N/A	D	N/A	90 dB	2 V
Yamaha	CD-400B	Front	5 Hz - 20 kHz	+0.5,-1.0	>95 dB	>98 dB	88.2	D	1	90 dB	2 V
Yamaha	CD-45	Front	5 Hz - 20 kHz	+0.5,-1.0	>95 dB	>98 dB	88.2	D	1	90 dB	2 V
Yamaha	CD-500B	Front	5 Hz - 20 kHz	+0.5,-1.0	>96 dB	>10 dB	88.2	D	1	92 dB	2 V
Yamaha	CD-55	Front	5 Hz - 20 kHz	+0.5,-1.0	>96 dB	>100 dB	88.2	D	1	92 dB	2 V
Yamaha	CD-56	Front	5 Hz - 20 kHz	+0.5,-1.0	>96 dB	>100 dB	88.2	D	1	92 dB	2 V
Yamaha	CD-700B	Front	4 Hz - 20 kHz	+0.5,-1.0	>96 dB	>100 dB	88.2	D	1	92 dB	2 V
Yamaha	CD-X2	Front	5 Hz - 20 kHz	+0.5,-1 dB	95 dB	95 dB	N/A	D	N/A	90 dB	2 V
Yamaha	CD-X3	Front	5 Hz - 20 kHz	+0.5,-1.0	>95 dB	>98 dB	88.2	D	1	90 dB	2 V
Yamaha	YCD-1000	Front	20 Hz - 20 kHz	-3.0 dB	>92 dB	>92 dB	88.2	D	1	75 dB	2 V

3	20	Yes	Yes	Optional	No	17x3.25x11.25	11 lbs.	
3	20	Yes	Yes	Yes	Yes, var	17x3.25x11.25	11 lbs.	
N/A	N/A	N/A	N/A	Yes	Yes	17x3.1x13	20.5 lbs.	
3	16	Yes	Yes	Yes	Yes	17x3.2x13.25	15 lbs.	
3	16	Yes	Yes	Yes	Yes, var	17x3.25x13.25	15 lbs.	
3	20	Yes	Yes	Yes	Yes, var	17x3.24x11.25	11 lbs.	
3	20	Yes	Yes	Yes	Yes	17x3.2x14	20 lbs.	
3	20	Yes	Yes	Yes	No	17x3.2x14	20 lbs.	Optional outboard D/A converter DAS-703ES
3	20	Yes	Yes	Yes	Yes, var	17x3.25x14	20 lbs.	Direct Digital Output
N/A	16	Yes	No	Optional	Yes	17x2.9x12	9 lbs.	
3	16	Yes	Yes	Optional	Yes,var	8.4x3.25x12	9 lbs.	
3	20	Yes	No	Yes	Yes, var	17x4.25x15	16 lbs.	10-Disc Changer, Cartridge
3	None	Yes	No	No	No	7.1x2x6.2	N/A	Car Player; CDX-R7 with AM/FM tuner
3	15	Yes	No	Yes	No	12.75x5.25x8.75	12.5 lbs.	Car Player; 10-Disc Changer, Cartridge
3	None	Yes	No	No	Yes, var	22x8x8	17.2 lbs.	Portable; with AM/FM & Cassette Deck
3	16	Yes	No	No	Yes, var	22x8x9	20 lbs.	Portable; AM/FM & Dual Cassette Deck
3	None	Yes	No	No	Yes, var	5x1.5x5.25	1.4 lbs.	Portable
N/A	N/A	N/A	N/A	No	Yes	5x1.5x5.2	1.4 lbs.	
3	16	Yes	No	No	Yes, var	5x1.3x5	1.5 lbs.	Portable; D-77 with AM/FM; D-55 with FM
3	20	Yes	Yes	Yes	Yes, var	17x3.25x14	20 lbs.	
3	16	Yes	Yes	Yes	Yes, var	17x3.5x13.25	15 lbs.	
3	16	Yes	No	No	Yes, var	7.5x2.25x9	10 lbs.	
N/A	20	Yes	No	No	No	12.5x3.5x11.75	7 lbs.	
N/A	20	Yes	Yes	No	Yes,fixed	16.5x3.5x11.75	8 lbs.	
N/A	20	Yes	Yes	Yes	No	16.5x3.5x11.75	8 lbs.	
N/A	20	Yes	Yes	Optional	No	12.5x11.75x3.5	N/A	
N/A	20	No	No	No	Yes	16.5x11.75x3.5	N/A	
N/A	16	Yes	Yes	No	No	13.9x1.7x3.2	10 lbs.	
N/A	20	Yes	Yes	Optional	N/A	17.1x13.75x3.5	12.5 lbs.	
3	15	Yes	Yes	Yes	Yes	N/A	N/A	CD/Cassette Deck
3	16	Yes	Yes	No	No	17x3x11	7.75 lbs.	
3	16	Yes	No	No	No	17.1x2.1x11.75	8.75 lbs.	
N/A	15	Yes	Yes	No	No	N/A	N/A	
N/A	15	Yes	Yes	Yes	Yes	17.2x3.7x11.3	10.7 lbs.	
3	20	Yes	Yes	Yes	Yes, var	17.5x3.5x13.5	17.5 lbs.	
3	20	Yes	Yes	Yes	Yes, var	17.5x4x13.5	20.1 lbs.	
3	16	Yes	Yes	Yes	Yes	17.1x2.2x11.5	16 lbs.	
1	15	Yes	No	No	No	N/A	N/A	Car Player; with AM/FM tuner
N/A	15	Yes	Yes	No	Yes	17x3.25x13.2	11.2 lbs.	
1	20	Yes	No	No	No	16.9x3.1x9.5	8 lbs.	
1	20	Yes	Yes	Yes	Yes	17x7x15	22 lbs.	
N/A	15	Yes	Yes	Yes	Yes	17x3.25x13.2	11.5 lbs.	
N/A	15	Yes	Yes	Yes	Yes	17x3.25x13.2	11.5 lbs.	
1	20	Yes	No	Yes	Yes	16.9x3.1x9.5	8 lbs.	
1	20	Yes	Yes	Yes	Yes	16.0x3.5x11	10.1 lbs.	
1	15	Yes	Yes	No	No	12.4x2.9x10.5	7.9 lbs.	
1	18	Yes	No	No	Yes, var	4.9x0.9x4.9	N/A	Portable
1	18	Yes	No	No	Yes, var	4.9x1.1x4.9	N/A	Portable; with AM/FM tuner
1	99	N/A	N/A	Yes	Yes	N/A	N/A	
3	16	No	No	No	No	16.5x3.2x12.1	9 lbs.	
3	16	No	No	No	No	16.5x3.2x12.1	9 lbs.	
N/A	8	No	Yes	No	Yes	16.5x12.2x13.2	10.6 lbs.	
3	16	No	No	No	Yes	9.8x1.8x5.1	2.9 lbs.	Portable
3	16	Yes	No	Yes	Yes,var	4.9x1.5x7.1	1.1 lbs.	Portable
N/A	8	No	Yes	No	No	13.3x12.2x3.3	9 lbs.	
3	30	No	No	No	No	13.2x4.4x14.1	13.4	Double Drawer Player
N/A	16	Yes	Yes	Optional	Yes	16.5x12.7x3.5	14 lbs.	
N/A	15	Yes	Yes	No	No	17x12.5x3.5	11 lbs.	
3	12	Yes	Yes	Yes	Yes, var	17.1x4x11.5	11.1 lbs.	
N/A	12	Yes	Yes	Yes	No	17.1x12.5x3.5	10.5 lbs.	
3	12	Yes	Yes	Yes, var	Yes, var	17.1x4x11.5	12.1 lbs.	M-Professional
3	12	Yes	Yes	Yes, var	Yes, var	17.1x4.11.5	11.4 lbs.	
N/A	9	Yes	Yes	Yes	Yes	17.1x3.7x11.4	11.2 lbs.	
3	9	Yes	Yes	No	Yes	13.3x3.6x11.25	7.7 lbs.	
N/A	9	Yes	Yes	No	Yes	17.1x12.5x3.5	9.75 lbs.	
3	9	Yes	Yes	No	Yes	17.1x3.75x11.25	9.25 lbs.	
3	9	Yes	Yes	No	Yes	17.1x3.75x11.25	9.25 lbs.	
3	9	Yes	Yes	Yes	Yes,var	17.1x3.7x11.25	10.5 lbs.	System Remote Independent
3	9	Yes	Yes	Optional	Yes, var	17.1x3.7x11.4	10.5 lbs.	System Remote
3	9	Yes	Yes	Yes	Yes, var	17.1x3.7x11.3	10.5 lbs.	System Remote Independent
3	12	Yes	Yes	Optional	Yes, var	17.1x3.7x11.4	10.5 lbs.	System Remote
N/A	9	Yes	Yes	No	Yes	17x3.6x11.4	8.4 lbs.	
3	9	Yes	Yes	No	Yes	13.3x3.6x11.25	7.7 lbs.	
3	None	Yes	No	No	No	7.1x2x7.1	3.4 lbs.	Car Player; cartridge

Glossary

A/B switch—1. A mechanical switch used to select between two incoming signal sources. 2. A method of testing the performance of a compact disc player by alternately switching between two machines playing simultaneously (usually the same musical selection).

ambiance—The feeling of space and surroundings; the sound environment of a given room.

ambiance simulation—An electrically synthesized approximation of room ambiance during compact disc playback.

amplitude—The relative strength (usually voltage) of an analog signal. Amplitude can be expressed as either a negative or positive number.

analog filter—A low-pass filtering system, placed in the analog stages of the CD player, where the spikes (noise transients) caused by the sampling process are blocked. Analog filters are placed after the D/A converter. Analog filters are sometimes called "brick-wall" filters, because they provide a sharp cut-off at 20 kHz, but frequencies before that are relatively unaffected.

auto space—A feature on some compact disc players where a blank three second space is inserted between music selections. Usually used for recording CDs onto cassettes when using a player with an automatic music search sensor.

Automatic Music Sensor (AMS)—A trademarked name for forward and reverse fast scan of a CD. AMS finds the beginning of each musical selection (either by track or index number). The feature, with various names on other players, is built into all CD players and works with all discs.

balance—Equal signal strength provided to both left and right stereo output channels. Balance can be adjusted to provide more signal strength to one channel than the other.

bit—A binary number—1 or 0. A number of bits make a word. With CD, one word is 16 bits, which permits 65,536 different binary combinations.

block—*See* frame.

block error— An error caused by dropouts or disc imperfections that occur anywhere within a block (or frame). If only one bit in the block of 588 bits is in error, the entire block is considered in error.

block error rate (BER)—The number of block errors that occur on the disc divided by the playing time (in seconds) of the disc. A block error rate of 30 to 40 is considered average.

CD-ROM—Similar to the compact disc in size and format, but designed specifically for computer data. In most cases, a CD-ROM disc requires a CD-ROM player.

clipping—An effect of distortion where the peaks of driven signals are clipped off. Clipping usually occurs in the amplifier when it's turned up too high.

clock—An electronic metronome used for the purpose of timing signals in compact disc player circuits. A master clock ensures that the sequence of signals occurs at the proper times.

CLV servo—An electrical system used in compact disc players to assure proper constant linear velocity during disc playback.

collimator—An optical component that forces a divergent light beam, usually from a laser, to travel in parallel lines.

compact disc (CD)—The compact disc is a worldwide standard for 2-channel and 4-channel stereo audio reproduction, using digital encoding techniques.

compact disc/interactive (CD/I)—Similar to the compact disc in size and data format, but designed specifically to mix audio, video, and computer information. In most cases, CD/I discs require CD/I players.

compander—Combination compressor and expander. A compressor is an electrical circuit that compresses the dynamic range of a musical selection just prior to recording. An expander circuit expands the dynamic range to its approximate original form. Used in analog recording, especially with cassette tape. Little used in compact disc, expected when making cassette tape copies of CDs.

constant linear velocity (CLV)—A system whereby the surface of the disc passes by the optical pickup at the same speed no matter where the pickup is located along the radius of the disc. The disc turns at its fastest when the pickup is tracking close to the inner circumference.

control code—Used to distinguish between 2-channel and 4-channel recording. Also used to detect whether preemphasis is given to a particular recording. If preemphasis is added, the player automatically switches in its preemphasis circuits, if so equipped.

cross interleave Reed Solomon code (CIRC)—An error correction scheme to eliminate or reduce errors caused by missing data.

crosstalk—A signal from one stereo channel that bleeds into the other. With compact disc players, crosstalk is minimal compared to other analog playback equipment.

cylindrical lens—A lens that expands or reduces an image in one axis only. In compact disc players, a cylindrical lens is used as a component in an astigmatic focusing system.

decibel (dB)—A unit of electrical measurement used extensively in audio applications. An increase of 3 dB is a doubling of electrical (or signal) strength; an increase of 10 dB is a doubling of perceived loudness. The decibel is not an absolute measurement, actually, but indicates the relationship between two signal levels.

diffraction grating—An optical component that splits a light beam into many discrete parts. As used in compact disc players, the diffraction grating splits the single laser beam into two secondary beams, which are used for tracking control. More than two secondary beams are created, actually, but these are very low in intensity.

digital—Information expressed in binary—on and off—form. The off state is usually indicated as a numeral 0; the on state is usually indicated as a numeral 1. Many 0's and 1's can be grouped together to represent any number or value.

digital filter—A low-pass filtering system, placed in the digital stages of the CD player, where the spikes (noise transients) caused by the sampling process are blocked. Digital filters are placed prior to the D/A converter. Digital filters are often supplemented by analog filters, which block higher frequency transients (in the 88 and 176 kHz range).

digital-to-analog converter (D/A converter)—An electrical circuit or component that transforms digital information into its analog equivalent. An A/D (analog-to-digital) converter was used when making the disc to transform the original music into digital data.

DIN—A European size and physical standard, pertains mostly to automotive applications. DIN-sized CD players fit into DIN-sized slots in car dashboards; DIN-sized electrical connectors fit into DIN-sized electrical jacks. DIN connectors are used mainly in automotive CD players. The graphics subcode output, available on some players, is usually a DIN-type connector.

dither—The process of adding intermediate signals between existing ones. Dithering is sometimes used in compact disc players to smooth out the analog waveform after digital-to-analog conversion.

dropout—Missing information. In CD, dropouts are usually caused by dirt and scratches on the disc.

dynamic range—The range of volume from softest to loudest sounds (the actual sound levels themselves are not a consideration, but it usually starts at "no sound" and goes from there). Expressed in dB (decibels). The higher the dB, the wider the dynamic range.

eight to fourteen modulation (EFM)—An encoding system developed for compact disc where eight bits of digital audio data is converted into a special fourteen bit code. The fourteen bits are then decoded into their original eight-bit form during playback on the compact disc player.

equalization—As used in audio output, the adjustment of frequency to tailor the sound to match personal preferences and room acoustics. Turning the Bass/Treble control on an amplifier is a kind of equalization. Higher-end stereo systems use a parametric or graphic equalizer, where the level of discrete frequency bands can be boosted or retarded individually.

eye pattern—A term used to describe the high frequency sine wave generated by the EFM data when read by the pickup.

filter—An electrical circuit designed to prevent the passage of certain frequencies. *See also* analog filter and digital filter.

flutter—A rapid up and down change in the speed of a playback mechanism. Unlike analog audio equipment, like cassette players and turntables, compact disc players exhibit almost no flutter (the actual amount is under 0.0001%). *See also* wow.

focus coil—An electromechanical coil used in CD players to move the objective lens up and down for proper focus.

focus servo—An electrical and mechanical system used in CD players to maintain absolute focus of the disc during playback. The servo detects errors and compensates for them.

Foucault focusing—A system of focusing, used in some CD players, where the separation of two beams changes according to variances in the distance of the focal point.

frame—A frame is the smallest recognizable data component in compact disc. It contains six samples of both the right and left stereo channels, plus synchronization, subcode, and parity bits. Also called a block.

frequency response—As used in compact disc applications, sonic range; the highest and lowest audio frequencies that can be accurately reproduced.

graphics subcode port—A special output port designed for CD graphics applications such as song titles, lyrics, and program (liner) notes.

ground—Refers to a point of (usually) zero voltage, and can pertain to a power circuit or a signal circuit.

harmonic—Basically, the multiple frequencies of a given sound. A "middle C" on the piano has a fundamental audio frequency of 256 Hertz, but also a number of secondary higher and lower frequencies (harmonics) that are multiples of this fundamental. The distribution and amplitude of the harmonics determines the true sonic nature of the sound.

harmonic distortion—Harmonics (frequencies) artificially added by an electrical circuit or speaker, and are generally undesirable. Expressed as a percentage.

hertz—Abbreviated Hz. A unit of measurement used for expressing cycles per second, named after German physicist H.R. Hertz. One hertz is equal to one cycle per second. Also used with the letters "k" and "M" as multipliers to indicate thousands and millions. One kHz is equal to one thousand cycles per second; one MHz is equal to one million cycles per second. (The letter "G" is used as a prefix for Giga, meaning billion: 1 GHz is one billion cycles per second. Speeds this high are not used in audio, CD, or digital applications—yet!)

high frequency (H.F.)—A radio signal that carries the EFM data read from the compact disc for processing by the digital circuits.

hiss—Audible high frequency noise, which sounds much like air passing through a hose. Hiss is common in analog recording and increases the more times the same signal is rerecorded. Hiss is caused by a number of factors, including electrical noise introduced during the recording process, and residual magnetism when the signal is stored on tape. The digital process of CD players eliminates the source of much hiss, most noise present in the original recording, in the analog output stages of the CD player, and in the amplifier, can cause hiss.

hum—A low-level, low-frequency electrical noise usually caused by the alternating current in household power wiring interfering with audio signal circuits. Hum is often picked up in cables extending between CD player and amplifier, but can be significantly reduced by using properly shielded cables and careful cable placement.

impedance—Technically, the degree of resistance that an electrical current will encounter when passing through a circuit, device, or wire. The amount of impedance is expressed in ohms.

integrated circuit (IC)—Also called a chip. A complete electrical circuit housed in a self-contained package. *See also* LSI.

interleave—A process whereby data is shifted, much like shuffling a card deck, from its original position. Data is interleaved as it is encoded on a compact disc, and de-interleaved during playback. Interleaving minimizes the effect of errors caused by dropouts or disc defects.

intermodulation distortion-Newly created frequencies which are the sum and difference of existing frequencies as well as the harmonics of the artificially added signals. Intermodulation distortion (IM) can be caused by an electrical circuit or speaker, and are generally undesirable. Expressed as a percentage.

jack—A term used for the cable connector on hi-fi equipment.

land—The flat areas between pits on the surface of a compact disc.

large scale integration (LSI)—A complex integrated circuit that is a combination of many ICs that are normally packaged separately. LSI (and VLSI, or Very Large Scale Integration) chips are used extensively in compact disc players, and are held proprietary by the manufacturer.

laser diode—The semiconductor laser used in compact disc players.

lead-in/lead-out signal—Codes placed at the beginning and end of selections, used to control the movement of the optical pickup.

logic—Primarily used to indicate digital circuits or components that accept one or more signals and act on those signals in a predefined, orderly fashion.

microprocessor—A special integrated circuit that performs semi-intelligent functions based on instructions written in a program. Fundamentally, a microprocessor is a hardware device that can be electrically "rewired" by using new software. Often considered the "brain" of a computer or circuit. All compact disc players have a microprocessor to control system operation.

modulation—A way in which one signal modifies or controls another signal for such purposes as enabling it to carry information. Often used to describe radio frequency (RF) transmission. FM is frequency modulation, AM is amplitude modulation. *See* EFM.

monitor photodiode—A special photodiode sandwiched behind the laser diode for the purpose of monitoring the light output of the laser.

music search—Audible fast forward search through a music selection. The pitch of the sound remains the same as during normal listening, because several tracks are skipped at a time, rather than speeding up the revolution of the disc.

music start flag—A code inserted in a blank space between selections to indicate the beginning of a new selection. Flags are counted sequentially to find any desired selection on the disc.

noise—An undesired signal. Noise is usually hiss and hum. In analog magnetic tape systems, noise can be caused by residual magnetism. In LP records, noise can be caused by surface scratches and blemishes.

objective lens—The lens used to focus the beam onto the surface of the disc.

oversampling—A technique used in digital filtering systems whereby the digital data retrieved from the disc is sampled at a rate higher than normal. Normally, audio data is sampled at a rate of 44.1 kHz; in oversampling, the audio is sampled at even multiples of this rate—usually 88.2 kHz and 176.4 kHz (called 2X and 4X oversampling, respectively).

peak—The highest level of an instantaneous burst of power or signal.

phase—The position in time of a sound wave in relation to another sound wave. Expressed in degrees. Sound waves are sinusoidal—with peaks and valleys. Zero degree phase is when the peaks and valleys of both waves are even. A phase of 180 degrees is when the peaks of one wave match up with the valleys of the other. Zero degree phase is usually desirable. In CD, the output of the right and left channel outputs are measured to reveal if they are in phase.

phone plug—A certain type of cable connector often used for headphone and microphone audio applications. It has a single stem, with parts of the stem insulated from others to provide a two or three line circuit. Phone plugs come in many sizes: 1/4″ phone plugs are large and are used for headphones and some microphones; 1/8″ (or miniature) phone plugs are smaller and mainly used for lightweight headsets. *See also* phono plug.

phono plug—A certain type of cable connector often used in home audio application. It is composed of a round center stem surrounded by a metal cap. Also called an RCA plug. *See also* phone plug.

photodiode—A light sensitive electrical component that registers the presence or absence of the laser beam in a compact disc player. Photodiodes are analog devices, and can relate the intensity of the beam to amplification circuits in the player, for use in tracking and focus control.

pickup—The optical and mechanical system comprising the laser diode, photodiode detectors, lenses, prisms, and other optical components for retrieving the encoded data on the compact disc.

pit—The tiny impressions on the surface of a compact disc. Pits are dug into a master disc by a high precision laser. The master disc is then used to make subsequent copies of the compact disc for distribution.

polarized beam splitter (PBS)—An optical component used in some compact disc players that consists of two prisms with a common 45 degree face. The PBS relays the light beam from the laser diode to the disc surface, then back through to the photodiode detectors.

quantization—The conversion of the amplitude of an instantaneous moment of sound (sample) into its approximate digital equivalent. In CD players, there are 65,536 possible levels of digital amplitude.

quarter wavelength plate (QWP)—An optical component used in some compact disc players to shift the polarized light from the laser beam 90 degrees.

radial arm—A mechanical motorized transport used in some CD players that swings the pickup along the radius of the disc in an arc. The other kind of pickup transport system is the slide.

random access memory (RAM)—As used in compact disc, electronic memory used to temporarily store system information and audio data.

sample and hold—An electronic circuit used to sample incoming data and hold it momentarily until the next sampling interval.

sampling—The measurement of the instantaneous amplitude of a signal. During the manufacture of a compact disc, sound is sampled at the rate of 44.1 kHz. The sample is then encoded as a digital number. During playback, the disc data is sampled at the same speed, or some even multiple thereof (oversampling).

separation—The complete electrical separation of two signals, and usually refers to right and left stereo channels. True separation is nearly impossible to achieve when two signals are sent through shared circuits, so some crosstalk is present.

shift register—A digital component or circuit that shifts a series of bits through sequential stages, for the purpose of timing, holding, and delaying data. Much like pouring water from one bucket to another until the water reaches its destination.

shuffle play—A technique of playing all the selections on a disc once, in a random order.

signal—The desired portion of electrical information.

signal-to-noise (S/N)—The relationship between the signal (sound you want) and noise (sound you don't want). Expressed in dB.

slide—Also called the sled. A mechanical motorized transport used to position the pickup along the radius of the disc. The other kind of pickup transport is the radial arm.

SPARS code—A code developed to indicate the recording process of the finished compact disc. It consists of three letters, and any of the letters can be either "A" or "D," as in "AAA" or "ADD." The letter A means analog; the letter D means digital. The codes represent the recording devices used in 1) making the original recording, 2) in re-mixing, and 3) in the final master.

symbol—A series of eight consecutive bits.

table of contents—Data that appears at the very beginning of a compact disc and includes the start time of each selection as well as the total number and playing time of selections. The data is displayed by some players.

total harmonic distortion (THD)—The percentage, in relation to a pure input signal, of harmonically derived frequencies introduced in the sound reproducing circuitry and equipment (including speakers).

track—1. One lane of the continuous spiral of pits impressed on the surface of a compact disc. 2. A music selection.

track number—The number of a selection. Compact discs can contain up to 99 selections.

tracking—The action of following the spiral of pits encoded on the surface of the compact disc.

tracking coil—An electromechanical coil used in CD players to move the objective lens about its axis for proper tracking.

tracking servo—An electrical and mechanical system used in CD players to maintain absolute tracking of the disc during playback. The servo detects errors and compensates for them.

wow—A slow up and down change in the speed of a playback mechanism. Compact disc players exhibit almost no wow (the actual amount is under 0.0001%). *See also* flutter.

Index